Java EE 8 Cookbook

Build reliable applications with the most robust and mature
technology for enterprise development

Elder Moraes

BIRMINGHAM - MUMBAI

Java EE 8 Cookbook

Commissioning Editor: Merint Mathew
Acquisition Editor: Isha Raval
Content Development Editor: Jason Pereira
Technical Editor: Prajakta Mhatre
Copy Editor: Safis Editing
Project Coordinator: Sheejal Shah
Proofreader: Safis Editing
Indexer: Mariammal Chettiyar
Production Coordinator: Deepika Naik

First published: April 2018
Production reference: 1060418

Published by Packt Publishing Ltd.
Livery Place
35 Livery Street
Birmingham
B3 2PB, UK.

ISBN 978-1-78829-303-7

www.packtpub.com

To Jesus Christ, my only source of eternal life and purpose.

To my beloved wife, Erica—thanks for your love and for sharing your life with me.

To my adorable daughter, Rebeca—if this book helps a single person, maybe it could help turning the world a better place for you.

To the memory of my mother, Matilde, who I miss every day.

To my brother, Marco, who introduced me to this incredible world of computers and software.

To my friend and guru, Bruno "Javaman" Souza—I would probably never have written this book if I hadn't meet you.

To the amazing team at SouJava—you folks really live the community thing.

To my peers at TCDB for all encouragement, tips, sharing, and feedbacks. Thank you!

– Elder Moraes

`mapt.io`

Mapt is an online digital library that gives you full access to over 5,000 books and videos, as well as industry leading tools to help you plan your personal development and advance your career. For more information, please visit our website.

Why subscribe?

- Spend less time learning and more time coding with practical eBooks and Videos from over 4,000 industry professionals

- Improve your learning with Skill Plans built especially for you

- Get a free eBook or video every month

- Mapt is fully searchable

- Copy and paste, print, and bookmark content

PacktPub.com

Did you know that Packt offers eBook versions of every book published, with PDF and ePub files available? You can upgrade to the eBook version at `www.PacktPub.com` and as a print book customer, you are entitled to a discount on the eBook copy. Get in touch with us at `service@packtpub.com` for more details.

At `www.PacktPub.com`, you can also read a collection of free technical articles, sign up for a range of free newsletters, and receive exclusive discounts and offers on Packt books and eBooks.

Foreword

It is a measure of the penetration, longevity, and quality of Java EE technology that in 2018 my friend Elder Moraes asked me to write the foreword for his book about Java EE 8. My personal involvement with Java EE goes back to the days preceding J2EE 1.4 in 2001. Since then, I have had the great honor of leading or co-leading the community teams that have developed JavaServer Faces and, later, servlet, two of the technologies Elder covers in this book. During that time, I tried to follow the model of servant-leader, and I think the result has been a very engaged community that has a real stake in the continued success of Java EE.

When writing this foreword, I want to focus on four Cs: Curation, Cohesion, Current, and Completeness. So much has been written about Java EE over the years, and continues to be written, that the task of writing a book, particularly one in the useful "cookbook" format, involves a lot of curation. From the set of all possible things that people are doing with Java EE, which is vast, Elder has presented a curation of what he thinks are the most useful and essential ones. Elder is well positioned to decide what goes in and what stays out. Elder has been consulting and working with Java EE for nearly as long as I have, but from the more practical perspective of the user.

Technical books that follow the cookbook pattern frequently suffer from a feeling of disjointness. Not this book. Elder has put a great deal of effort into ensuring cohesion. Over the years, the technologies of Java EE have sometimes been criticized for not being cohesive enough with each other. This is something Sun made a conscious effort to address starting with Java EE 6, and which Oracle continued on to Java EE 8. Elder has leveraged this effort to seek out and present the best way to leverage the synergy of all the technologies of Java EE 8 to maximum effect.

The world outside Java EE has continued to evolve, and this has changed the way people use Java EE dramatically. The challenge for any architect on a multiyear software effort, with a service lifetime of at least a decade, is how to keep it maintainable even while the surrounding technology landscape changes. Elder has accounted for this with two excellent chapters about microservices and Docker. These two technologies provide a great complement to the power of Java EE, but also have numerous pitfalls. Elder helps you avoid the pitfalls while getting the most out of these current trends.

Finally, completeness. Many technology cookbooks stop short of providing "complete reference" sort of material, but Elder goes much deeper. It's almost to the point that the term "cookbook" does not do this book justice. Perhaps, a more correct label would be "complete restaurant management with supply chain logistics and a cookbook on top." Elder covers the current popular app servers on which people are running Java EE, continuous integration and pipelines, reactive programming, and more. Coming back to the curation point, it's all there, and in depth.

I hope you have success with Java EE and with its successor, Jakarta EE from the Eclipse Foundation.

Ed Burns

Consulting Member of Technical Staff at *Oracle*

Specification Lead of JSF and Servlet

Contributors

About the author

Elder Moraes helps Java EE developers build and deliver secure, fast, and available applications so that they are able to work on great projects. He is passionate about content sharing; he does it by speaking at international events, blogging, and writing articles. He has been working with Java since 2002 and has developed applications for different industries. As a board member at SouJava, he led the *Java EE 8 - The Next Frontier* initiative, interviewing some of the world class Java EE experts.

> *First, I have to thank my wife and daughter, Erica and Rebeca, respectively, for all the time they allowed me to put into writing this book. It was not easy for any of us. Also, thank you to my friends, Lucas and Mari, for all the support and encouragement since day one. Last but not least, thank you to all the Packt team (Isha, Sreeja, Jason, Prajakta, and others that I haven't talked personally). You folks rock!*

About the reviewers

Romain Manni Bucau is a senior software engineer who has been involved in Java EE and more particularly Apache projects as a committer (Apache TomEE, OpenWebBeans, Johnzon, BatchEE, OpenJPA, BVal, Meecrowave, and many more) since 2011. He also wrote *JavaEE 8 High Performance* for Packt. He now works at Talend on Big Data and API projects. You can follow him on Twitter at `@rmannibucau` or on his blog at `rmannibucau.metawerx.net`.

Omar El-Prince is an experienced software engineer with a computer engineering graduate degree and master's degree in computer science from Johns Hopkins University. He has wide experience on working in large Java EE projects at CSRA, Booz Allen Hamilton, HP, EDS, and other companies. He enjoys programming and technology blogging, focused on agile culture, software development, and architecture. He is Java EE enthusiastic and loves learning, mentoring, and helping others.

Bauke Scholtz is an Oracle Java champion and the main creator of the award-winning JSF helper library OmniFaces. On the internet, he is more commonly known as BalusC, who is among the top contributors on Stack Overflow. He is a web application specialist and consults for clients from fintech, affiliate marketing, social media, and more as part of his 17 years of experience. Bauke has previously reviewed *Mastering OmniFaces* and wrote *The Definitive Guide to JSF in Java EE 8*.

Packt is searching for authors like you

If you're interested in becoming an author for Packt, please visit `authors.packtpub.com` and apply today. We have worked with thousands of developers and tech professionals, just like you, to help them share their insight with the global tech community. You can make a general application, apply for a specific hot topic that we are recruiting an author for, or submit your own idea.

Table of Contents

Preface

Java EE is a mature platform that's widely used around the world. It is also a standard that has evolved through the hard work of individuals, vendors, groups leaders, and communities. It has a whole market and ecosystem around it, with millions of users, which also means a big and active community that is always willing to help it move forward.

For those reasons, the purpose of this book is to meet the needs of those professionals who depend on Java EE to deliver really awesome enterprise solutions, not only talking about real solutions for real problems, but also showing how to do it in a practical way.

The book starts with a quick overview of what Java EE and the improvements in version 8. Then, it takes you on a hands-on journey through the most important APIs.

You will learn how to use Java EE for server-side development, web services, and web applications. You will also take a look at how you can properly improve the security of your enterprise solutions.

No Java EE application is good enough if it doesn't follow the standards, and for that, you can count on the Java EE application servers. This book will teach you how to use the most important servers on the market and take the best they have to offer for your project.

From an architectural point of view, the book will cover microservices, cloud computing, and containers. Also, it will not forget to give you all tools for building a reactive Java EE application using not only Java EE features, but also Java core features such as lambdas and completable future.

The whole Java world is all about the community, so we will also show you how community-driven professionals can improve the results of their projects and even go to higher levels in their careers.

The book was based on a concept that I call "*The Five Mistakes That Keep Java EE Professionals Away From Great Projects.*" I am ruining my career when I don't do the following things:

- Keep myself up to date
- Know the APIs (an overview of all of them and master the most important ones)
- Know the most commonaly used Java EE application servers
- Know advanced architectures
- Share what I know

So, the book is a straight, practical, and helpful solution to each one of these mistakes. I can say with confidence that dealing with them properly can change the careers and lives of many developers around the world. I know because they've changed mine, for good.

Who this book is for

This book is made for developers who would like to learn how to meet real enterprise application needs using Java EE 8. They should be familiar with application development and need to have knowledge of least basic Java, the basic concepts of cloud computing, and web services.

The readers should want to learn how to combine a bunch of APIs in a secure and fast solution, and for this, they need to know how the APIs work and when to use each one.

What this book covers

Chapter 1, *New Features and Improvements*, explains the main changes to the Java EE 8 specification and what the reader can do with them. It also shows the new features and briefly explores the benefits of them. All these topics are supported by code examples.

Chapter 2, *Server-Side Development*, deep dives into the most important APIs and most commonly used features for server-side development. The readers here will go through real recipes for solving real problems.

Chapter 3, *Building Powerful Services with JSON and RESTful Features*, creates web services for different enterprise scenarios. Readers will go deep into the JAX-RS, JSON-P, and JSON-B APIs.

Chapter 4, *Web- and Client-Server Communication*, deals with the communication generated by web applications in a fast and reliable way using the latest Java EE 8 features, such as HTTP2 and Server Push.

Chapter 5, *Security of Enterprise Architecture*, gives the readers information on the tools using the best Java EE features to create secure architectures.

Chapter 6, *Reducing the Coding Effort by Relying on Standards*, describes the services and features that Java EE application servers give to the applications they host. Those features not only let the readers rely on a standard and build their application based on it, but also allow them to write less code, as they don't need to implement features that have been already implemented by the server.

Chapter 7, *Deploying and Managing Applications on Major Java EE Servers*, describes the use of each of the most commonly used Java EE application servers on the market, giving special attention to the way you deploy and manage them.

Chapter 8, *Building Lightweight Solutions Using Microservices*, makes you understand how microservice architectures work and how readers can easily use Java EE 8 to build microservice and/or break down their monoliths in order to implement this paradigm.

Continuous Delivery and Continuous Deployment are also described, as no successful microservice project is complete without a mature building and deployment process.

Chapter 9, *Using Multithreading on Enterprise Context*, describes the use of multithreading and concurrency when building enterprise applications.

Chapter 10, *Using Event-Driven Programming to Build Reactive Applications*, describes the use of Java EE 8 and core Java to create low-latency, efficient, and high-throughput applications.

Chapter 11, *Rising to the Cloud – Java EE, Containers, and Cloud Computing*, describes how to combine Java EE and containers to run applications on the cloud.

Appendix, *The Power of Sharing Knowledge*, describes how the community is vital for the whole Java EE ecosystem (even if readers don't know about it) and how they can improve their own daily work by joining the Adopt a JSR initiative.

It also describes how sharing knowledge is a powerful tool for improving their careers and what it has to do with Java EE (and it has everything to do with Java EE!).

To get the most out of this book

Readers should be familiar with application development and need to have at least basic knowledge of Java. Basic knowledge of cloud computing and web services are also assumed.

Download the example code files

You can download the example code files for this book from your account at www.packtpub.com. If you purchased this book elsewhere, you can visit www.packtpub.com/support and register to have the files emailed directly to you.

You can download the code files by following these steps:

1. Log in or register at www.packtpub.com.
2. Select the **SUPPORT** tab.
3. Click on **Code Downloads & Errata**.
4. Enter the name of the book in the **Search** box and follow the onscreen instructions.

Once the file is downloaded, please make sure that you unzip or extract the folder using the latest version of:

- WinRAR/7-Zip for Windows
- Zipeg/iZip/UnRarX for Mac
- 7-Zip/PeaZip for Linux

The code bundle for the book is also hosted on GitHub at https://github.com/PacktPublishing/Java-EE-8-Cookbook. In case there's an update to the code, it will be updated on the existing GitHub repository.

We also have other code bundles from our rich catalog of books and videos available at https://github.com/PacktPublishing/. Check them out!

Conventions used

There are a number of text conventions used throughout this book.

`CodeInText`: Indicates code words in text, database table names, folder names, filenames, file extensions, pathnames, dummy URLs, user input, and Twitter handles. Here is an example: "Then two key methods from `SseResource` take place."

A block of code is set as follows:

```
<dependency>
    <groupId>javax</groupId>
    <artifactId>javaee-api</artifactId>
    <version>8.0</version>
    <scope>provided</scope>
</dependency>
```

Any command-line input or output is written as follows:

```
Info:    destroy
```

Bold: Indicates a new term, an important word, or words that you see onscreen. For example, words in menus or dialog boxes appear in the text like this. Here is an example: "Now let's move to the **Additional Properties** section."

Warnings or important notes appear like this.

Tips and tricks appear like this.

Sections

In this book, you will find several headings that appear frequently (*Getting ready, How to do it..., How it works..., There's more...,* and *See also*).

To give clear instructions on how to complete a recipe, use these sections as follows:

Getting ready

This section tells you what to expect in the recipe and describes how to set up any software or any preliminary settings required for the recipe.

How to do it...

This section contains the steps required to follow the recipe.

How it works...

This section usually consists of a detailed explanation of what happened in the previous section.

There's more...

This section consists of additional information about the recipe in order to make you more knowledgeable about the recipe.

See also

This section provides helpful links to other useful information for the recipe.

Get in touch

Feedback from our readers is always welcome.

General feedback: Email `feedback@packtpub.com` and mention the book title in the subject of your message. If you have questions about any aspect of this book, please email us at `questions@packtpub.com`.

Errata: Although we have taken every care to ensure the accuracy of our content, mistakes do happen. If you have found a mistake in this book, we would be grateful if you would report this to us. Please visit `www.packtpub.com/submit-errata`, selecting your book, clicking on the Errata Submission Form link, and entering the details.

Piracy: If you come across any illegal copies of our works in any form on the internet, we would be grateful if you would provide us with the location address or website name. Please contact us at copyright@packtpub.com with a link to the material.

If you are interested in becoming an author: If there is a topic that you have expertise in and you are interested in either writing or contributing to a book, please visit authors.packtpub.com.

Reviews

Please leave a review. Once you have read and used this book, why not leave a review on the site that you purchased it from? Potential readers can then see and use your unbiased opinion to make purchase decisions, we at Packt can understand what you think about our products, and our authors can see your feedback on their book. Thank you!

For more information about Packt, please visit packtpub.com.

1
New Features and Improvements

Java EE 8 is a big release, desired and anticipated by the global community for about four years. More than ever before, the whole platform is now even more robust, mature, and stable.

This chapter will cover the main APIs that we can highlight for Java EE 8. Not that they are the only topics covered by this release—far from it—but they have a big role in the enterprise context and are worthy of a careful look inside.

In this chapter, we will cover the following recipes:

- Running your first Bean Validation 2.0 code
- Running your first CDI 2.0 code
- Running your first JAX-RS 2.1 code
- Running your first JSF 2.3 code
- Running your first JSON-P 1.1 code
- Running your first JSON-B 1.0
- Running your first Servlet 4.0 code
- Running your first Security API 1.0
- Running your first MVC 1.0 code

Running your first Bean Validation 2.0 code

Bean Validation is a Java specification that basically helps you to protect your data. Through its API, you can validate fields and parameters, express constraints using annotations, and extend your customs' validation rules.

It can be used both with Java SE and Java EE.

In this recipe, you will have a glimpse of Bean Validation 2.0. It doesn't matter whether you are new to it or already using version 1.1; this content will help you get familiar with some of its new features.

Getting ready

First, you need to add the right Bean Validation dependency to your project, as follows:

```
<dependencies>
    <dependency>
        <groupId>junit</groupId>
        <artifactId>junit</artifactId>
        <version>4.12</version>
        <scope>test</scope>
    </dependency>
    <dependency>
        <groupId>org.hamcrest</groupId>
        <artifactId>hamcrest-core</artifactId>
        <version>1.3</version>
        <scope>test</scope>
    </dependency>
    <dependency>
        <groupId>javax</groupId>
        <artifactId>javaee-api</artifactId>
        <version>8.0</version>
        <scope>provided</scope>
    </dependency>
    <dependency>
        <groupId>org.hibernate.validator</groupId>
        <artifactId>hibernate-validator</artifactId>
        <version>6.0.8.Final</version>
    </dependency>
    <dependency>
        <groupId>org.glassfish</groupId>
        <artifactId>javax.el</artifactId>
        <version>3.0.1-b10</version>
    </dependency>
</dependencies>
```

How to do it...

1. First, we need to create an object with some fields to be validated:

```java
public class User {

    @NotBlank
    private String name;
    @Email
    private String email;
    @NotEmpty
    private List<@PositiveOrZero Integer> profileId;
    public User(String name, String email, List<Integer> profileId)
{
        this.name = name;
        this.email = email;
        this.profileId = profileId;
    }
}
```

2. Then we create a `test` class to validate those constraints:

```java
public class UserTest {

    private static Validator validator;

    @BeforeClass
    public static void setUpClass() {
        validator = Validation.buildDefaultValidatorFactory()
        .getValidator();
    }

    @Test
    public void validUser() {
        User user = new User(
            "elder",
            "elder@eldermoraes.com",
            asList(1,2));

            Set<ConstraintViolation<User>> cv = validator
            .validate(user);
            assertTrue(cv.isEmpty());
    }

    @Test
    public void invalidName() {
        User user = new User(
```

```
                        "",
                        "elder@eldermoraes.com",
                        asList(1,2));

                        Set<ConstraintViolation<User>> cv = validator
                        .validate(user);
                        assertEquals(1, cv.size());
            }

            @Test
            public void invalidEmail() {
                User user = new User(
                "elder",
                "elder-eldermoraes_com",
                asList(1,2));

                        Set<ConstraintViolation<User>> cv = validator
                        .validate(user);
                        assertEquals(1, cv.size());
            }

            @Test
            public void invalidId() {
                User user = new User(
                    "elder",
                    "elder@eldermoraes.com",
                    asList(-1,-2,1,2));

                        Set<ConstraintViolation<User>> cv = validator
                        .validate(user);
                        assertEquals(2, cv.size());
            }
    }
```

How it works...

Our `User` class uses three of the new constraints introduced by Bean Validation 2.0:

- `@NotBlank`: Assures that the value is not null, empty, or an empty string (it trims the value before evaluation, to make sure there aren't spaces).
- `@Email`: Allows only a valid email format. Forget those crazy JavaScript functions!
- `@NotEmpty`: Ensures that a list has at least one item.
- `@PositiveOrZero`: Guarantees that a number is equal or greater than zero.

Then we create a `test` class (using JUnit) to test our validations. It first instantiates `Validator`:

```
@BeforeClass
public static void setUpClass() {
    validator = Validation.buildDefaultValidatorFactory().getValidator();
}
```

`Validator` is an API that validates beans according to the constraints defined for them.

Our first `test` method tests a valid user, which is a `User` object that has:

- Name not empty
- Valid email
- `profileId` list only with integers greater than zero:

```
User user = new User(
    "elder",
    "elder@eldermoraes.com",
    asList(1,2));
```

And finally, the validation:

```
Set<ConstraintViolation<User>> cv = validator.validate(user);
```

The `validate()` method from `Validator` returns a set of constraint violations found, if any, or an empty set if there are no violations at all.

So, for a valid user it should return an empty set:

```
assertTrue(cv.isEmpty());
```

And the other methods work with variations around this model:

- `invalidName()`: Uses an empty name
- `invalidEmail()`: Uses a malformed email
- `invalidId()`: Adds some negative numbers to the list

Note that the `invalidId()` method adds two negative numbers to the list:

```
asList(-1,-2,1,2));
```

So, we expect two constraint violations:

```
assertEquals(2, cv.size());
```

In other words, `Validator` checks not only the constraints violated, but how many times they are violated.

See also

- You can check the Bean Validation 2.0 specification at `http://beanvalidation.org/2.0/spec/`
- The full source code of this recipe is at `https://github.com/eldermoraes/javaee8-cookbook/tree/master/chapter01/ch01-beanvalidation/`

Running your first CDI 2.0 code

Context and Dependency Injection (CDI) is certainly one of the most important APIs for the Java EE platform. In version 2.0, it also works with Java SE.

Nowadays, CDI has an impact on many other APIs in the Java EE platform. As said in an interview for *Java EE 8 – The Next Frontier* project:

> *"If there was CDI by the time we created JSF, it would be made completely different."*
> – Ed Burns, JSF Spec Lead

There is a lot of new features in CDI 2.0. This recipe will cover Observer Ordering to give you a quick start.

Getting ready

First, you need to add the right CDI 2.0 dependency to your project. To make things easier at this point, we are going to use CDI SE, the dependency that allows you to use CDI without a Java EE server:

```
<dependency>
    <groupId>org.jboss.weld.se</groupId>
    <artifactId>weld-se-shaded</artifactId>
    <version>3.0.0.Final</version>
</dependency>
```

How to do it...

This recipe will show you one of the main features introduced by CDI 2.0: Ordered Observers. Now, you can turn the observers job into something predictable:

1. First, let's make an event to be observed:

```
public class MyEvent {
    private final String value;
    public MyEvent(String value){
        this.value = value;
    }
    public String getValue(){
        return value;
    }
}
```

2. Now, we build our observers and the server that will fire them:

```
public class OrderedObserver {

    public static void main(String[] args){
        try(SeContainer container =
        SeContainerInitializer.newInstance().initialize()){
            container
                .getBeanManager()
                .fireEvent(new MyEvent("event: " +
                System.currentTimeMillis()));
        }
    }

    public void thisEventBefore(
            @Observes @Priority(Interceptor.Priority
            .APPLICATION - 200)
            MyEvent event){
        System.out.println("thisEventBefore: " + event.getValue());
    }

    public void thisEventAfter(
            @Observes @Priority(Interceptor.Priority
            .APPLICATION + 200)
            MyEvent event){
        System.out.println("thisEventAfter: " + event.getValue());
    }
}
```

Also, don't forget to add the `beans.xml` file into the `META-INF` folder:

```xml
<?xml version="1.0" encoding="UTF-8"?>
<beans xmlns="http://xmlns.jcp.org/xml/ns/javaee"
       xmlns:xsi="http://www.w3.org/2001/XMLSchema-instance"
       xsi:schemaLocation="http://xmlns.jcp.org/xml/ns/javaee
       http://xmlns.jcp.org/xml/ns/javaee/beans_1_1.xsd"
       bean-discovery-mode="all">
</beans>
```

3. Once you run it, you should see a result like this:

```
INFO: WELD-ENV-002003: Weld SE container
353db40d-e670-431d-b7be-4275b1813782 initialized
 thisEventBefore: event -> 1501818268764
 thisEventAfter: event -> 1501818268764
```

How it works...

First, we are building a server to manage our event and observers:

```java
public static void main(String[] args){
    try(SeContainer container =
    SeContainerInitializer.newInstance().initialize()){
        container
            .getBeanManager()
            .fireEvent(new ExampleEvent("event: "
            + System.currentTimeMillis()));
    }
}
```

This will give us all the resources needed to run the recipe as if it was a Java EE server.

Then we build an observer:

```java
public void thisEventBefore(
        @Observes @Priority(Interceptor.Priority.APPLICATION - 200)
        MyEvent event){
    System.out.println("thisEventBefore: " + event.getValue());
}
```

So, we have three important topics:

- `@Observes`: This annotation is used to tell the server that it needs to watch the events fired with `MyEvent`
- `@Priority`: This annotation informs in which priority order this observer needs to run; it receives an `int` parameter, and the execution order is ascendant
- `MyEvent event`: The event being observed

On the `thisEventBefore` method and `thisEventAfter`, we only changed the `@Priority` value and the server took care of running it in the right order.

There's more...

The behavior would be exactly the same in a Java EE 8 server. You just wouldn't need `SeContainerInitializer` and would need to change the dependencies to the following:

```
<dependency>
    <groupId>javax</groupId>
    <artifactId>javaee-api</artifactId>
    <version>8.0</version>
    <scope>provided</scope>
</dependency>
```

See also

- You can stay tuned with everything related to the CDI Specification at http://www.cdi-spec.org/
- The source code of this recipe is at https://github.com/eldermoraes/javaee8-cookbook/tree/master/chapter01/ch01-cdi

Running your first JAX-RS 2.1 code

JAX-RS is an API designed to give a portable and standard way for building RESTful web services in Java. This is one of the most used technologies for data transporting between different applications that uses some network (internet included) for communication.

One of the coolest features introduced by the 2.1 release is **Server-Sent Events** (**SSE**), which will be covered in this recipe. SSE is a specification created by HTML5 where it has established a channel between server and client, one way only from server to client. It is a protocol that transports a message containing some data.

Getting ready

Let's start by adding the right dependency to our project:

```
<dependencies>
    <dependency>
        <groupId>org.glassfish.jersey.containers</groupId>
        <artifactId>jersey-container-grizzly2-http</artifactId>
        <version>2.26-b09</version>
    </dependency>
    <dependency>
        <groupId>org.glassfish.jersey.inject</groupId>
        <artifactId>jersey-hk2</artifactId>
        <version>2.26-b09</version>
    </dependency>
    <dependency>
        <groupId>org.glassfish.jersey.media</groupId>
        <artifactId>jersey-media-sse</artifactId>
        <version>2.26-b09</version>
    </dependency>
    <dependency>
        <groupId>javax</groupId>
        <artifactId>javaee-api</artifactId>
        <version>8.0</version>
        <scope>provided</scope>
    </dependency>
</dependencies>
```

You surely noticed that we are using Jersey here. Why? Because Jersey is the reference implementation for JAX-RS, which means that all JAX-RS specifications are first implemented through Jersey.

Moreover, with Jersey we can use Grizzly to start a small local server, which will be useful for this recipe, as we need just a few server features to show the SSE behavior.

Further on in this book, we will use a full GlassFish to build more JAX-RS recipes.

How to do it...

1. First, we create a class that will be our server:

```
public class ServerMock {

    public static final URI CONTEXT =
    URI.create("http://localhost:8080/");
    public static final String BASE_PATH = "ssevents";

    public static void main(String[] args) {
        try {
            final ResourceConfig resourceConfig = new
            ResourceConfig(SseResource.class);

            final HttpServer server =
            GrizzlyHttpServerFactory.createHttpServer(CONTEXT,
            resourceConfig, false);
            server.start();

            System.out.println(String.format("Mock Server started
            at %s%s", CONTEXT, BASE_PATH));

            Thread.currentThread().join();
        } catch (IOException | InterruptedException ex) {
            System.out.println(ex.getMessage());
        }
    }
}
```

2. Then, we create a JAX-RS endpoint to send the events to the clients:

```
@Path(ServerMock.BASE_PATH)
public class SseResource {

    private static volatile SseEventSink SINK = null;

    @GET
    @Produces(MediaType.SERVER_SENT_EVENTS)
    public void getMessageQueue(@Context SseEventSink sink) {
        SseResource.SINK = sink;
    }

    @POST
    public void addMessage(final String message, @Context Sse sse)
    throws IOException {
        if (SINK != null) {
```

```
                    SINK.send(sse.newEventBuilder()
                        .name("sse-message")
                        .id(String.valueOf(System.currentTimeMillis()))
                        .data(String.class, message)
                        .comment("")
                        .build());
                }
            }
        }
```

3. Then, we create a client class to consume the events generated from the server:

```
public class ClientConsumer {

    public static final Client CLIENT = ClientBuilder.newClient();
    public static final WebTarget WEB_TARGET =
    CLIENT.target(ServerMock.CONTEXT
    + BASE_PATH);
    public static void main(String[] args) {
        consume();
    }

    private static void consume() {

        try (final SseEventSource sseSource =
                    SseEventSource
                        .target(WEB_TARGET)
                        .build()) {

            sseSource.register(System.out::println);
            sseSource.open();

            for (int counter=0; counter < 5; counter++) {
                System.out.println(" ");
                for (int innerCounter=0; innerCounter < 5;
                innerCounter++) {
                    WEB_TARGET.request().post(Entity.json("event "
                    + innerCounter));
                }
                Thread.sleep(1000);
            }
            CLIENT.close();
            System.out.println("\n All messages consumed");
        } catch (InterruptedException e) {
            System.out.println(e.getMessage());
        }
    }
}
```

To try it out, you have to first run the `ServerMock` class and then the `ClientConsumer` class. If everything worked well, you should see something like this:

```
InboundEvent{name='sse-message', id='1502228257736', comment='',
data=event 0}
  InboundEvent{name='sse-message', id='1502228257753', comment='',
data=event 1}
  InboundEvent{name='sse-message', id='1502228257758', comment='',
data=event 2}
  InboundEvent{name='sse-message', id='1502228257763', comment='',
data=event 3}
  InboundEvent{name='sse-message', id='1502228257768', comment='',
data=event 4}
```

These are the messages sent from the server to the client.

How it works...

This recipe is made up of three parts:

- The server, represented by the `ServerMock` class
- The SSE engine, represented by the `SseResource` class
- The client, represented by the `ClientConsumer` class

So once `ServerMock` is instantiated, it registers the `SseResource` class:

```
final ResourceConfig resourceConfig = new
ResourceConfig(SseResource.class);
final HttpServer server =
GrizzlyHttpServerFactory.createHttpServer(CONTEXT, resourceConfig, false);
server.start();
```

Then two key methods from `SseResource` take place. The first one adds messages to the server queue:

```
addMessage(final String message, @Context Sse sse)
```

The second one consumes this queue and sends the messages to the clients:

```
@GET
@Produces(MediaType.SERVER_SENT_EVENTS)
public void getMessageQueue(@Context SseEventSink sink)
```

Note that this one has a media type `SERVER_SENT_EVENTS`, introduced in this version for this very purpose. And finally, we have our client. In this recipe, it is both posting and consuming messages.

It consumes here:

```
sseSource.register(System.out::println);
sseSource.open();
```

It posts here:

```
ServerMock.WEB_TARGET.request().post(Entity.json("event " + innerCounter));
```

See also

- You can stay tuned with everything related to JAX-RS at `https://github.com/jax-rs`
- The source code of this recipe is at `https://github.com/eldermoraes/javaee8-cookbook/tree/master/chapter01/ch01-jaxrs`

Running your first JSF 2.3 code

JavaServer Faces (JSF) is the Java technology made to simplify the process of building a UIs, despite how it's made for the frontend and the UI is built in the backend.

With JSF, you can build components and use (or reuse) them in the UI in an extensible way. You can also use other powerful APIs, such as CDI and Bean Validation, to improve your application and its architecture.

In this recipe, we will use the `Validator` and `Converter` interfaces with the new feature introduced by version 2.3, which is the possibility of using them with generic parameters.

Getting ready

First, we need to add the dependencies needed:

```xml
<dependency>
    <groupId>javax</groupId>
    <artifactId>javaee-api</artifactId>
    <version>8.0</version>
    <scope>provided</scope>
</dependency>
```

How to do it...

1. Let's create a `User` class as the main object of our recipe:

```java
public class User implements Serializable {

    private String name;
    private String email;

    public User(String name, String email) {
        this.name = name;
        this.email = email;
    }
    //DON'T FORGET THE GETTERS AND SETTERS
    //THIS RECIPE WON'T WORK WITHOUT THEM
}
```

2. Now, we create a `UserBean` class to manage our UI:

```java
@Named
@ViewScoped
public class UserBean implements Serializable {

    private User user;
    public UserBean(){
        user = new User("Elder Moraes", "elder@eldermoraes.com");
    }

    public void userAction(){
        FacesContext.getCurrentInstance().addMessage(null,
                new FacesMessage("Name|Password welformed"));
    }

    //DON'T FORGET THE GETTERS AND SETTERS
```

```
            //THIS RECIPE WON'T WORK WITHOUT THEM
    }
```

3. Now, we implement the `Converter` interface with a `User` parameter:

```
@FacesConverter("userConverter")
public class UserConverter implements Converter<User> {

    @Override
    public String getAsString(FacesContext fc, UIComponent uic,
    User user) {
        return user.getName() + "|" + user.getEmail();
    }

    @Override
    public User getAsObject(FacesContext fc, UIComponent uic,
    String string) {
        return new User(string.substring(0, string.indexOf("|")),
        string.substring(string.indexOf("|") + 1));
    }

}
```

4. Now, we implement the `Validator` interface with a `User` parameter:

```
@FacesValidator("userValidator")
public class UserValidator implements Validator<User> {

    @Override
    public void validate(FacesContext fc, UIComponent uic,
    User user)
    throws ValidatorException {
        if(!user.getEmail().contains("@")){
            throw new ValidatorException(new FacesMessage(null,
                                         "Malformed e-mail"));
        }
    }
}
```

5. And then we create our UI using all of them:

```
<h:body>
    <h:form>
        <h:panelGrid columns="3">
            <h:outputLabel value="Name|E-mail:"
            for="userNameEmail"/>
            <h:inputText id="userNameEmail"
            value="#{userBean.user}"
```

```
                converter="userConverter" validator="userValidator"/>
                <h:message for="userNameEmail"/>
            </h:panelGrid>
            <h:commandButton value="Validate"
            action="#{userBean.userAction()}"/>
        </h:form>
    </h:body>
```

Don't forget to run it in a Java EE 8 server.

How it works...

The UserBean class manages the communication between the UI and the server. Once you instantiate the user object, it is available for both of them.

That's why when you run it, the Name | E-mail is already filled (the user object is instantiated when the UserBean class is created by the server).

We associated the userAction() method from the UserBean class to the Validate button of the UI:

```
<h:commandButton value="Validate" action="#{userBean.userAction()}"/>
```

You can create other methods in UserBean and do the same to empower your application.

The whole core of our recipe is represented by just a single line in the UI:

```
<h:inputText id="userNameEmail" value="#{userBean.user}"
converter="userConverter" validator="userValidator"/>
```

So, our two implemented interfaces used here are userConverter and userValidator.

Basically, the UserConverter class (with getAsString and getAsObject methods) converts an object to/from a string and vice versa, according to the logic defined by you.

We have just mentioned it in the preceding code snippet:

```
value="#{userBean.user}"
```

The server uses the userConverter object, calls the getAsString method, and prints the result using the preceding expression language.

Finally, the `UserValidator` class is automatically called when you submit the form, by calling its `validate` method, and applying the rules defined by you.

There's more...

You could increase the validators by adding a Bean Validation on it and, for example, defining the `email` property from `User` with an `@Email` constraint.

See also

- You can stay tuned with everything related to JSF at `https://javaserverfaces.github.io/`
- The source code of this recipe is at `https://github.com/eldermoraes/javaee8-cookbook/tree/master/chapter01/ch01-jsf`

Running your first JSON-P 1.1 code

JSON-Pointer is the Java API for JSON processing. By processing, we mean generating, transforming, parsing, and querying JSON strings and/or objects.

In this recipe, you will learn how to use JSON Pointer to get a specific value from a JSON message in a very easy way.

Getting ready

Let's get our `dependency`:

```
<dependency>
      <dependency>
          <groupId>javax</groupId>
          <artifactId>javaee-api</artifactId>
          <version>8.0</version>
          <scope>provided</scope>
      </dependency>
</dependency>
```

How to do it...

1. First, we define a JSON message to represent a `User` object:

```
{
  "user": {
    "email": "elder@eldermoraes.com",
    "name": "Elder",
    "profile": [
      {
        "id": 1
      },
      {
        "id": 2
      },
      {
        "id": 3
      }
    ]
  }
}
```

2. Now, we create a method to read it and print the values we want:

```
public class JPointer {

    public static void main(String[] args) throws IOException{
        try (InputStream is =
JPointer.class.getClassLoader().getResourceAsStream("user.json");
                JsonReader jr = Json.createReader(is)) {

            JsonStructure js = jr.read();
            JsonPointer jp = Json.createPointer("/user/profile");
            JsonValue jv = jp.getValue(js);
            System.out.println("profile: " + jv);
        }
    }
}
```

The execution of this code prints the following:

```
profile: [{"id":1},{"id":2},{"id":3}]
```

How it works...

The JSON Pointer is a standard defined by the **Internet Engineering Task Force** (**IETF**) under **Request for Comments** (**RFC**) 6901. The standard basically says that a JSON Pointer is a string that identifies a specific value in a JSON document.

Without a JSON Pointer, you would need to parse the whole message and iterate through it until you find the desired value; probably lots of ifs, elses, and things like that.

So, JSON Pointer helps you to decrease the written code dramatically by doing this kind of operation in a very elegant way.

See also

- You can stay tuned with everything related to JSON-P at `https://javaee.github.io/jsonp/`
- The source code of this recipe is at `https://github.com/eldermoraes/javaee8-cookbook/tree/master/chapter01/ch01-jsonp`

Running your first JSON-B code

JSON-B is an API for converting Java objects to/from JSON messages in a standardized way. It defines a default mapping algorithm to convert Java classes to JSON and still lets you customize your own algorithms.

With JSON-B, Java EE now has a complete set of tools to work with JSON, such as JSON API, and JSON-P. No third-party frameworks are needed anymore (although you are still free to use them).

This quick recipe will show you how to use JSON-B to convert a Java object to and from a JSON message.

Getting ready

Let's add our dependencies to the project:

```
<dependencies>
    <dependency>
        <groupId>org.eclipse</groupId>
```

```
        <artifactId>yasson</artifactId>
        <version>1.0</version>
    </dependency>
    <dependency>
        <groupId>org.glassfish</groupId>
        <artifactId>javax.json</artifactId>
        <version>1.1</version>
    </dependency>
</dependencies>
```

How to do it...

1. Let's create a `User` class as a model for our JSON message:

```
public class User {

    private String name;
    private String email;

    public User(){
    }

    public User(String name, String email) {
        this.name = name;
        this.email = email;
    }

    @Override
    public String toString() {
        return "User{" + "name=" + name + ", email=" + email + '}';
    }

    //DON'T FORGET THE GETTERS AND SETTERS
    //THIS RECIPE WON'T WORK WITHOUT THEM

}
```

2. Then, let's create a class to use JSON-B to transform an object:

```
public class JsonBUser {
    public static void main(String[] args) throws Exception {
        User user = new User("Elder", "elder@eldermoraes.com");
        Jsonb jb = JsonbBuilder.create();
        String jsonUser = jb.toJson(user);
        User u = jb.fromJson(jsonUser, User.class);
        jb.close();
```

```
                    System.out.println("json: " + jsonUser);
                    System.out.println("user: " + u);
             }
         }
```

The result printed is:

```
json: {"email":"elder@eldermoraes.com","name":"Elder"}
 user: User{name=Elder, email=elder@eldermoraes.com}
```

The first line is the object transformed into a JSON string. The second is the same string converted into an object.

How it works...

It uses the getters and setters defined in the User class to transform both ways and that's why they are so important.

See also

- You can stay tuned with everything related to JSON-B at http://json-b.net/
- The source code of this recipe is at https://github.com/eldermoraes/javaee8-cookbook/tree/master/chapter01/ch01-jsonb

Running your first Servlet 4.0 code

Servlet 4.0 is one the of biggest APIs of Java EE 8. Since the very beginning of the Java EE platform (the old J2EE), the Servlet specification has always played a key role.

The coolest additions of this version are surely HTTP/2.0 and Server Push. Both of them bring performance improvements to your application.

This recipe will use Server Push to do one of the most basic tasks in a web page—loading an image.

Getting ready

Let's add the dependencies that we need:

```xml
<dependency>
    <groupId>javax</groupId>
    <artifactId>javaee-api</artifactId>
    <version>8.0</version>
    <scope>provided</scope>
</dependency>
```

How to do it...

1. We will create a servlet:

```java
@WebServlet(name = "ServerPush", urlPatterns = {"/ServerPush"})
public class ServerPush extends HttpServlet {

    @Override
    protected void doGet(HttpServletRequest request,
    HttpServletResponse
    response) throws ServletException, IOException {

        PushBuilder pb = request.newPushBuilder();
        if (pb != null) {
            pb.path("images/javaee-logo.png")
              .addHeader("content-type", "image/png")
              .push();
        }

        try (PrintWriter writer = response.getWriter();) {
            StringBuilder html = new StringBuilder();
            html.append("<html>");
            html.append("<center>");
            html.append("<img src='images/javaee-logo.png'><br>");
            html.append("<h2>Image pushed by ServerPush</h2>");
            html.append("</center>");
            html.append("</html>");
            writer.write(html.toString());
        }
    }
}
```

2. To try it, run the project in a Java EE 8 server and open this URL:

```
https://localhost:8080/ch01-servlet/ServerPush
```

How it works...

We use the `PushBuilder` object to send an image to the client before it is requested by the `img src` tag. In other words, the browser doesn't need to do another request (what it usually does with `img src`) to have an image available for rendering.

It might seem as if it doesn't make too much difference for a single image, but it would with dozens, hundreds, or thousands of images. Less traffic for your client and from your server. Better performance for all!

There's more...

If you are using JSF, you can get the benefits from Server Push for free! You don't even need to rewrite a single line of your code, as JSF relies on the Server Push specification.

Just make sure that you run it under the HTTPS protocol, as HTTP/2.0 only works under it.

See also

- You can stay tuned with everything related to the Servlet specification at `https://github.com/javaee/servlet-spec`
- The source code of this recipe is at `https://github.com/eldermoraes/javaee8-cookbook/tree/master/chapter01/ch01-servlet`

Running your first Security API code

Security is one of the top concerns when you build an enterprise application. Luckily, the Java EE platform now has this API that handles many of the enterprise requirements in a standardized way.

In this recipe, you will learn how to define roles and give them the right authorization based on rules defined in the methods that manage sensitive data.

Getting ready

We start by adding our dependencies to the project:

```xml
<dependency>
    <groupId>junit</groupId>
    <artifactId>junit</artifactId>
    <version>4.12</version>
    <scope>test</scope>
</dependency>
<dependency>
    <groupId>org.apache.tomee</groupId>
    <artifactId>openejb-core</artifactId>
    <version>7.0.4</version>
</dependency>
<dependency>
    <groupId>javax</groupId>
    <artifactId>javaee-api</artifactId>
    <version>8.0</version>
    <scope>provided</scope>
</dependency>
```

How to do it...

1. We first create a User entity:

```java
@Entity
public class User implements Serializable{

    @Id
    private Long id;
    private String name;
    private String email;

    public User(){
    }

    public User(Long id, String name, String email) {
        this.id = id;
        this.name = name;
        this.email = email;
    }
    //DON'T FORGET THE GETTERS AND SETTERS
    //THIS RECIPE WON'T WORK WITHOUT THEM
}
```

2. Here, we create a class to store our security roles:

```
public class Roles {
    public static final String ADMIN = "ADMIN";
    public static final String OPERATOR = "OPERATOR";
}
```

3. Then, we create a stateful bean to manage our user operations:

```
@Stateful
public class UserBean {

    @PersistenceContext(unitName = "ch01-security-pu",
    type = PersistenceContextType.EXTENDED)
    private EntityManager em;

    @RolesAllowed({Roles.ADMIN, Roles.OPERATOR})
    public void add(User user){
        em.persist(user);
    }

    @RolesAllowed({Roles.ADMIN})
    public void remove(User user){
        em.remove(user);
    }

    @RolesAllowed({Roles.ADMIN})
    public void update(User user){
        em.merge(user);
    }

    @PermitAll
    public List<User> get(){
        Query q = em.createQuery("SELECT u FROM User as u ");
        return q.getResultList();
    }
```

4. Now, we need to create an executor for each role:

```
public class RoleExecutor {

    public interface Executable {
        void execute() throws Exception;
    }

    @Stateless
    @RunAs(Roles.ADMIN)
    public static class AdminExecutor {
```

```
        public void run(Executable executable) throws Exception {
            executable.execute();
        }
    }

    @Stateless
    @RunAs(Roles.OPERATOR)
    public static class OperatorExecutor {
        public void run(Executable executable) throws Exception {
            executable.execute();
        }
    }
}
```

5. And finally, we create a test class to try our security rules.

Our code uses three test methods: asAdmin(), asOperator(), and asAnonymous().

1. First, it tests asAdmin():

```
//Lot of setup code before this point

@Test
public void asAdmin() throws Exception {
    adminExecutor.run(() -> {
        userBean.add(new User(1L, "user1", "user1@user.com"));
        userBean.add(new User(2L, "user2", "user2@user.com"));
        userBean.add(new User(3L, "user3", "user3@user.com"));
        userBean.add(new User(4L, "user4", "user4@user.com"));

        List<User> list = userBean.get();

        list.forEach((user) -> {
            userBean.remove(user);
        });

        Assert.assertEquals("userBean.get()", 0,
        userBean.get().size());
    });
}
```

2. Then it tests asOperator():

```
@Test
public void asOperator() throws Exception {

    operatorExecutor.run(() -> {
        userBean.add(new User(1L, "user1", "user1@user.com"));
```

```
                userBean.add(new User(2L, "user2", "user2@user.com"));
                userBean.add(new User(3L, "user3", "user3@user.com"));
                userBean.add(new User(4L, "user4", "user4@user.com"));

                List<User> list = userBean.get();

                list.forEach((user) -> {
                    try {
                        userBean.remove(user);
                        Assert.fail("Operator was able to remove user " +
                        user.getName());
                    } catch (EJBAccessException e) {
                    }
                });
                Assert.assertEquals("userBean.get()", 4,
                userBean.get().size());
        });
    }
```

4. And, finally it tests `asAnonymous()`:

```
@Test
public void asAnonymous() {

    try {
        userBean.add(new User(1L, "elder",
        "elder@eldermoraes.com"));
        Assert.fail("Anonymous user should not add users");
    } catch (EJBAccessException e) {
    }

    try {
        userBean.remove(new User(1L, "elder",
        "elder@eldermoraes.com"));
        Assert.fail("Anonymous user should not remove users");
    } catch (EJBAccessException e) {
    }

    try {
        userBean.get();
    } catch (EJBAccessException e) {
        Assert.fail("Everyone can list users");
    }
}
```

This class is huge! For the full source code, check the link at the end of the recipe.

How it works...

The whole point in this recipe is to do with the @RolesAllowed, @RunsAs, and @PermitAll annotations. They define what operations each role can do and what happens when a user tries an operation using the wrong role.

There's more...

What we did here is called **programmatic security;** that is, we defined the security rules and roles through our code (the program). There's another approach called **declarative security**, where you declare the rules and roles through application and server configurations.

One good step up for this recipe is if you evolve the roles management to a source outside the application, such as a database or a service.

See also

- You can stay tuned with everything related to Security API at https://github. com/javaee-security-spec
- The source code of this recipe is at https://github.com/eldermoraes/javaee8-cookbook/tree/master/chapter01/ch01-security

Running your first MVC 1.0 code

If you are following the news about Java EE 8, you may now be wondering: *why is MVC 1.0 here if it was dropped from the Java EE 8 umbrella?*

Yes, it is true. MVC 1.0 doesn't belong (anymore) to the Java EE 8 release. But it didn't reduce the importance of this great API and I'm sure it will change the way some other APIs work in future releases (for example, JSF).

So why not cover it here? You will use it anyway.

This recipe will show you how to use a Controller (the C) to inject a Model (the M) into the View (the V). It also brings some CDI and JAX-RS to the party.

Getting ready

Add the proper dependencies to your project:

```
<dependency>
    <groupId>javax</groupId>
    <artifactId>javaee-api</artifactId>
    <version>8.0</version>
    <scope>provided</scope>
</dependency>
<dependency>
    <groupId>javax.mvc</groupId>
    <artifactId>javax.mvc-api</artifactId>
    <version>1.0-pr</version>
</dependency>
```

How to do it...

1. Start by creating a root for your JAX-RS endpoints:

```
@ApplicationPath("webresources")
public class AppConfig extends Application{
}
```

2. Create a User class (this will be your MODEL):

```
public class User {

    private String name;
    private String email;

    public User(String name, String email) {
        this.name = name;
        this.email = email;
    }

    //DON'T FORGET THE GETTERS AND SETTERS
    //THIS RECIPE WON'T WORK WITHOUT THEM
}
```

3. Now, create a Session Bean, which will be injected later in your Controller:

```
@Stateless
public class UserBean {
    public User getUser(){
        return new User("Elder", "elder@eldermoraes.com");
    }
}
```

4. Then, create the Controller:

```
@Controller
@Path("userController")
public class UserController {
    @Inject
    Models models;
    @Inject
    UserBean userBean;
    @GET
    public String user(){
        models.put("user", userBean.getUser());
        return "/user.jsp";
    }
}
```

5. And finally, the web page (the View):

```
<head>
    <meta http-equiv="Content-Type" content="text/html;
    charset=UTF-8">
    <title>User MVC</title>
</head>
<body>
    <h1>${user.name}/${user.email}</h1>
</body>
```

Run it on a Java EE 8 server and access this URL:

```
http://localhost:8080/ch01-mvc/webresources/userController
```

How it works...

The main actor in this whole scenario is the `Models` class injected into the Controller:

```
@Inject
Models models;
```

It's a class from MVC 1.0 API that owns the responsibility, in this recipe, of letting the User object be available for the View layer. It's injected (using CDI) and uses another injected bean, userBean, to do it:

```
models.put("user", userBean.getUser());
```

So, the View can easily access the values from the User object using expression language:

```
<h1>${user.name}/${user.email}</h1>
```

See also

- You can stay tuned with everything related to MVC specification at https://github.com/mvc-spec
- The source code of this recipe is at https://github.com/eldermoraes/javaee8-cookbook/tree/master/chapter01/ch01-mvc

2
Server-Side Development

Java EE can be seen as being **made for server-side development**. Most of the APIs are powerful for server-side processing and managing.

This chapter will provide you with some common and useful scenarios that you may face as a Java EE developer and will show you how you should deal with them.

In this chapter, we will cover the following recipes:

- Using CDI to inject context and dependency
- Using Bean Validation for data validation
- Using servlet for request and response management
- Using Server Push to make objects available beforehand
- Using EJB and JTA for transaction management
- Using EJB to deal with concurrency
- Using JPA for smart data persistence
- Using EJB and JPA for data caching
- Using batch processing

Using CDI to inject context and dependency

Context and Dependency Injection for Java EE (CDI) is one of the most important APIs under the Java EE umbrella. Introduced in Java EE 6, it now has a big influence over many other APIs.

In the recipe, you will learn how to use CDI in a couple of different ways and situations.

Getting ready

First, let's add the required dependency needed:

```
<dependency>
    <groupId>javax.enterprise</groupId>
    <artifactId>cdi-api</artifactId>
    <version>2.0</version>
    <scope>provided</scope>
</dependency>
<dependency>
    <groupId>javax</groupId>
    <artifactId>javaee-web-api</artifactId>
    <version>7.0</version>
    <scope>provided</scope>
</dependency>
```

How to do it...

1. We are going to build a JAX-RS based application, so we will start by preparing the application to perform:

```
@ApplicationPath("webresources")
public class Application extends javax.ws.rs.core.Application {
}
```

2. Then, we create a User application as our main object:

```
public class User implements Serializable {

    private String name;
    private String email;

    //DO NOT FORGET TO ADD THE GETTERS AND SETTERS
}
```

Our User class doesn't have a default constructor, so CDI doesn't know how to construct the class when it tries to inject it. So, we create a factory class and use the @Produces annotation over its methods:

```
public class UserFactory implements Serializable{

    @Produces
    public User getUser() {
        return new User("Elder Moraes", "elder@eldermoraes.com");
```

3. Let's create an enumeration to list our profile types:

```
public enum ProfileType {
    ADMIN, OPERATOR;
}
```

4. Here, we create a custom annotation:

```
@Qualifier
@Retention(RetentionPolicy.RUNTIME)
@Target({ElementType.TYPE, ElementType.FIELD, ElementType.METHOD,
ElementType.PARAMETER})
public @interface Profile {
    ProfileType value();
}
```

5. Add them to an interface to prototype the user profile behavior:

```
public interface UserProfile {
    ProfileType type();
}
```

Now that we have defined the profile list and its behavior with respect to the user, we can give it a proper implementation for an admin profile:

```
@Profile(ProfileType.ADMIN)
public class ImplAdmin implements UserProfile{

    @Override
    public ProfileType type() {
        System.out.println("User is admin");
        return ProfileType.ADMIN;
    }
}
```

And the same can be done for an operator profile:

```
@Profile(ProfileType.OPERATOR)
@Default
public class ImplOperator implements UserProfile{

    @Override
    public ProfileType type() {
        System.out.println("User is operator");
```

```
                    return ProfileType.OPERATOR;
        }
    }
```

6. Then, we create a REST endpoint by injecting all the objects that we are going to use into it:

```
@Path("userservice/")
@RequestScoped
public class UserService {
    @Inject
    private User user;
    @Inject
    @Profile(ProfileType.ADMIN)
    private UserProfile userProfileAdmin;
    @Inject
    @Profile(ProfileType.OPERATOR)
    private UserProfile userProfileOperator;
    @Inject
    private UserProfile userProfileDefault;
    @Inject
    private Event<User> userEvent;

        . . .
```

7. This method gets the user injected by CDI and sends it to the result page:

```
@GET
@Path("getUser")
public Response getUser(@Context HttpServletRequest request,
        @Context HttpServletResponse response)
        throws ServletException, IOException{
    request.setAttribute("result", user);
    request.getRequestDispatcher("/result.jsp")
    .forward(request, response);
    return Response.ok().build();
}
```

8. This one does the same with an admin profile:

```
@GET
@Path("getProfileAdmin")
public Response getProfileAdmin(@Context HttpServletRequest request,
        @Context HttpServletResponse response)
        throws ServletException, IOException{
        request.setAttribute("result",
        fireUserEvents(userProfileAdmin.type()));
         request.getRequestDispatcher("/result.jsp")
```

```
        .forward(request, response);
    return Response.ok().build();
}
```

9. And this one does the same with an operator profile:

```
@GET
@Path("getProfileOperator")
public Response getProfileOperator(@Context HttpServletRequest request,
        @Context HttpServletResponse response)
        throws ServletException, IOException{
        request.setAttribute("result",
        fireUserEvents(userProfileOperator.type()));
        request.getRequestDispatcher("/result.jsp")
        .forward(request, response);
    return Response.ok().build();
}
```

10. Finally, we send the default profile to the result page:

```
@GET
@Path("getProfileDefault")
public Response getProfileDefault(@Context HttpServletRequest request,
        @Context HttpServletResponse response)
        throws ServletException, IOException{
        request.setAttribute("result",
        fireUserEvents(userProfileDefault.type()));
        request.getRequestDispatcher("/result.jsp")
        .forward(request, response);
        return Response.ok().build();
}
```

11. We use the `fireUserEvents` method to fire an event and async events over a previously injected `User` object:

```
private ProfileType fireUserEvents(ProfileType type){
    userEvent.fire(user);
    userEvent.fireAsync(user);
    return type;
}
public void sendUserNotification(@Observes User user){
    System.out.println("sendUserNotification: " + user);
}
public void sendUserNotificationAsync(@ObservesAsync User user){
    System.out.println("sendUserNotificationAsync: " + user);
}
```

12. So, we build a page to call each endpoint method:

```
<body>
 <a href="http://localhost:8080/ch02-
 cdi/webresources/userservice/getUser">getUser</a>
 <br>
 <a href="http://localhost:8080/ch02-
 cdi/webresources/userservice/getProfileAdmin">getProfileAdmin</a>
 <br>
 <a href="http://localhost:8080/ch02-
 cdi/webresources/userservice/getProfileOperator">getProfileOperator
 </a>
 <br>
 <a href="http://localhost:8080/ch02-
 cdi/webresources/userservice/getProfileDefault">getProfileDefault</
 a>
</body>
```

13. And finally, we use an expression language to print the result at the result page:

```
<body>
    <h1>${result}</h1>
    <a href="javascript:window.history.back();">Back</a>
</body>
```

How it works...

Well, there's a lot happening in the previous section! We should first have a look at the @Produces annotation. It is a CDI annotation that says to the server: *"Hey! This method knows how to construct a User object."*

As we didn't create a default constructor for the User class, the getUser method from our factory will be injected into our context as one.

The second annotation is our custom annotation @Profile that has our enumeration ProfileType as a parameter. It is the qualifier of our UserProfile objects.

Now, let's have a look at these declarations:

```
@Profile(ProfileType.ADMIN)
public class ImplAdmin implements UserProfile{
    ...
}

@Profile(ProfileType.OPERATOR)
```

```
@Default
public class ImplOperator implements UserProfile{
    ...
}
```

This code will *teach* CDI how to inject a `UserProfile` object:

- If the object is annotated as `@Profile(ProfileType.ADMIN)`, use `ImplAdmin`
- If the object is annotated as `@Profile(ProfileType.OPERATOR)`, use `ImplOperator`
- If the object is not annotated, use `ImplOperator`, as it has the `@Default` annotation

We can see them in action in our endpoint declaration:

```
@Inject
@Profile(ProfileType.ADMIN)
private UserProfile userProfileAdmin;
@Inject
@Profile(ProfileType.OPERATOR)
private UserProfile userProfileOperator;
@Inject
private UserProfile userProfileDefault;
```

So CDI is helping us to use the context to inject the right implementation of our `UserProfile` interface.

Looking at the endpoint methods, we see this:

```
@GET
@Path("getUser")
public Response getUser(@Context HttpServletRequest request,
        @Context HttpServletResponse response)
        throws ServletException, IOException{
    request.setAttribute("result", user);
    request.getRequestDispatcher("/result.jsp")
    .forward(request, response);
    return Response.ok().build();
}
```

Note that we included `HttpServletRequest` and `HttpServletResponse` as parameters for our method, but annotated them as `@Context`. So even though this is not a servlet context (when we have easy access to request and response references), we can ask CDI to give us a proper reference to them.

And finally, we have our user event engine:

```
@Inject
private Event<User> userEvent;

...

private ProfileType fireUserEvents(ProfileType type){
    userEvent.fire(user);
    userEvent.fireAsync(user);
    return type;
}
public void sendUserNotification(@Observes User user){
    System.out.println("sendUserNotification: " + user);
}
public void sendUserNotificationAsync(@ObservesAsync User user){
    System.out.println("sendUserNotificationAsync: " + user);
}
```

So, we are using the `@Observes` and `@ObserversAsync` annotations to say to CDI: "*Hey CDI! Watch over User object... when somebody fires an event over it, I want you to do something.*"

And for "something," CDI understands this as calling the `sendUserNotification` and `sendUserNotificationAsync` methods. Try it!

Obviously, `@Observers` will be executed synchronously and `@ObservesAsync` asynchronously.

There's more...

We used a GlassFish 5 to run this recipe. You can do it with whatever Java EE 8 compatible server you want, and you can even use CDI with Java SE without any server. Have a look at the CDI recipe from `Chapter 1`, *New Features and Improvements*.

See also

- You can see the full source code of this recipe at `https://github.com/eldermoraes/javaee8-cookbook/tree/master/chapter02/ch02-cdi`

Using Bean Validation for data validation

You can use Bean Validation to constrain your data in many different ways. In this recipe, we are going to use it to validate a JSF form, so we can validate it as soon as the user tries to submit it, and avoid any invalid data right away.

Getting ready

First, we add our dependencies:

```
<dependency>
    <groupId>javax.validation</groupId>
    <artifactId>validation-api</artifactId>
    <version>2.0.0.Final</version>
</dependency>
<dependency>
    <groupId>org.hibernate.validator</groupId>
    <artifactId>hibernate-validator</artifactId>
    <version>6.0.1.Final</version>
</dependency>
<dependency>
    <groupId>javax</groupId>
    <artifactId>javaee-web-api</artifactId>
    <version>7.0</version>
    <scope>provided</scope>
</dependency>
```

How to do it...

1. Let's create a `User` object that will be attached to our JSF page:

```
@Named
@RequestScoped
public class User {
    @NotBlank (message = "Name should not be blank")
    @Size (min = 4, max = 10,message = "Name should be between
    4 and 10 characters")
    private String name;
    @Email (message = "Invalid e-mail format")
    @NotBlank (message = "E-mail shoud not be blank")
    private String email;
    @PastOrPresent (message = "Created date should be
    past or present")
```

```
@NotNull (message = "Create date should not be null")
private LocalDate created;
@Future (message = "Expires should be a future date")
@NotNull (message = "Expires should not be null")
private LocalDate expires;

//DO NOT FORGET TO IMPLEMENT THE GETTERS AND SETTERS

...
```

2. Then we define the method that will be fired once all data is valid:

```
public void valid(){
    FacesContext
            .getCurrentInstance()
            .addMessage(
                null,
                new FacesMessage(FacesMessage.SEVERITY_INFO,
                "Your data is valid", ""));
}
```

3. And now our JSF page references each `User` class fields declared:

```
<h:body>
 <h:form>
 <h:outputLabel for="name" value="Name" />
 <h:inputText id="name" value="#{user.name}" />
 <br/>
 <h:outputLabel for="email" value="E-mail" />
 <h:inputText id="email" value="#{user.email}" />
 <br/>
 <h:outputLabel for="created" value="Created" />
 <h:inputText id="created" value="#{user.created}">
     <f:convertDateTime type="localDate" pattern="dd/MM/uuuu" />
 </h:inputText>
 <br/>
 <h:outputLabel for="expire" value="Expire" />
 <h:inputText id="expire" value="#{user.expires}">
     <f:convertDateTime type="localDate" pattern="dd/MM/uuuu" />
 </h:inputText>
 <br/>
 <h:commandButton value="submit" type="submit"
action="#{user.valid()}" />
 </h:form>
</h:body>
```

Now, if you run this code, you will get all fields validated once you click the **Submit** button. Try it!

How it works...

Let's check each declared constraint:

```
@NotBlank (message = "Name should not be blank")
@Size (min = 4, max = 10,message = "Name should be between
       4 and 10 characters")
private String name;
```

The @NotBlank annotation will deny not only null values, but also white spaces values, and @Size speaks for itself:

```
@Email (message = "Invalid e-mail format")
@NotBlank (message = "E-mail shoud not be blank")
private String email;
```

The @Email constraint will check the email string format:

```
@PastOrPresent (message = "Created date should be past or present")
@NotNull (message = "Create date should not be null")
private LocalDate created;
```

@PastOrPresent will constrain LocalDate to be in the past or until the present date. It can't be in the future.

Here we can't use @NotBlank, as there is no blank date, only null, so we avoid it using @NotNull:

```
@Future (message = "Expires should be a future date")
@NotNull (message = "Expires should not be null")
private LocalDate expires;
```

This is the same as the last one, but constraints for a future date.

In our UI, there are two places worth a careful look:

```
<h:inputText id="created" value="#{user.created}">
   <f:convertDateTime type="localDate" pattern="dd/MM/uuuu" />
</h:inputText>

...

<h:inputText id="expire" value="#{user.expires}">
   <f:convertDateTime type="localDate" pattern="dd/MM/uuuu" />
</h:inputText>
```

We are using `convertDateTime` to automatically convert the data inputted into `inputText` according to the `dd/MM/uuuu` pattern.

See also

- You can check the full source code of this recipe at `https://github.com/eldermoraes/javaee8-cookbook/tree/master/chapter02/ch02-beanvalidation`

Using servlet for request and response management

The Servlet API was created even before Java EE exists—actually before J2EE existed! It became part of EE in J2EE 1.2 (Servlet 2.2) in 1999.

This is a powerful tool to deal with a request/response context and this recipe will show you an example of how to do it.

Getting ready

Let's add our dependencies:

```
<dependency>
    <groupId>javax.servlet</groupId>
    <artifactId>javax.servlet-api</artifactId>
    <version>4.0.0-b05</version>
    <scope>provided</scope>
</dependency>
<dependency>
    <groupId>javax</groupId>
    <artifactId>javaee-web-api</artifactId>
    <version>7.0</version>
    <scope>provided</scope>
</dependency>
```

How to do it...

1. Let's create a User class for our recipe:

```
public class User {

    private String name;
    private String email;

    //DO NOT FORGET TO IMPLEMENT THE GETTERS AND SETTERS

}
```

2. And then our servlet:

```
@WebServlet(name = "UserServlet", urlPatterns = {"/UserServlet"})
public class UserServlet extends HttpServlet {
    private User user;
    @PostConstruct
    public void instantiateUser(){
        user = new User("Elder Moraes", "elder@eldermoraes.com");
    }

    . . .
```

 We use the @PostConstruct annotation over the instantiateUser() method. It says to the server that whenever this servlet is constructed (a new instance is up), it can run this method.

3. We also implement the init() and destroy() super methods:

```
@Override
public void init() throws ServletException {
    System.out.println("Servlet " + this.getServletName() +
                        " has started");
}

@Override
public void destroy() {
    System.out.println("Servlet " + this.getServletName() +
                        " has destroyed");
}
```

4. And we also implemented `doGet()` and `doPost()`:

```
@Override
protected void doGet(HttpServletRequest request,
HttpServletResponse response)
        throws ServletException, IOException {
    doRequest(request, response);
}

@Override
protected void doPost(HttpServletRequest request,
HttpServletResponse response)
        throws ServletException, IOException {
    doRequest(request, response);
}
```

5. Both `doGet()` and `doPost()` will call our custom method `doRequest()`:

```
protected void doRequest(HttpServletRequest request,
HttpServletResponse response)
        throws ServletException, IOException {
    response.setContentType("text/html;charset=UTF-8");
    try (PrintWriter out = response.getWriter()) {
        out.println("<html>");
        out.println("<head>");
        out.println("<title>Servlet UserServlet</title>");
        out.println("</head>");
        out.println("<body>");
        out.println("<h2>Servlet UserServlet at " +
                    request.getContextPath() + "</h2>");
        out.println("<h2>Now: " + new Date() + "</h2>");
        out.println("<h2>User: " + user.getName() + "/" +
                    user.getEmail() + "</h2>");
        out.println("</body>");
        out.println("</html>");
    }
}
```

6. And we finally have a web page to call our servlet:

```
<body>
    <a href="<%=request.getContextPath()%>/UserServlet">
    <%=request.getContextPath() %>/UserServlet</a>
</body>
```

How it works...

The Java EE server itself will call doGet() or doPost() methods, depending on the HTTP method used by the caller. In our recipe, we are redirecting them both to the same doRequest() method.

The init() method belongs to the servlet life cycle managed by the server and is executed as a first method after the servlet instantiation.

The destroy() method also belongs to the servlet life cycle and it's executed as the last method before the instance deallocation.

There's more...

The init() behavior seems like @PostConstruct, but this last one is executed before init(), so keep it in mind when using both.

The @PostConstruct is executed right after the default constructor.

Be careful when using the destroy() method and avoid holding any memory reference; otherwise, you can mess up with the servlet life cycle and run into memory leaks.

See also

- Check the full source code of this recipe at https://github.com/eldermoraes/javaee8-cookbook/tree/master/chapter02/ch02-servlet

Using Server Push to make objects available beforehand

One of the most important new features of Servlet 4.0 is the HTTP/2.0 support. It brings another cool and reliable feature—the Server Push.

This recipe will show you how to use Server Push in a filter and push the resources needed in every request that we want.

Getting ready

We should first add the dependencies needed:

```xml
<dependency>
    <groupId>javax.servlet</groupId>
    <artifactId>javax.servlet-api</artifactId>
    <version>4.0.0-b07</version>
    <scope>provided</scope>
</dependency>
<dependency>
    <groupId>javax</groupId>
    <artifactId>javaee-web-api</artifactId>
    <version>7.0</version>
    <scope>provided</scope>
</dependency>
```

How to do it...

1. We first create `UserServlet` that calls `user.jsp`:

```java
@WebServlet(name = "UserServlet", urlPatterns = {"/UserServlet"})
public class UserServlet extends HttpServlet {

    protected void doRequest(HttpServletRequest request,
                             HttpServletResponse response)
        throws ServletException, IOException {
        request.getRequestDispatcher("/user.jsp")
        .forward(request, response);
        System.out.println("Redirected to user.jsp");
    }

    @Override
    protected void doGet(HttpServletRequest request,
                         HttpServletResponse response)
        throws ServletException, IOException {
        doRequest(request, response);
    }

    @Override
    protected void doPost(HttpServletRequest request,
                          HttpServletResponse response)
        throws ServletException, IOException {
        doRequest(request, response);
    }
```

```
}
```

2. And we do the same with `ProfileServlet`, but by calling `profile.jsp`:

```java
@WebServlet(name = "ProfileServlet", urlPatterns =
{"/ProfileServlet"})
public class ProfileServlet extends HttpServlet {

    protected void doRequest(HttpServletRequest request,
                              HttpServletResponse response)
        throws ServletException, IOException {
      request.getRequestDispatcher("/profile.jsp").
      forward(request, response);
      System.out.println("Redirected to profile.jsp");
    }

    @Override
    protected void doGet(HttpServletRequest request,
                         HttpServletResponse response)
        throws ServletException, IOException {
      doRequest(request, response);
    }

    @Override
    protected void doPost(HttpServletRequest request,
                          HttpServletResponse response)
        throws ServletException, IOException {
      doRequest(request, response);
    }
}
```

3. And then we create a filter that will be executed on every request (`urlPatterns = {"/*"}`):

```java
@WebFilter(filterName = "PushFilter", urlPatterns = {"/*"})
public class PushFilter implements Filter {
    @Override
    public void doFilter(ServletRequest request,
    ServletResponse response,
        FilterChain chain)
        throws IOException, ServletException {
      HttpServletRequest httpReq = (HttpServletRequest)request;
      PushBuilder builder = httpReq.newPushBuilder();
      if (builder != null){
          builder
              .path("resources/javaee-logo.png")
              .path("resources/style.css")
```

```
                .path("resources/functions.js")
                .push();
            System.out.println("Resources pushed");
        }

        chain.doFilter(request, response);
    }
}
```

4. Here we create a page to call our servlets:

```html
<body>
 <a href="UserServlet">User</a>
 <br/>
 <a href="ProfileServlet">Profile</a>
</body>
```

5. And here are the pages called by the servlets. First is the `user.jsp` page:

```html
<head>
    <meta http-equiv="Content-Type" content="text/html;
     charset=UTF-8">
    <link rel="stylesheet" type="text/css"
     href="resources/style.css">
    <script src="resources/functions.js"></script>
    <title>User Push</title>
</head>

<body>
    <h1>User styled</h1>
    <img src="resources/javaee-logo.png">
    <br />
    <button onclick="message()">Message</button>
    <br />
    <a href="javascript:window.history.back();">Back</a>
</body>
```

6. Second, the `profile.jsp` page is called:

```html
<head>
    <meta http-equiv="Content-Type" content="text/html; charset=UTF-8">
    <link rel="stylesheet" type="text/css" href="resources/style.css">
    <script src="resources/functions.js"></script>
    <title>User Push</title>
</head>

<body>
    <h1>Profile styled</h1>
```

```
<img src="resources/javaee-logo.png">
<br />
<button onclick="message()">Message</button>
<br />
<a href="javascript:window.history.back();">Back</a>
</body>
```

How it works...

A web application running under HTTP/1.0 sends a request to the server when it finds references for an image file, CSS file, and any other resources needed to render a web page.

With HTTP/2.0 you still can do it, but now you can do better: the server can now push the resources beforehand, avoiding unnecessary new requests, decreasing the server load, and improving performance.

In this recipe, our resources are represented by the following:

```
<meta http-equiv="Content-Type" content="text/html; charset=UTF-8">
<link rel="stylesheet" type="text/css" href="resources/style.css">
<script src="resources/functions.js"></script>
```

And the push happens at this part of our filter:

```
HttpServletRequest httpReq = (HttpServletRequest)request;
PushBuilder builder = httpReq.newPushBuilder();
if (builder != null){
    builder
        .path("resources/javaee-logo.png")
        .path("resources/style.css")
        .path("resources/functions.js")
        .push();
    System.out.println("Resources pushed");
}
```

So when the browser needs those resources to render the web page, they are already available.

There's more...

Note that your browser needs to support the Server Push feature; otherwise, your page will work as usual. So make sure you check if PushBuilder is null before using it and ensure all users will have the working application.

Note that JSF 2.3 is built over the Server Push feature, so if you just migrate your JSF application to a Java EE 8 compatible server, you get its performance boost for free!

See also

- View the full source code of this recipe at `https://github.com/eldermoraes/javaee8-cookbook/tree/master/chapter02/ch02-serverpush`

Using EJB and JTA for transaction management

The Java Transaction API, or JTA, is an API that enables distributed transactions over the Java EE environment. It is most powerful when you delegate the transaction management to the server.

This recipe will show you how to do it!

Getting ready

First, add the dependencies:

```
<dependency>
    <groupId>org.hibernate</groupId>
    <artifactId>hibernate-entitymanager</artifactId>
    <version>4.3.1.Final</version>
</dependency>
<dependency>
    <groupId>junit</groupId>
    <artifactId>junit</artifactId>
    <version>4.12</version>
    <scope>test</scope>
</dependency>
<dependency>
    <groupId>org.hamcrest</groupId>
    <artifactId>hamcrest-core</artifactId>
    <version>1.3</version>
    <scope>test</scope>
</dependency>
<dependency>
    <groupId>javax</groupId>
```

```
        <artifactId>javaee-web-api</artifactId>
        <version>7.0</version>
        <scope>provided</scope>
    </dependency>
    <dependency>
        <groupId>org.apache.openejb</groupId>
        <artifactId>openejb-core</artifactId>
        <version>4.7.4</version>
        <scope>test</scope>
    </dependency>
```

How to do it...

1. First, we need to create our persistence unit (at `persistence.xml`):

```xml
<persistence-unit name="ch02-jta-pu" transaction-type="JTA">
    <provider>org.hibernate.ejb.HibernatePersistence</provider>
    <jta-data-source>userDb</jta-data-source>
    <non-jta-data-source>userDbNonJta</non-jta-data-source>
    <exclude-unlisted-classes>false</exclude-unlisted-classes>

    <properties>
        <property name="javax.persistence.schema-
          generation.database.action"
          value="create"/>
    </properties>
</persistence-unit>
```

2. Then we create a `User` class as an entity (`@Entity`):

```java
@Entity
public class User implements Serializable {

    private static final long serialVersionUID = 1L;

    @Id
    @GeneratedValue(strategy = GenerationType.AUTO)
    private Long id;
    private String name;
    private String email;

    protected User() {
    }
    public User(Long id, String name, String email) {
        this.id = id;
```

```
        this.name = name;
        this.email = email;
    }

    //DO NOT FORGET TO IMPLEMENT THE GETTERS AND SETTERS
}
```

3. We also need an EJB to perform the operations over the `User` entity:

```
@Stateful
public class UserBean {

    @PersistenceContext(unitName = "ch02-jta-pu",
    type = PersistenceContextType.EXTENDED)
    private EntityManager em;
    public void add(User user){
        em.persist(user);
    }
    public void update(User user){
        em.merge(user);
    }
    public void remove(User user){
        em.remove(user);
    }
    public User findById(Long id){
        return em.find(User.class, id);
    }

}
```

4. And then we create our unit test:

```
public class Ch02JtaTest {
    private EJBContainer ejbContainer;
    @EJB
    private UserBean userBean;
    public Ch02JtaTest() {
    }
    @Before
    public void setUp() throws NamingException {
        Properties p = new Properties();
        p.put("userDb", "new://Resource?type=DataSource");
        p.put("userDb.JdbcDriver", "org.hsqldb.jdbcDriver");
        p.put("userDb.JdbcUrl", "jdbc:hsqldb:mem:userdatabase");

        ejbContainer = EJBContainer.createEJBContainer(p);
        ejbContainer.getContext().bind("inject", this);
    }
    @After
```

```
public void tearDown() {
    ejbContainer.close();
}
@Test
public void validTransaction() throws Exception{
    User user = new User(null, "Elder Moraes",
                            "elder@eldermoraes.com");
    userBean.add(user);
    user.setName("John Doe");
    userBean.update(user);
    User userDb = userBean.findById(1L);
    assertEquals(userDb.getName(), "John Doe");
}
}
```

How it works...

The key code line in this recipe for JTA is right here:

```
<persistence-unit name="ch02-jta-pu" transaction-type="JTA">
```

When you use `transaction-type='JTA'`, you are saying to the server that it should take care of all transactions made under this context. If you use `RESOURCE-LOCAL` instead, you are saying that you are taking care of the transactions:

```
@Test
public void validTransaction() throws Exception{
    User user = new User(null, "Elder Moraes",
    "elder@eldermoraes.com");
    userBean.add(user);
    user.setName("John Doe");
    userBean.update(user);
    User userDb = userBean.findById(1L);
    assertEquals(userDb.getName(), "John Doe");
}
```

Each called method of `UserBean` starts a transaction to be completed and would run into a rollback if there's any issue while the transaction is alive would commit to the end of it.

There's more...

Another important piece of code is the following:

```
@Stateful
public class UserBean {

    @PersistenceContext(unitName = "ch02-jta-pu",
                         type = PersistenceContextType.EXTENDED)
    private EntityManager em;

    ...

}
```

So, here we are defining our `PersistenceContext` as `EXTENDED`. It means that this persistence context is bound to the `@Stateful` bean until it is removed from the container.

The other option is `TRANSACTION`, which means the persistence context would live only by the time of transaction.

See also

- Check the full source code of this recipe at `https://github.com/eldermoraes/javaee8-cookbook/tree/master/chapter02/ch02-jta`

Using EJB to deal with concurrency

Concurrency management is one of the biggest advantages supplied by a Java EE server. You can rely on a ready environment to deal with this tricky topic.

This recipe will show you how you can set up your beans to use it!

Getting ready

Just add a Java EE dependency to your project:

```
<dependency>
    <groupId>javax</groupId>
    <artifactId>javaee-web-api</artifactId>
    <version>7.0</version>
    <scope>provided</scope>
```

```
</dependency>
```

How to do it...

The recipe will show you three scenarios.

In the first scenario, LockType is defined at the class level:

```
@Singleton
@ConcurrencyManagement(ConcurrencyManagementType.CONTAINER)
@Lock(LockType.READ)
@AccessTimeout(value = 10000)
public class UserClassLevelBean {

    private int userCount;

    public int getUserCount() {
        return userCount;
    }
    public void addUser(){
        userCount++;
    }

}
```

In the second scenario, LockType is defined at the method level:

```
@Singleton
@ConcurrencyManagement(ConcurrencyManagementType.CONTAINER)
@AccessTimeout(value = 10000)
public class UserMethodLevelBean {

    private int userCount;
    @Lock(LockType.READ)
    public int getUserCount(){
        return userCount;
    }
    @Lock(LockType.WRITE)
    public void addUser(){
        userCount++;
    }
}
```

The third scenario is a self-managed bean:

```
@Singleton
@ConcurrencyManagement(ConcurrencyManagementType.BEAN)
public class UserSelfManagedBean {

    private int userCount;

    public int getUserCount() {
        return userCount;
    }
    public synchronized void addUser(){
        userCount++;
    }
}
```

How it works...

The first thing to have a look at the following:

```
@ConcurrencyManagement(ConcurrencyManagementType.CONTAINER)
```

This is completely redundant! Singleton beans are container-managed by default, so you don't need to specify them.

Singletons are designed for concurrent access, so they are the perfect use case for this recipe.

Now let's check the LockType defined at the class level:

```
@Lock(LockType.READ)
@AccessTimeout(value = 10000)
public class UserClassLevelBean {
    ...
}
```

When we use the @Lock annotation at the class level, the informed LockType will be used for all class methods.

In this case, LockType.READ means that many clients can access a resource at the same time. It is usual for reading data.

In case of some kind of locking, LockType will use the @AccessTimeout annotation time defined to run into a timeout or not.

Now, let's check `LockType` defined at the method level:

```
@Lock(LockType.READ)
public int getUserCount(){
    return userCount;
}
@Lock(LockType.WRITE)
public void addUser(){
    userCount++;
}
```

So, here we are basically saying that `getUserCount()` can be accessed by many users at once (`LockType.READ`), but `addUser()` will be accessed just by one user at a time (`LockType.WRITE`).

The last case is the self-managed bean:

```
@ConcurrencyManagement(ConcurrencyManagementType.BEAN)
public class UserSelfManagedBean{

    ...

    public synchronized void addUser(){
        userCount++;
    }

    ...
}
```

In this case, you have to manage all the concurrency issues for your bean in your code. We used a synchronized qualifier as an example.

There's more...

Unless you really *really* need to, don't use self-managed beans. The Java EE container is (well) designed to do it in a very efficient and elegant way.

See also

- Check the full source code of this recipe at `https://github.com/eldermoraes/javaee8-cookbook/tree/master/chapter02/ch02-ejb-concurrency`

Using JPA for smart data persistence

The Java Persistence API is a specification that describes an interface for managing relational databases using Java EE.

It eases data manipulation and reduces a lot of the code written for it, especially if you are used to SQL ANSI.

This recipe will show you how to use it to persist your data.

Getting ready

Let's first add the dependencies needed:

```
<dependency>
    <groupId>org.hibernate</groupId>
    <artifactId>hibernate-entitymanager</artifactId>
    <version>4.3.1.Final</version>
</dependency>
<dependency>
    <groupId>junit</groupId>
    <artifactId>junit</artifactId>
    <version>4.12</version>
    <scope>test</scope>
</dependency>
<dependency>
    <groupId>org.hamcrest</groupId>
    <artifactId>hamcrest-core</artifactId>
    <version>1.3</version>
    <scope>test</scope>
</dependency>
<dependency>
    <groupId>javax</groupId>
    <artifactId>javaee-web-api</artifactId>
    <version>7.0</version>
    <scope>provided</scope>
</dependency>
<dependency>
    <groupId>org.apache.openejb</groupId>
    <artifactId>openejb-core</artifactId>
    <version>4.7.4</version>
    <scope>test</scope>
</dependency>
```

How to do it...

1. Let's begin by creating an entity (you can see it as a table):

```java
@Entity
public class User implements Serializable {

    private static final long serialVersionUID = 1L;

    @Id
    @GeneratedValue(strategy = GenerationType.AUTO)
    private Long id;
    private String name;
    private String email;

    protected User() {
    }
    public User(Long id, String name, String email) {
        this.id = id;
        this.name = name;
        this.email = email;
    }

    //DO NOT FORGET TO IMPLEMENT THE GETTERS AND SETTERS
}
```

2. Here we declare our persistence unit (at `persistence.xml`):

```xml
<persistence-unit name="ch02-jpa-pu" transaction-type="JTA">
    <provider>org.hibernate.ejb.HibernatePersistence</provider>
    <jta-data-source>userDb</jta-data-source>
    <exclude-unlisted-classes>false</exclude-unlisted-classes>

    <properties>
        <property name="javax.persistence.schema-
         generation.database.action"
         value="create"/>
    </properties>
</persistence-unit>
```

3. Then we create a session bean to manage our data:

```java
@Stateless
public class UserBean {

    @PersistenceContext(unitName = "ch02-jpa-pu",
    type = PersistenceContextType.TRANSACTION)
```

```
        private EntityManager em;
        public void add(User user){
            em.persist(user);
        }
        public void update(User user){
            em.merge(user);
        }
        public void remove(User user){
            em.remove(user);
        }
        public User findById(Long id){
            return em.find(User.class, id);
        }
    }
```

4. And here we use a unit test to try it out:

```
    public class Ch02JpaTest {
        private EJBContainer ejbContainer;
        @EJB
        private UserBean userBean;
        public Ch02JpaTest() {
        }
        @Before
        public void setUp() throws NamingException {
            Properties p = new Properties();
            p.put("userDb", "new://Resource?type=DataSource");
            p.put("userDb.JdbcDriver", "org.hsqldb.jdbcDriver");
            p.put("userDb.JdbcUrl", "jdbc:hsqldb:mem:userdatabase");

            ejbContainer = EJBContainer.createEJBContainer(p);
            ejbContainer.getContext().bind("inject", this);
        }
        @After
        public void tearDown() {
            ejbContainer.close();
        }
        @Test
        public void persistData() throws Exception{
            User user = new User(null, "Elder Moraes",
            "elder@eldermoraes.com");
            userBean.add(user);
            user.setName("John Doe");
            userBean.update(user);
            User userDb = userBean.findById(1L);
            assertEquals(userDb.getName(), "John Doe");
        }
    }
```

How it works...

Let's break down our **persistence unit (pu)**.

This line defines the pu name and the transaction type used:

```
<persistence-unit name="ch02-jpa-pu" transaction-type="JTA">
```

The following line shows the provider the JPA implementation used:

```
<provider>org.hibernate.ejb.HibernatePersistence</provider>
```

It is the datasource name that will be accessed through JNDI:

```
<jta-data-source>userDb</jta-data-source>
```

This line lets all your entities be available for this pu, so you don't need to declare each one:

```
<exclude-unlisted-classes>false</exclude-unlisted-classes>
```

This block allows the database objects to be created if they don't exist:

```
<properties>
    <property name="javax.persistence.schema-
    generation.database.action"
    value="create"/>
</properties>
```

And now let's have a look at `UserBean`:

```
@Stateless
public class UserBean {

    @PersistenceContext(unitName = "ch02-jpa-pu",
                        type = PersistenceContextType.TRANSACTION)
    private EntityManager em;

    ...

}
```

`EntityManager` is the object responsible for the interface between the bean and the datasource. It's bound to the context by the `@PersistenceContext` annotation.

And we check the `EntityManager` operations as follows:

```
public void add(User user){
    em.persist(user);
}
```

The `persist()` method is used to add new data to the datasource. At the end of the execution, the object is attached to the context:

```
public void update(User user){
    em.merge(user);
}
```

The `merge()` method is used to update existing data on the datasource. The object is first found at the context, then updated at the database and attached to the context with the new state:

```
public void remove(User user){
    em.remove(user);
}
```

The `remove()` method, guess what is it?

```
public User findById(Long id){
    return em.find(User.class, id);
}
```

And finally the `find()` method uses the `id` parameter to search a database object with the same ID. That's why JPA demands your entities have an ID declared with the `@Id` annotation.

See also

- Check the full source code of this recipe at `https://github.com/eldermoraes/javaee8-cookbook/tree/master/chapter02/ch02-jpa`

Using EJB and JPA for data caching

Knowing how to build a simple and local cache for your application is an important skill. It may have a big impact on some data access performance and it is quite easy to do.

This recipe will show you how.

Getting ready

Simply add a Java EE dependency to your project:

```xml
<dependency>
    <groupId>javax</groupId>
    <artifactId>javaee-web-api</artifactId>
    <version>7.0</version>
    <scope>provided</scope>
</dependency>
```

How to do it...

1. Let's create a `User` class to be our cached object:

```java
public class User {
    private String name;
    private String email;
    //DO NOT FORGET TO IMPLEMENT THE GETTERS AND SETTERS
}
```

2. And then create a singleton to hold our user list cache:

```java
@Singleton
@Startup
public class UserCacheBean {

    protected Queue<User> cache = null;
    @PersistenceContext
    private EntityManager em;

    public UserCacheBean() {
    }

    protected void loadCache() {
        List<User> list = em.createQuery("SELECT u FROM USER
                                          as u").getResultList();

        list.forEach((user) -> {
            cache.add(user);
        });
    }

    @Lock(LockType.READ)
    public List<User> get() {
```

```
                    return cache.stream().collect(Collectors.toList());
        }

        @PostConstruct
        protected void init() {
            cache = new ConcurrentLinkedQueue<>();
            loadCache();
        }
    }
```

How it works...

Let's first understand our bean declaration:

```
@Singleton
@Startup
public class UserCacheBean {
    ...

    @PostConstruct
    protected void init() {
        cache = new ConcurrentLinkedQueue<>();
        loadCache();
    }
}
```

We are using a singleton because it has one and only one instance in the application context. And that's the way we want a data cache because we don't want to allow the possibility of different data being shared.

Also note that we used the `@Startup` annotation. It says to the server that this bean should be *executed* once it is loaded and the method annotated with `@PostConstruct` is used for it.

So we take the startup time to load our cache:

```
protected void loadCache() {
    List<User> list = em.createQuery("SELECT u FROM USER
                                      as u").getResultList();

    list.forEach((user) -> {
        cache.add(user);
    });
}
```

Now let's check the object holding our cache:

```
protected Queue<User> cache = null;

...

cache = new ConcurrentLinkedQueue<>();
```

`ConcurrentLinkedQueue` is a list built with one main purpose—being accessed by multiple processes in a thread-safe environment. That's exactly what we need and also it offers great performance on accessing its members.

And finally, let's check the access to our data cache:

```
@Lock(LockType.READ)
public List<User> get() {
    return cache.stream().collect(Collectors.toList());
}
```

We annotated the `get()` method with `LockType.READ`, so it says to the concurrency manager that it can be accessed by multiple processes at once in a thread-safe way.

There's more...

If you need big and complex caches in your application, you should use some enterprise cache solutions for better results.

See also

- Check the full source code of this recipe at `https://github.com/eldermoraes/javaee8-cookbook/tree/master/chapter02/ch02-datacache`

Using batch processing

Batch processing is the last recipe of this chapter. Running background tasks is a useful and important skill in an enterprise context.

You could use it to process data in bulk or just to separate it from the UI processes. This recipe will show you how to do it.

Getting ready

Let's add our dependencies:

```
<dependency>
    <groupId>org.hibernate</groupId>
    <artifactId>hibernate-entitymanager</artifactId>
    <version>5.2.10.Final</version>
    <scope>runtime</scope>
</dependency>
<dependency>
    <groupId>javax</groupId>
    <artifactId>javaee-api</artifactId>
    <version>7.0</version>
    <scope>provided</scope>
</dependency>
```

How to do it...

1. We first define our persistence unit:

```
<persistence-unit name="ch02-batch-pu" >
<provider>org.hibernate.jpa.HibernatePersistenceProvider</provider>
    <jta-data-source>java:app/userDb</jta-data-source>
    <exclude-unlisted-classes>false</exclude-unlisted-classes>
    <properties>
      <property name="javax.persistence.schema-
      generation.database.action"
      value="create"/>
      <property name="hibernate.transaction.jta.platform"
      value="org.hibernate.service.jta.platform
      .internal.SunOneJtaPlatform"/>
    </properties>
  </persistence-unit>
```

2. Then we declare a `User` entity:

```
@Entity
@Table(name = "UserTab")
public class User implements Serializable {

    private static final long serialVersionUID = 1L;

    @Id
    @NotNull
```

```java
    private Integer id;

    private String name;

    private String email;

    public User() {
    }

    //DO NOT FORGET TO IMPLEMENT THE GETTERS AND SETTERS
}
```

3. Here we create a job reader:

```java
@Named
@Dependent
public class UserReader extends AbstractItemReader {

    private BufferedReader br;

    @Override
    public void open(Serializable checkpoint) throws Exception {
        br = new BufferedReader(
                new InputStreamReader(
                        Thread.currentThread()
                        .getContextClassLoader()
                        .getResourceAsStream
                        ("META-INF/user.txt")));
    }

    @Override
    public String readItem() {
        String line = null;

        try {
            line = br.readLine();
        } catch (IOException ex) {
            System.out.println(ex.getMessage());
        }

        return line;
    }
}
```

4. Then we create a job processor:

```java
@Named
@Dependent
public class UserProcessor implements ItemProcessor {

    @Override
    public User processItem(Object line) {
        User user = new User();

        StringTokenizer tokens = new StringTokenizer((String)
        line, ",");
        user.setId(Integer.parseInt(tokens.nextToken()));
        user.setName(tokens.nextToken());
        user.setEmail(tokens.nextToken());
        return user;
    }
}
```

5. And here we create a job writer:

```java
@Named
@Dependent
public class UserWriter extends AbstractItemWriter {

    @PersistenceContext
    EntityManager entityManager;

    @Override
    @Transactional
    public void writeItems(List list) {
        for (User user : (List<User>) list) {
            entityManager.persist(user);
        }
    }
}
```

The processor, reader, and writer are referenced by the `acess-user.xml` file located at `META-INF.batch-jobs`:

```xml
<?xml version="1.0" encoding="windows-1252"?>
<job id="userAccess"
    xmlns="http://xmlns.jcp.org/xml/ns/javaee"
    version="1.0">
    <step id="loadData">
        <chunk item-count="3">
            <reader ref="userReader"/>
```

```
            <processor ref="userProcessor"/>
            <writer ref="userWriter"/>
        </chunk>
    </step>
</job>
```

6. And finally, we create a bean to interact with the batch engine:

```
@Named
@RequestScoped
public class UserBean {

    @PersistenceContext
    EntityManager entityManager;

    public void run() {
        try {
            JobOperator job = BatchRuntime.getJobOperator();
            long jobId = job.start("acess-user", new Properties());
            System.out.println("Job started: " + jobId);
        } catch (JobStartException ex) {
            System.out.println(ex.getMessage());
        }
    }

    public List<User> get() {
        return entityManager
                .createQuery("SELECT u FROM User as u", User.class)
                .getResultList();
    }
}
```

For the purpose of this example, we are going to use a JSF page to run the job and load the data:

```
<h:body>
 <h:form>
 <h:outputLabel value="#{userBean.get()}" />
 <br />
 <h:commandButton value="Run" action="index"
actionListener="#{userBean.run()}"/>
 <h:commandButton value="Reload" action="index"/>
 </h:form>
</h:body>
```

Run it on a Java EE server, click on the **Run** button and then the **Reload** button.

How it works...

To understand what is happening:

1. `UserReader` extends the `AbstractItemReader` class that has two key methods: `open()` and `readItem()`. In our case, the first one opens the `META-INF/user.txt` and the second one reads each line of the file.

2. The `UserProcessor` class extends the `ItemProcessor` class that has a `processItem()` method. It gets the item read by `readItem()` (from `UserReader`) to generate the `User` object that we want.

3. Once all items are processed and available in a list (in memory) we use the `UserWriter` class; that extends the `AbstractItemWriter` class and has the `writeItems` method. We use it, in our case, to persist the data read from the `user.txt` file.

All set so, we just use `UserBean` to run the job:

```
public void run() {
    try {
        JobOperator job = BatchRuntime.getJobOperator();
        long jobId = job.start("acess-user", new Properties());
        System.out.println("Job started: " + jobId);
    } catch (JobStartException ex) {
        System.out.println(ex.getMessage());
    }
}
```

The `job.start()` method is referencing the `acess-user.xml` file, enabling our reader, processor, and writer to work together.

See also

- Check the full source code of this recipe at `https://github.com/eldermoraes/javaee8-cookbook/tree/master/chapter02/ch02-batch`

Building Powerful Services with JSON and RESTful Features

3

Nowadays, using REST services with JSON is the most common method for data transfer between applications over the HTTP protocol and this is not a coincidence—this is fast and easy to do. It's an easy to read, easy to parse and, with JSON-P, easy to code!

The following recipes will show you some common scenarios and how to apply Java EE to deal with them.

This chapter covers the following recipes:

- Building server-side events with JAX-RS
- Improving a service's capabilities with JAX-RS and CDI
- Easing data and object representation with JSON-B
- Parsing, generating, transforming, and querying JSON objects using JSON-P

Building server-side events with JAX-RS

Usually, web applications rely on the events sent by the client side. So, basically the server will only do something if it is asked to.

But with the evolution of the technologies surrounding the internet (HTML5, mobile clients, smartphones, and so on), the server side also had to evolve. So that gave birth to the server-side events, events fired by the server (as the name suggests).

With this recipe, you will learn how to use the server-side event to update a user view.

Getting ready

Start by adding the Java EE dependency:

```
<dependencies>
    <dependency>
        <groupId>javax</groupId>
        <artifactId>javaee-api</artifactId>
        <version>8.0</version>
        <scope>provided</scope>
    </dependency>
</dependencies>
```

How to do it...

First, we build a REST endpoint to manage the server events we are going to use, and to use REST we should start by properly configuring it:

```
@ApplicationPath("webresources")
public class ApplicationConfig extends Application {

}
```

The following is quite a big chunk of code, but don't worry, we are going to split it up and understand each piece:

```
@Path("serverSentService")
@RequestScoped
public class ServerSentService {

    private static final Map<Long, UserEvent> POOL =
    new ConcurrentHashMap<>();

    @Resource(name = "LocalManagedExecutorService")
    private ManagedExecutorService executor;

    @Path("start")
    @POST
    public Response start(@Context Sse sse) {

        final UserEvent process = new UserEvent(sse);

        POOL.put(process.getId(), process);
        executor.submit(process);

        final URI uri =
```

```
UriBuilder.fromResource(ServerSentService.class).path
        ("register/{id}").build(process.getId());
        return Response.created(uri).build();
    }

    @Path("register/{id}")
    @Produces(MediaType.SERVER_SENT_EVENTS)
    @GET
    public void register(@PathParam("id") Long id,
            @Context SseEventSink sseEventSink) {
        final UserEvent process = POOL.get(id);

        if (process != null) {
            process.getSseBroadcaster().register(sseEventSink);
        } else {
            throw new NotFoundException();
        }
    }

    static class UserEvent implements Runnable {

        private final Long id;
        private final SseBroadcaster sseBroadcaster;
        private final Sse sse;

        UserEvent(Sse sse) {
            this.sse = sse;
            this.sseBroadcaster = sse.newBroadcaster();
            id = System.currentTimeMillis();
        }

        Long getId() {
            return id;
        }

        SseBroadcaster getSseBroadcaster() {
            return sseBroadcaster;
        }

        @Override
        public void run() {
            try {
                TimeUnit.SECONDS.sleep(5);
                sseBroadcaster.broadcast(sse.newEventBuilder().
                name("register").data(String.class, "Text from event "
                                    + id).build());
                sseBroadcaster.close();
            } catch (InterruptedException e) {
```

```
                    System.out.println(e.getMessage());
            }
        }
    }
}
```

Here, we have a bean to manage the UI and help us with a better view of what is happening in the server:

```
@ViewScoped
@Named
public class SseBean implements Serializable {

    @NotNull
    @Positive
    private Integer countClient;
    private Client client;
    @PostConstruct
    public void init(){
        client = ClientBuilder.newClient();
    }
    @PreDestroy
    public void destroy(){
        client.close();
    }

    public void sendEvent() throws URISyntaxException, InterruptedException
{

        WebTarget target = client.target(URI.create("http://localhost:8080/
                                        ch03-sse/"));
        Response response =
        target.path("webresources/serverSentService/start")
                .request()
                .post(Entity.json(""), Response.class);

        FacesContext.getCurrentInstance().addMessage(null,
                new FacesMessage("Sse Endpoint: " +
                response.getLocation()));

        final Map<Integer, String> messageMap = new ConcurrentHashMap<>
        (countClient);
        final SseEventSource[] sources = new
        SseEventSource[countClient];

        final String processUriString =
        target.getUri().relativize(response.getLocation()).
        toString();
        final WebTarget sseTarget = target.path(processUriString);
```

```java
        for (int i = 0; i < countClient; i++) {
            final int id = i;
            sources[id] = SseEventSource.target(sseTarget).build();
            sources[id].register((event) -> {
                final String message = event.readData(String.class);

                if (message.contains("Text")) {
                    messageMap.put(id, message);
                }
            });
            sources[i].open();
        }

        TimeUnit.SECONDS.sleep(10);

        for (SseEventSource source : sources) {
            source.close();
        }

        for (int i = 0; i < countClient; i++) {
            final String message = messageMap.get(i);

            FacesContext.getCurrentInstance().addMessage(null,
                    new FacesMessage("Message sent to client " +
                                    (i + 1) + ": " + message));
        }
    }

    public Integer getCountClient() {
        return countClient;
    }

    public void setCountClient(Integer countClient) {
        this.countClient = countClient;
    }

}
```

And finally, the UI is code a simple JSF page:

```
<h:body>
    <h:form>
        <h:outputLabel for="countClient" value="Number of Clients" />
        <h:inputText id="countClient" value="#{sseBean.countClient}" />
        <br />
        <h:commandButton type="submit" action="#{sseBean.sendEvent()}"
         value="Send Events" />
    </h:form>
</h:body>
```

How it works...

We started with our SSE engine, the `ServerEvent` class, and a JAX-RS endpoint—these hold all the methods that we need for this recipe.

Let's understand the first one:

```
@Path("start")
@POST
public Response start(@Context Sse sse) {

    final UserEvent process = new UserEvent(sse);

    POOL.put(process.getId(), process);
    executor.submit(process);

    final URI uri = UriBuilder.fromResource(ServerSentService.class).
    path("register/{id}").build(process.getId());
    return Response.created(uri).build();
}
```

Following are the main points:

1. First things first—this method will create and prepare an event to be sent by the server to the clients.
2. Then, the just created event is put in a HashMap called POOL.
3. Then our event is attached to a URI that represents another method in this same class (details are provided next).

Pay attention to this parameter:

```
@Context Sse sse
```

It brings the server-side events feature from the server context and lets you use it as you need and, of course, it is injected by CDI (yes, CDI is everywhere!).

Now we see our `register()` method:

```
@Path("register/{id}")
@Produces(MediaType.SERVER_SENT_EVENTS)
@GET
public void register(@PathParam("id") Long id,
        @Context SseEventSink sseEventSink) {
    final UserEvent event = POOL.get(id);

    if (event != null) {
        event.getSseBroadcaster().register(sseEventSink);
    } else {
        throw new NotFoundException();
    }
}
```

This is the very method that sends the events to your clients—check the `@Produces` annotation; it uses the new media type `SERVER_SENT_EVENTS`.

The engine works, thanks to this small piece of code:

```
@Context SseEventSink sseEventSink

...

event.getSseBroadcaster().register(sseEventSink);
```

The `SseEventSink` is a queue of events managed by the Java EE server, and it is served to you by injection from the context.

Then you get the process broadcaster and register it to this sink, which means that everything that this process broadcasts will be sent by the server from `SseEventSink`.

And now we check our event setup:

```java
static class UserEvent implements Runnable {

    ...

    UserEvent(Sse sse) {
        this.sse = sse;
        this.sseBroadcaster = sse.newBroadcaster();
        id = System.currentTimeMillis();
    }

    ...

    @Override
    public void run() {
        try {
            TimeUnit.SECONDS.sleep(5);
            sseBroadcaster.broadcast(sse.newEventBuilder().
            name("register").data(String.class, "Text from event "
            + id).build());
            sseBroadcaster.close();
        } catch (InterruptedException e) {
            System.out.println(e.getMessage());
        }
    }
}
```

If you pay attention to this line:

```java
this.sseBroadcaster = sse.newBroadcaster();
```

You'll remember that we've just used this broadcaster in the last class. Here we see that this broadcaster is brought by the `Sse` object injected by the server.

This event implements the `Runnable` interface so we can use it with the executor (as explained before), so once it runs, you can broadcast to your clients:

```java
sseBroadcaster.broadcast(sse.newEventBuilder().name("register").
data(String.class, "Text from event " + id).build());
```

This is exactly the message sent to the client. This could be whatever message you need.

For this recipe, we used another class to interact with Sse. Let's highlight the most important parts:

```
WebTarget target = client.target(URI.create
("http://localhost:8080/ch03-sse/"));
Response response = target.path("webresources/serverSentService
                                /start")
        .request()
        .post(Entity.json(""), Response.class);
```

This is a simple code that you can use to call any JAX-RS endpoint.

And finally, the most important part of this mock client:

```
for (int i = 0; i < countClient; i++) {
    final int id = i;
    sources[id] = SseEventSource.target(sseTarget).build();
    sources[id].register((event) -> {
        final String message = event.readData(String.class);

        if (message.contains("Text")) {
            messageMap.put(id, message);
        }
    });
    sources[i].open();
}
```

Each message that is broadcast is read here:

```
final String message = messageMap.get(i);
```

It could be any client you want, another service, a web page, a mobile client, or anything.

Then we check our UI:

```
<h:inputText id="countClient" value="#{sseBean.countClient}" />
...
<h:commandButton type="submit" action="#{sseBean.sendEvent()}"
value="Send Events" />
```

We are using the countClient field to fill the countClient value in the client, so you can play around with as many threads as you want.

There's more...

It's important to mention that SSE is not supported in MS IE/Edge web browsers and that it is not as scalable as web sockets. In case you want to have full cross-browser support in the desktop side and/or better scalability (so, not only mobile apps, but also web apps which can open many more connections per instance), then **WebSockets** should be considered instead. Fortunately, standard Java EE has supported WebSockets since 7.0.

See also

- The full source code of this recipe is at `https://github.com/eldermoraes/` `javaee8-cookbook/tree/master/chapter03/ch03-sse`

Improving service's capabilities with JAX-RS and CDI

This recipe will show you how to take advantage of CDI and JAX-RS features to reduce the effort and lower the complexity of writing powerful services.

Getting ready

Start by adding the Java EE dependency:

```
<dependencies>
    <dependency>
        <groupId>javax</groupId>
        <artifactId>javaee-api</artifactId>
        <version>8.0</version>
        <scope>provided</scope>
    </dependency>
</dependencies>
```

How to do it...

1. We first create a `User` class to be managed through our service:

```java
public class User implements Serializable{

    private String name;
    private String email;

    public User(){
    }

    public User(String name, String email) {
        this.name = name;
        this.email = email;
    }

    //DO NOT FORGET TO IMPLEMENT THE GETTERS AND SETTERS

}
```

2. To have multiple sources of `User` objects, we create a `UserBean` class:

```java
@Stateless
public class UserBean {
    public User getUser(){
        long ts = System.currentTimeMillis();
        return new User("Bean" + ts, "user" + ts +
                        "@eldermoraes.com");
    }
}
```

3. And finally, we create our `UserService` endpoint:

```java
@Path("userservice")
public class UserService implements Serializable{
    @Inject
    private UserBean userBean;
    private User userLocal;
    @Inject
    private void setUserLocal(){
        long ts = System.currentTimeMillis();
        userLocal = new User("Local" + ts, "user" + ts +
                        "@eldermoraes.com");
    }
    @GET
    @Path("getUserFromBean")
```

```
@Produces(MediaType.APPLICATION_JSON)
public Response getUserFromBean(){
    return Response.ok(userBean.getUser()).build();
}

@GET
@Path("getUserFromLocal")
@Produces(MediaType.APPLICATION_JSON)
public Response getUserFromLocal(){
    return Response.ok(userLocal).build();
}
}
```

4. To load our UI, we have the `UserView` class that will be like a Controller between the UI and the service:

```
@ViewScoped
@Named
public class UserView implements Serializable {

    public void loadUsers() {
        Client client = ClientBuilder.newClient();
        WebTarget target = client.target(URI.create
        ("http://localhost:8080/ch03-rscdi/"));
        User response = target.path("webresources/userservice/
                                    getUserFromBean")
                    .request()
                    .accept(MediaType.APPLICATION_JSON)
                    .get(User.class);

        FacesContext.getCurrentInstance()
                    .addMessage(null,
                        new FacesMessage("userFromBean: " +
                                            response));

        response = target.path("webresources/userservice
                            /getUserFromLocal")
                    .request()
                    .accept(MediaType.APPLICATION_JSON)
                    .get(User.class);

        FacesContext.getCurrentInstance()
                    .addMessage(null,
                        new FacesMessage("userFromLocal:
                                        " + response));
```

```
        client.close();
    }

}
```

5. And we add simple JSF page just to show the results:

```
<h:body>
<h:form>
<h:commandButton type="submit"
action="#{userView.loadUsers()}"
value="Load Users" />
</h:form>
</h:body>
```

How it works...

We used two kinds of injection:

- From `UserBean`, when `UserService` is attached to the context
- From `UserService` itself

Injection from `UserBean` is the simplest possible to perform:

```
@Inject
private UserBean userBean;
```

Injection from `UserService` itself is also simple:

```
@Inject
private void setUserLocal(){
    long ts = System.currentTimeMillis();
    userLocal = new User("Local" + ts, "user" + ts +
                         "@eldermoraes.com");
}
```

Here, the `@Inject` works like the `@PostConstruct` annotation, with the difference begin in the server context running the method. But the result is quite the same.

Everything is injected, so now it's just a matter of getting the results:

```
response = target.path("webresources/userservice/getUserFromBean")
                .request()
                .accept(MediaType.APPLICATION_JSON)
                .get(User.class);
```

```
...

response = target.path("webresources/userservice/getUserFromLocal")
                  .request()
                  .accept(MediaType.APPLICATION_JSON)
                  .get(User.class);
```

There's more...

As you can see, JAX-RS eases a lot of the objects parsing and represention:

```
@GET
@Path("getUserFromBean")
@Produces(MediaType.APPLICATION_JSON)
public Response getUserFromBean(){
    userFromBean = userBean.getUser();
    return Response.ok(userFromBean).build();
}

@GET
@Path("getUserFromLocal")
@Produces(MediaType.APPLICATION_JSON)
public Response getUserFromLocal(){
    return Response.ok(userLocal).build();
}
```

By using a `Response` returning object and
`@Produces(MediaType.APPLICATION_JSON)`, you give the framework the hard job of
parsing your `user` object to a JSON representation. Lots of effort saved in a few lines!

You could also inject the user using a producer (the `@Produces` annotation). Check the CDI
recipe from `Chapter 1`, *New Features and Improvements,* for more details.

See also

- Check the full source code of this recipe at `https://github.com/eldermoraes/`
  `javaee8-cookbook/tree/master/chapter03/ch03-rscdi`

Easing data and objects representation with JSON-B

This recipe will show you how you can use the power of the new JSON-B API to give some flexibility to your data representation, and also help to transform your objects into JSON messages.

Getting ready

Start by adding the Java EE dependency:

```
<dependencies>
    <dependency>
        <groupId>javax</groupId>
        <artifactId>javaee-api</artifactId>
        <version>8.0</version>
        <scope>provided</scope>
    </dependency>
</dependencies>
```

How to do it...

1. We first create a User class with some customization (details ahead):

```
public class User {

    private Long id;
    @JsonbProperty("fullName")
    private String name;
    private String email;
    @JsonbTransient
    private Double privateNumber;
    @JsonbDateFormat(JsonbDateFormat.DEFAULT_LOCALE)
    private Date dateCreated;
    public User(Long id, String name, String email,
                Double privateNumber, Date dateCreated) {
        this.id = id;
        this.name = name;
        this.email = email;
        this.privateNumber = privateNumber;
        this.dateCreated = dateCreated;
    }
```

```
private User(){
}

//DO NOT FORGET TO IMPLEMENT THE GETTERS AND SETTERS
}
```

2. Here we use `UserView` to return the user JSON to the UI:

```
@ViewScoped
@Named
public class UserView implements Serializable{
    private String json;
    public void loadUser(){
        long now = System.currentTimeMillis();
        User user = new User(now,
                "User" + now,
                "user" + now + "@eldermoraes.com",
                Math.random(),
                new Date());
        Jsonb jb = JsonbBuilder.create();
        json = jb.toJson(user);
        try {
            jb.close();
        } catch (Exception ex) {
            System.out.println(ex.getMessage());
        }
    }

    public String getJson() {
        return json;
    }

    public void setJson(String json) {
        this.json = json;
    }
}
```

3. And we add JSF page just to show the results:

```
<h:body>
<h:form>
<h:commandButton type="submit" action="#{userView.loadUser()}"
 value="Load User" />

<br />

<h:outputLabel for="json" value="User JSON" />
<br />
<h:inputTextarea id="json" value="#{userView.json}"
 style="width: 300px; height: 300px;" />
</h:form>
</h:body>
```

How it works...

We are using some JSON-B annotations to customize our user data representation:

```
@JsonbProperty("fullName")
private String name;
```

The @JsonbProperty is used to change the field name to some other value:

```
@JsonbTransient
private Double privateNumber;
```

Use @JsonbTransient when you want to prevent some property appearing at the JSON representation:

```
@JsonbDateFormat(JsonbDateFormat.DEFAULT_LOCALE)
private Date dateCreated;
```

With @JsonbDateFormat, you use the API to automatically format your dates.

And then we use our UI manager to update the view:

```
public void loadUser(){
    long now = System.currentTimeMillis();
    User user = new User(now,
            "User" + now,
            "user" + now + "@eldermoraes.com",
            Math.random(),
            new Date());
    Jsonb jb = JsonbBuilder.create();
```

```
        json = jb.toJson(user);
    }
```

See also

- The full source code of this recipe is at `https://github.com/eldermoraes/javaee8-cookbook/tree/master/chapter03/ch03-jsonb`

Parsing, generating, transforming, and querying on JSON objects using JSON-P

Dealing with JSON objects is an activity that you can't avoid anymore. So if you can do it by relying on a powerful and easy to use framework—even better!

This recipe will show you how you can use JSON-P to carry out some different operations using or generating JSON objects.

Getting ready

Start by adding the Java EE dependency:

```
<dependencies>
    <dependency>
        <groupId>javax</groupId>
        <artifactId>javaee-api</artifactId>
        <version>8.0</version>
        <scope>provided</scope>
    </dependency>
</dependencies>
```

How to do it...

1. Let's create a `User` class to support our operations:

```
public class User {

    private String name;
    private String email;
    private Integer[] profiles;
    public User(String name, String email, Integer[] profiles) {
        this.name = name;
        this.email = email;
        this.profiles = profiles;
    }

    //DO NOT FORGET TO IMPLEMENT THE GETTERS AND SETTERS
}
```

2. Then a `UserView` class to do all the JSON operations:

```
@ViewScoped
@Named
public class UserView implements Serializable{
    private static final JsonBuilderFactory BUILDERFACTORY =
    Json.createBuilderFactory(null);
    private final Jsonb jsonbBuilder = JsonbBuilder.create();
    private String fromArray;
    private String fromStructure;
    private String fromUser;
    private String fromJpointer;
    public void loadUserJson(){
        loadFromArray();
        loadFromStructure();
        loadFromUser();
    }
    private void loadFromArray(){
        JsonArray array = BUILDERFACTORY.createArrayBuilder()
                .add(BUILDERFACTORY.createObjectBuilder()
                        .add("name", "User1")
                        .add("email", "user1@eldermoraes.com"))
                .add(BUILDERFACTORY.createObjectBuilder()
                        .add("name", "User2")
                        .add("email", "user2@eldermoraes.com"))
                .add(BUILDERFACTORY.createObjectBuilder()
                        .add("name", "User3")
                        .add("email", "user3@eldermoraes.com"))
                .build();
```

```
                         fromArray = jsonbBuilder.toJson(array);
                }
                private void loadFromStructure(){
                        JsonStructure structure =
                        BUILDERFACTORY.createObjectBuilder()
                                .add("name", "User1")
                                .add("email", "user1@eldermoraes.com")
                                .add("profiles",
    BUILDERFACTORY.createArrayBuilder()
                                        .add(BUILDERFACTORY.createObjectBuilder()
                                                .add("id", "1")
                                                .add("name", "Profile1"))
                                        .add(BUILDERFACTORY.createObjectBuilder()
                                                .add("id", "2")
                                                .add("name", "Profile2")))
                                .build();
                        fromStructure = jsonbBuilder.toJson(structure);

                        JsonPointer pointer = Json.createPointer("/profiles");
                        JsonValue value = pointer.getValue(structure);
                        fromJpointer = value.toString();
                }
                private void loadFromUser(){
                        User user = new User("Elder Moraes",
                        "elder@eldermoraes.com",
                        new Integer[]{1,2,3});
                        fromUser = jsonbBuilder.toJson(user);
                }

                //DO NOT FORGET TO IMPLEMENT THE GETTERS AND SETTERS
        }
```

3. Then we create a JSF page to show the results:

```
<h:body>
<h:form>
<h:commandButton type="submit" action="#{userView.loadUserJson()}"
value="Load JSONs" />

<br />

<h:outputLabel for="fromArray" value="From Array" />
<br />
<h:inputTextarea id="fromArray" value="#{userView.fromArray}"
style="width: 300px; height: 150px" />
<br />

<h:outputLabel for="fromStructure" value="From Structure" />
```

```
<br />
<h:inputTextarea id="fromStructure"
value="#{userView.fromStructure}"
style="width: 300px; height: 150px" />
<br />

<h:outputLabel for="fromUser" value="From User" />
<br />
<h:inputTextarea id="fromUser" value="#{userView.fromUser}"
style="width: 300px; height: 150px" />

 <br />
 <h:outputLabel for="fromJPointer" value="Query with JSON Pointer
 (from JsonStructure Above)" />
 <br />
 <h:inputTextarea id="fromJPointer"
  value="#{userView.fromJpointer}"
 style="width: 300px; height: 100px" />
</h:form>
</h:body>
```

How it works...

First, the `loadFromArray()` method:

```
private void loadFromArray(){
    JsonArray array = BUILDERFACTORY.createArrayBuilder()
            .add(BUILDERFACTORY.createObjectBuilder()
                    .add("name", "User1")
                    .add("email", "user1@eldermoraes.com"))
            .add(BUILDERFACTORY.createObjectBuilder()
                    .add("name", "User2")
                    .add("email", "user2@eldermoraes.com"))
            .add(BUILDERFACTORY.createObjectBuilder()
                    .add("name", "User3")
                    .add("email", "user3@eldermoraes.com"))
            .build();
    fromArray = jsonbBuilder.toJson(array);
}
```

It uses the `BuilderFactory` and the `createArrayBuilder` method to easily build an array of JSONs (each call of `createObjectBuilder` creates another array member). At the end, we use the JSON-B to convert it to a JSON string:

```
private void loadFromStructure(){
    JsonStructure structure = BUILDERFACTORY.createObjectBuilder()
            .add("name", "User1")
            .add("email", "user1@eldermoraes.com")
            .add("profiles", BUILDERFACTORY.createArrayBuilder()
                    .add(BUILDERFACTORY.createObjectBuilder()
                            .add("id", "1")
                            .add("name", "Profile1"))
                    .add(BUILDERFACTORY.createObjectBuilder()
                            .add("id", "2")
                            .add("name", "Profile2")))
            .build();
    fromStructure = jsonbBuilder.toJson(structure);

    JsonPointer pointer = new JsonPointerImpl("/profiles");
    JsonValue value = pointer.getValue(structure);
    fromJpointer = value.toString();
}
```

Here, instead of an array, we are building a single JSON structure. Again, we use JSON-B to convert the `JsonStructure` to a JSON string.

We also took advantage of having this `JsonStructure` ready and used it to query the user profiles using the `JsonPointer` object:

```
private void loadFromUser(){
    User user = new User("Elder Moraes", "elder@eldermoraes.com",
            new Integer[]{1,2,3});
    fromUser = jsonbBuilder.toJson(user);
}
```

And here was the simplest: creating an object and asking JSON-B to convert it to a JSON string.

See also

- Check the full source code of this recipe at https://github.com/eldermoraes/ javaee8-cookbook/tree/master/chapter03/ch03-jsonp

4
Web- and Client-Server Communication

Web development is one of the greatest ways to use Java EE. Actually, since before J2EE times, we could use JSP and servlets, and that's how web development using Java began.

This chapter will show some advanced features for web development that will make your application faster and better—for you and for your client!

This chapter covers the following recipes:

- Using servlet for request and response management
- Building UI with template features using JSF
- Improving response performance with Server Push

Using servlets for request and response management

Servlets are the core place to deal with requests and responses using Java EE. If you are still not familiar with it, know that even a JSP is nothing more than a way to build a servlet once the page is called.

This recipe will show you three features you can use when using servlets:

- Load on startup
- Parameterized servlets
- Asynchronous servlets

Getting ready

Start by adding the dependency to your project:

```
<dependency>
    <groupId>javax</groupId>
    <artifactId>javaee-api</artifactId>
    <version>8.0</version>
    <scope>provided</scope>
</dependency>
```

How to do it...

The load on startup servlet

Let's start with our servlet that will load on the server's start up:

```
@WebServlet(name = "LoadOnStartupServlet", urlPatterns =
{"/LoadOnStartupServlet"},
loadOnStartup = 1)
public class LoadOnStartupServlet extends HttpServlet {

    @Override
    public void init() throws ServletException {
        System.out.println("*******SERVLET LOADED
                        WITH SERVER's STARTUP*******");
    }

}
```

A servlet with init params

Now we add a servlet with some parameters for its own initialization:

```
@WebServlet(name = "InitConfigServlet", urlPatterns =
{"/InitConfigServlet"},
        initParams = {
                @WebInitParam(name = "key1", value = "value1"),
                @WebInitParam(name = "key2", value = "value2"),
                @WebInitParam(name = "key3", value = "value3"),
                @WebInitParam(name = "key4", value = "value4"),
                @WebInitParam(name = "key5", value = "value5")
        }
```

```
)
public class InitConfigServlet extends HttpServlet {

    Map<String, String> param = new HashMap<>();
    @Override
    protected void doPost(HttpServletRequest req,
    HttpServletResponse resp)
    throws ServletException, IOException {
        doProcess(req, resp);
    }

    @Override
    protected void doGet(HttpServletRequest req,
    HttpServletResponse resp)
    throws ServletException, IOException {
        doProcess(req, resp);
    }
    private void doProcess(HttpServletRequest req,
    HttpServletResponse resp)
    throws IOException{
        resp.setContentType("text/html");
        PrintWriter out = resp.getWriter();
        if (param.isEmpty()){
            out.println("No params to show");
        } else{
            param.forEach((k,v) -> out.println("param: " + k + ",
                                    value: " + v + "<br />"));
        }
    }

    @Override
    public void init(ServletConfig config) throws ServletException {
        System.out.println("init");
        List<String> list =
        Collections.list(config.getInitParameterNames());
        list.forEach((key) -> {
            param.put(key, config.getInitParameter(key));
        });
    }

}
```

The asynchronous servlet

And then we implement our asynchronous servlet:

```java
@WebServlet(urlPatterns = "/AsyncServlet", asyncSupported = true)
public class AsyncServlet extends HttpServlet {

    private static final long serialVersionUID = 1L;

    @Override
    protected void doGet(HttpServletRequest request,
            HttpServletResponse response) throws ServletException,
            IOException {
        long startTime = System.currentTimeMillis();
        System.out.println("AsyncServlet Begin, Name="
                + Thread.currentThread().getName() + ", ID="
                + Thread.currentThread().getId());

        String time = request.getParameter("timestamp");
        AsyncContext asyncCtx = request.startAsync();

        asyncCtx.start(() -> {
            try {
                Thread.sleep(Long.valueOf(time));
                long endTime = System.currentTimeMillis();
                long timeElapsed = endTime - startTime;
                System.out.println("AsyncServlet Finish, Name="
                        + Thread.currentThread().getName() + ", ID="
                        + Thread.currentThread().getId() + ", Duration="
                        + timeElapsed + " milliseconds.");

                asyncCtx.getResponse().getWriter().write
                ("Async process time: " + timeElapsed + " milliseconds");
                asyncCtx.complete();
            } catch (InterruptedException | IOException ex) {
                System.err.println(ex.getMessage());
            }
        });
    }
}
```

And finally, we need a simple web page to try all those servlets:

```
<body>
    <a href="${pageContext.request.contextPath}/InitConfigServlet">
    InitConfigServlet</a>
    <br />
    <br />
    <form action="${pageContext.request.contextPath}/AsyncServlet"
     method="GET">
        <h2>AsyncServlet</h2>
        Milliseconds
        <br />
        <input type="number" id="timestamp" name="timestamp"
        style="width: 200px" value="5000"/>
        <button type="submit">Submit</button>
    </form>

</body>
```

How it works...

The load on startup servlet

If you want your servlet to be initialized when the server starts, then this is what you need. Usually you will use it to load some cache, start a background process, log some information, or whatever you need to do when the server has just started and can't wait until somebody calls the servlet.

The key points of this kind of servlet are:

- The loadOnStartup param: Accepts any number of servlets. This number defines the order used by the server to run all the servlets that will run in the startup. So if you have more than one servlet running this way, remember to define the right order (if there is any). If there's no number defined or a negative one, the server will choose the default order.
- The init method: Remember to override the init method with the operation you would like to do at the start up time, otherwise your servlet will do nothing.

A servlet with init params

Sometimes you need to define some parameters for your servlet that goes beyond local variables – `initParams` is the place to do it:

```
@WebServlet(name = "InitConfigServlet", urlPatterns =
{"/InitConfigServlet"},
        initParams = {
                @WebInitParam(name = "key1", value = "value1"),
                @WebInitParam(name = "key2", value = "value2"),
                @WebInitParam(name = "key3", value = "value3"),
                @WebInitParam(name = "key4", value = "value4"),
                @WebInitParam(name = "key5", value = "value5")
        }
)
```

The `@WebInitParam` annotation will handle them for you and those parameters will be available for the server through the `ServletConfig` object.

Asynchronous servlet

Let's split our `AsyncServlet` class into pieces so we can understand it:

```
@WebServlet(urlPatterns = "/AsyncServlet", asyncSupported = true)
```

Here, we defined our servlet for accepting async behavior by using the `asyncSupported` param:

```
AsyncContext asyncCtx = request.startAsync();
```

We used the request being processed to start a new async context.

Then we start our async process:

```
asyncCtx.start(() -> {...
```

And here we print our output to see the response and finish the async process:

```
asyncCtx.getResponse().getWriter().write("Async
process time: "
+ timeElapsed + " milliseconds");
asyncCtx.complete();
```

See also

- To get the full source code of this recipe, check `https://github.com/eldermoraes/javaee8-cookbook/tree/master/chapter04/ch04-servlet`

Building UI with template's features using JSF

The **JavaServer Faces** (**JSF**) is a powerful Java EE API for building outstanding UIs, using both client and server features.

It goes much further than when you are using JSP, as you are not only using Java code inside HTML code, but actually really referencing code injected in the server context.

This recipe will show you how to use the Facelet's template feature to get more flexibility and reusability from your layout template.

Getting ready

Start by adding the dependency to your project:

```
<dependency>
    <groupId>javax</groupId>
    <artifactId>javaee-api</artifactId>
    <version>8.0</version>
    <scope>provided</scope>
</dependency>
```

How to do it...

1. Let's first create our page layout with a header, content section, and footer:

```
<h:body>
    <div id="layout">
        <div id="header">
            <ui:insert name="header" >
                <ui:include src="header.xhtml" />
            </ui:insert>
        </div>
```

```
            <div id="content">
                <ui:insert name="content" >
                    <ui:include src="content.xhtml" />
                </ui:insert>
            </div>
            <div id="footer">
                <ui:insert name="footer" >
                    <ui:include src="footer.xhtml" />
                </ui:insert>
            </div>
        </div>
    </h:body>
```

2. Define the default header section:

```
<body>
    <h1>Template header</h1>
</body>
```

3. The default content section:

```
<body>
    <h1>Template content</h1>
</body>
```

4. The default footer section:

```
<body>
    <h1>Template content</h1>
</body>
```

5. And then a simple page using our default template:

```
<h:body>
    <ui:composition template="WEB-INF/template/layout.xhtml">

    </ui:composition>
</h:body>
```

6. Now, let's create another page and override just the content section:

```
<h:body>
    <ui:composition template="/template/layout.xhtml">
        <ui:define name="content">
            <h1><p style="color:red">User content. Timestamp: #
            {userBean.timestamp}</p></h1>
        </ui:define>
    </ui:composition>
</h:body>
```

7. As this code is calling UserBean, let's define it:

```
@Named
@RequestScoped
public class UserBean implements Serializable{

    public Long getTimestamp(){
        return new Date().getTime();
    }
}
```

8. Also, don't forget to include the beans.xml file inside the WEB-INF folder; otherwise, this bean will not work as expected:

```
<?xml version="1.0" encoding="UTF-8"?>
<beans xmlns="http://xmlns.jcp.org/xml/ns/javaee"
        xmlns:xsi="http://www.w3.org/2001/XMLSchema-instance"
        xsi:schemaLocation="http://xmlns.jcp.org/xml/ns/javaee
        http://xmlns.jcp.org/xml/ns/javaee/beans_1_1.xsd"
        bean-discovery-mode="all">
</beans>
```

If you want to try this code, run it in a Java EE compatible server and access the following URLs:

- http://localhost:8080/ch04-jsf/
- http://localhost:8080/ch04-jsf/user.xhtml

How it works...

The explanation is as simple as possible: the layout.xhtml is our template. As long as you name each section (in our case its header, content, and footer), whatever JSF page that uses it will inherit its layout.

Any page using this layout and wanting to customize some of those defined sections, should just describe the desired section like we did in the `user.xhtml` file:

```
<ui:composition template="/template/layout.xhtml">
    <ui:define name="content">
        <h1><font color="red">User content. Timestamp: #
            {userBean.timestamp}
        </font></h1>
    </ui:define>
</ui:composition>
```

See also

- To get the full source code of this recipe, check `https://github.com/eldermoraes/javaee8-cookbook/tree/master/chapter04/ch04-jsf`

Improving the response performance with Server Push

One of the main features of HTTP/2.0 is the Server Push. When it is available, that means, being supported by the protocol, the server, and the browser client—it lets the server send ("push") data to the client before it asks for it.

It is one of the most wanted features in JSF 2.3 and probably the one that demands less effort to use if your application is based on JSF—just migrate to a Java EE 8 compatible server and then you are done.

This recipe will show you how to use it in your application and will even let you compare the performance between HTTP/1.0 and HTTP/2.0 in the same scenario.

Getting ready

Start by adding the dependency to your project:

```
<dependency>
    <groupId>javax</groupId>
    <artifactId>javaee-api</artifactId>
    <version>8.0</version>
    <scope>provided</scope>
```

```
</dependency>
```

How to do it...

This recipe has only this single servlet:

```java
@WebServlet(name = "ServerPushServlet", urlPatterns =
{"/ServerPushServlet"})
public class ServerPushServlet extends HttpServlet {

    @Override
    protected void doGet(HttpServletRequest request,
    HttpServletResponse response)
            throws ServletException, IOException {
        doRequest(request, response);
    }

    private void doRequest(HttpServletRequest request,
    HttpServletResponse response) throws IOException{
        String usePush = request.getParameter("usePush");
        if ("true".equalsIgnoreCase(usePush)){
            PushBuilder pb = request.newPushBuilder();
            if (pb != null) {
                for(int row=0; row < 5; row++){
                    for(int col=0; col < 8; col++){
                        pb.path("image/keyboard_buttons/keyboard_buttons-"
                                + row + "-" + col + ".jpeg")
                            .addHeader("content-type", "image/jpeg")
                            .push();
                    }
                }
            }
        }

        try (PrintWriter writer = response.getWriter()) {
            StringBuilder html = new StringBuilder();
            html.append("<html>");
            html.append("<center>");
            html.append("<table cellspacing='0' cellpadding='0'
                    border='0'>");

            for(int row=0; row < 5; row++){
                html.append(" <tr>");
                for(int col=0; col < 8; col++){
                    html.append(" <td>");
                    html.append("<img
```

```
                        src='image/keyboard_buttons/keyboard_buttons-" +
                            row + "-" + col + ".jpeg' style='width:100px;
                            height:106.25px;'>");
                    html.append("  </td>");
                }
                html.append("  </tr>");
            }
            html.append("</table>");
            html.append("<br>");
            if ("true".equalsIgnoreCase(usePush)){
                html.append("<h2>Image pushed by ServerPush</h2>");
            } else{
                html.append("<h2>Image loaded using HTTP/1.0</h2>");
            }
            html.append("</center>");
            html.append("</html>");
            writer.write(html.toString());
        }
    }

}
```

And we creat a simple page to call both HTTP/1.0 and HTTP/2.0 cases:

```
<body>
    <a href="ServerPushServlet?usePush=true">Use HTTP/2.0 (ServerPush)</a>
    <br />
    <a href="ServerPushServlet?usePush=false">Use HTTP/1.0</a>
</body>
```

And try it on a Java EE 8 compatible server using this URL:

```
https://localhost:8181/ch04-serverpush
```

How it works...

The image loaded in this recipe was shared in 25 pieces. When there's no HTTP/2.0 available, the server will wait for 25 requests made by img src (from HTML) and then reply to each one of them with the proper image.

With HTTP/2.0, the server can push them all beforehand. The "magic" is done here:

```
PushBuilder pb = request.newPushBuilder();
if (pb != null) {
    for(int row=0; row < 5; row++){
        for(int col=0; col < 8; col++){
            pb.path("image/keyboard_buttons/keyboard_buttons-"
                    + row + "-" + col + ".jpeg")
              .addHeader("content-type", "image/jpeg")
              .push();
        }
    }
}
```

To check if your images are loaded using Server Push or not, open the developer console of your browser, go to network monitoring, and then load the page. One of the pieces of information about each image should be who sent it to the browser. If there's something like **Push** or **ServerPush**, you are using it!

There's more...

Server Push will only work under SSL. In other words, if you are using GlassFish 5 and try to run this recipe, your URL should be something like this:

```
https://localhost:8181/ch04-serverpush
```

If you miss it, the code will still work, but using HTTP/1.0. means that when the code asks for `newPushBuilder,` it will return null (not available):

```
if (pb != null) {
    ...
}
```

See also

- To get the full source code of this recipe, check `https://github.com/eldermoraes/javaee8-cookbook/tree/master/chapter04/ch04-serverpush`

5
Security of Enterprise Architecture

This chapter covers the following recipes:

- Domain protection with authentication
- Granting rights through authorization
- Protecting data confidentiality and integrity with SSL/TLS
- Using declarative security
- Using programmatic security

Introduction

Security is surely one of the hottest topics of all time in the software industry, and there's no reason for that to change any time soon. Actually, it will probably become even hotter as time goes on.

With all your data being streamed through the cloud, passing through uncountable servers, links, databases, sessions, devices, and so on, what you would expect, at least, is that it is well-protected, secured, and that its integrity is kept.

Now, finally, Java EE has its own Security API, with Soteria being its reference implementation.

Security is a subject worthy of dozens of books; that's a fact. But this chapter will cover some common use cases that you may come across in your daily projects.

Domain protection with authentication

Authentication is whatever process, task, and/or policy is used to define who can access your domain. It's like, for example, a badge that you use to access your office.

In applications, the most common use of authentication is to allow access to your domain to users who are already registered.

This recipe will show you how to use a simple code and configuration to control who can and who cannot access some of the resources of your application.

Getting ready

We begin by adding our dependency:

```
<dependency>
    <groupId>javax</groupId>
    <artifactId>javaee-api</artifactId>
    <version>8.0</version>
    <scope>provided</scope>
</dependency>
```

How to do it

1. First, we do some configuration in the web.xml file:

```
<security-constraint>
    <web-resource-collection>
        <web-resource-name>CH05-Authentication</web-resource-name>
        <url-pattern>/authServlet</url-pattern>
    </web-resource-collection>
    <auth-constraint>
        <role-name>role1</role-name>
    </auth-constraint>
</security-constraint>

<security-role>
    <role-name>role1</role-name>
</security-role>
```

2. Then we create a servlet to deal with our user access:

```java
@DeclareRoles({"role1", "role2", "role3"})
@WebServlet(name = "/UserAuthenticationServlet", urlPatterns =
{"/UserAuthenticationServlet"})
public class UserAuthenticationServlet extends HttpServlet {

    private static final long serialVersionUID = 1L;

    @Inject
    private javax.security.enterprise.SecurityContext
    securityContext;

    @Override
    public void doGet(HttpServletRequest request,
    HttpServletResponse response) throws ServletException,
    IOException {

        String name = request.getParameter("name");
        if (null != name || !"".equals(name)) {
            AuthenticationStatus status =
            securityContext.authenticate(
                    request, response,
AuthenticationParameters.withParams().credential
                    (new CallerOnlyCredential(name)));

            response.getWriter().write("Authentication status: "
            + status.name() + "\n");
        }

        String principal = null;
        if (request.getUserPrincipal() != null) {
            principal = request.getUserPrincipal().getName();
        }

        response.getWriter().write("User: " + principal + "\n");
        response.getWriter().write("Role \"role1\" access: " +
        request.isUserInRole("role1") + "\n");
        response.getWriter().write("Role \"role2\" access: " +
        request.isUserInRole("role2") + "\n");
        response.getWriter().write("Role \"role3\" access: " +
        request.isUserInRole("role3") + "\n");
        response.getWriter().write("Access to /authServlet? " +
        securityContext.hasAccessToWebResource("/authServlet") +
        "\n");
    }
}
```

3. And finally, we create the class that will define our authentication policy:

```
@ApplicationScoped
public class AuthenticationMechanism implements
HttpAuthenticationMechanism {

    @Override
    public AuthenticationStatus validateRequest(HttpServletRequest
    request,
    HttpServletResponse response, HttpMessageContext
    httpMessageContext)
    throws AuthenticationException {

        if (httpMessageContext.isAuthenticationRequest()) {

            Credential credential =
            httpMessageContext.getAuthParameters().getCredential();
            if (!(credential instanceof CallerOnlyCredential)) {
                throw new IllegalStateException("Invalid
                mechanism");
            }

            CallerOnlyCredential callerOnlyCredential =
            (CallerOnlyCredential) credential;

            if ("user".equals(callerOnlyCredential.getCaller())) {
                return
                httpMessageContext.notifyContainerAboutLogin
                (callerOnlyCredential.getCaller(), new HashSet<>
                (Arrays.asList("role1","role2")));
            } else{
                throw new AuthenticationException();
            }

        }

        return httpMessageContext.doNothing();
    }

}
```

If you run this project in a Java EE 8-compatible server, you should use this URL (assuming that you are running locally. If not, make the appropriate changes):

```
http://localhost:8080/ch05-authentication/UserAuthenticationServlet?nam
e=user
```

This should result in a page with these messages:

```
Authentication status: SUCCESS
User: user
Role "role1" access: true
Role "role2" access: true
Role "role3" access: false
Access to /authServlet? true
```

Try making any change to the name parameter, such as this:

```
http://localhost:8080/ch05-authentication/UserAuthenticationServlet?nam
e=anotheruser
```

Then the result will be as follows:

```
Authentication status: SEND_FAILURE
User: null
Role "role1" access: false
Role "role2" access: false
Role "role3" access: false
Access to /authServlet? false
```

How it works...

Let's split up the code shown earlier, so that we can better understand what's happening.

In the web.xml file, we are creating a security constraint:

```
<security-constraint>
    ...
</security-constraint>
```

We're defining a resource inside it:

```
<web-resource-collection>
    <web-resource-name>CH05-Authentication</web-resource-name>
    <url-pattern>/authServlet</url-pattern>
</web-resource-collection>
```

And we're defining an authorization policy. In this case, it's a role:

```
<auth-constraint>
    <role-name>role1</role-name>
</auth-constraint>
```

Now we have `UserAuthenticationServlet`. We should pay attention to this annotation:

```
@DeclareRoles({"role1", "role2", "role3"})
```

It defines which roles are part of the context of this particular servlet.

Another important actor in this scene is this one:

```
@Inject
private SecurityContext securityContext;
```

Here, we are asking the server to give us a security context so that we can use it for our purpose. It will make sense in a minute.

Then, if the `name` parameter is filled, we reach this line:

```
AuthenticationStatus status = securityContext.authenticate(
    request, response, withParams().credential(new
    CallerOnlyCredential(name)));
```

This will ask the Java EE server to process an authentication. But...based on what? That's where our `HttpAuthenticationMechanism` implementation comes in.

As the preceding code created `CallerOnlyCredential`, our authentication mechanism will be based on it:

```
Credential credential = httpMessageContext.getAuthParameters()
.getCredential();
if (!(credential instanceof CallerOnlyCredential)) {
    throw new IllegalStateException("Invalid mechanism");
}

CallerOnlyCredential callerOnlyCredential =
(CallerOnlyCredential) credential;
```

And once we have a `credential` instance, we can check if the user "exists":

```
if ("user".equals(callerOnlyCredential.getCaller())) {
    ...
} else{
    throw new AuthenticationException();
}
```

As an example, we have just compared the names, but in a real case you could search your database, an LDAP server, and so on.

If the user exists, we proceed with the authentication based on some rules:

```
return httpMessageContext.notifyContainerAboutLogin
(callerOnlyCredential.getCaller(), new HashSet<>(asList("role1","role2")));
```

In this case, we have said that the user has access to `"role1"` and `"role2"`.

Once the authentication is done, it comes back to the servlet and uses the result to finish the process:

```
response.getWriter().write("Role \"role1\" access: " +
request.isUserInRole("role1") + "\n");
response.getWriter().write("Role \"role2\" access: " +
request.isUserInRole("role2") + "\n");
response.getWriter().write("Role \"role3\" access: " +
request.isUserInRole("role3") + "\n");
response.getWriter().write("Access to /authServlet? " +
securityContext.hasAccessToWebResource("/authServlet") + "\n");
```

So, this code will print `true` for `"role1"` and `"role2"`, and `false` for `"role3"`. Because `"/authServlet"` is allowed for `"role1"`, the user will have access to it.

See also

- The full source code of this recipe is available at `https://github.com/eldermoraes/javaee8-cookbook/tree/master/chapter05/ch05-authentication`.

Granting rights through authorization

If authentication is the way to define who can access a particular resource, authorization is the way to define what a user can and cannot do once they have access to the domain.

It's like allowing someone to get into your house, but denying them access to the remote control for your TV (very important access, by the way). Or, allowing access to the remote control, but denying access to adult channels.

One way to do it is through profiles, and that's what we are going to do in this recipe.

Getting ready

Let's start by adding the dependency:

```
<dependency>
    <groupId>javax</groupId>
    <artifactId>javaee-api</artifactId>
    <version>8.0</version>
    <scope>provided</scope>
</dependency>
```

How to do it...

1. First, we define some roles in a separate class so that we can reuse it:

```
public class Roles {
    public static final String ROLE1 = "role1";
    public static final String ROLE2 = "role2";
    public static final String ROLE3 = "role3";
}
```

2. Then we define some things that the application's users can do:

```
@Stateful
public class UserActivity {
    @RolesAllowed({Roles.ROLE1})
    public void role1Allowed(){
        System.out.println("role1Allowed executed");
    }
    @RolesAllowed({Roles.ROLE2})
    public void role2Allowed(){
        System.out.println("role2Allowed executed");
    }

    @RolesAllowed({Roles.ROLE3})
    public void role3Allowed(){
        System.out.println("role3Allowed executed");
    }

    @PermitAll
    public void anonymousAllowed(){
        System.out.println("anonymousAllowed executed");
```

```
    }

    @DenyAll
    public void noOneAllowed(){
        System.out.println("noOneAllowed executed");
    }
}
```

3. Let's create an interface for executable tasks:

```
public interface Executable {
    void execute() throws Exception;
}
```

4. And let's create another for the roles that will execute them:

```
public interface RoleExecutable {
    void run(Executable executable) throws Exception;
}
```

5. For each role, we create an executor. It will be like an environment that owns the rights of that role:

```
@Named
@RunAs(Roles.ROLE1)
public class Role1Executor implements RoleExecutable {

    @Override
    public void run(Executable executable) throws Exception {
        executable.execute();
    }
}

@Named
@RunAs(Roles.ROLE2)
public class Role2Executor implements RoleExecutable {

    @Override
    public void run(Executable executable) throws Exception {
        executable.execute();
    }
}

@Named
@RunAs(Roles.ROLE3)
public class Role3Executor implements RoleExecutable {

    @Override
```

```
            public void run(Executable executable) throws Exception {
                executable.execute();
            }
        }
```

6. **Then we implement** HttpAuthenticationMechanism:

```
@ApplicationScoped
public class AuthenticationMechanism implements
HttpAuthenticationMechanism {

    @Override
    public AuthenticationStatus validateRequest(HttpServletRequest
     request, HttpServletResponse response, HttpMessageContext
     httpMessageContext) throws AuthenticationException {

        if (httpMessageContext.isAuthenticationRequest()) {

            Credential credential =
            httpMessageContext.getAuthParameters()
            .getCredential();
            if (!(credential instanceof CallerOnlyCredential)) {
                throw new IllegalStateException("Invalid
                mechanism");
            }

            CallerOnlyCredential callerOnlyCredential =
            (CallerOnlyCredential) credential;

            if (null == callerOnlyCredential.getCaller()) {
                throw new AuthenticationException();
            } else switch (callerOnlyCredential.getCaller()) {
                case "user1":
                    return
                    httpMessageContext.
                    notifyContainerAboutLogin
                    (callerOnlyCredential.getCaller(),
                     new HashSet<>
                    (asList(Roles.ROLE1)));
                case "user2":
                    return
                    httpMessageContext.
                    notifyContainerAboutLogin
                    (callerOnlyCredential.getCaller(),
                     new HashSet<>
                    (asList(Roles.ROLE2)));
                case "user3":
                    return
```

```
                        httpMessageContext.
                        notifyContainerAboutLogin
                        (callerOnlyCredential.getCaller(),
                         new HashSet<>
                        (asList(Roles.ROLE3)));
                    default:
                        throw new AuthenticationException();
                }

            }

            return httpMessageContext.doNothing();
        }

    }
```

7. And finally, we create the servlet that will manage all these resources:

```
@DeclareRoles({Roles.ROLE1, Roles.ROLE2, Roles.ROLE3})
@WebServlet(name = "/UserAuthorizationServlet", urlPatterns =
{"/UserAuthorizationServlet"})
public class UserAuthorizationServlet extends HttpServlet {

    private static final long serialVersionUID = 1L;

    @Inject
    private SecurityContext securityContext;
    @Inject
    private Role1Executor role1Executor;
    @Inject
    private Role2Executor role2Executor;
    @Inject
    private Role3Executor role3Executor;
    @Inject
    private UserActivity userActivity;
    @Override
    public void doGet(HttpServletRequest request,
    HttpServletResponse
    response) throws ServletException, IOException {

        try {
            String name = request.getParameter("name");
            if (null != name || !"".equals(name)) {
                AuthenticationStatus status =
                securityContext.authenticate(
                        request, response, withParams().credential(
                        new CallerOnlyCredential(name)));
```

```
        response.getWriter().write("Authentication
        status: " + status.name() + "\n");
    }

    String principal = null;
    if (request.getUserPrincipal() != null) {
        principal = request.getUserPrincipal().getName();
    }

    response.getWriter().write("User: " + principal +
    "\n");
    response.getWriter().write("Role \"role1\" access: " +
    request.isUserInRole(Roles.ROLE1) + "\n");
    response.getWriter().write("Role \"role2\" access: " +
    request.isUserInRole(Roles.ROLE2) + "\n");
    response.getWriter().write("Role \"role3\" access: " +
    request.isUserInRole(Roles.ROLE3) + "\n");

    RoleExecutable executable = null;

    if (request.isUserInRole(Roles.ROLE1)) {
        executable = role1Executor;
    } else if (request.isUserInRole(Roles.ROLE2)) {
        executable = role2Executor;
    } else if (request.isUserInRole(Roles.ROLE3)) {
        executable = role3Executor;
    }

    if (executable != null) {
        executable.run(() -> {
            try {
                userActivity.role1Allowed();
                response.getWriter().write("role1Allowed
                executed: true\n");
            } catch (Exception e) {
                response.getWriter().write("role1Allowed
                executed: false\n");
            }

            try {
                userActivity.role2Allowed();
                response.getWriter().write("role2Allowed
                executed: true\n");
            } catch (Exception e) {
                response.getWriter().write("role2Allowed
                executed: false\n");
            }
```

```
                    try {
                        userActivity.role3Allowed();
                        response.getWriter().write("role2Allowed
                        executed: true\n");
                    } catch (Exception e) {
                        response.getWriter().write("role2Allowed
                        executed: false\n");
                    }

                });

            }

            try {
                userActivity.anonymousAllowed();
                response.getWriter().write("anonymousAllowed
                executed: true\n");
            } catch (Exception e) {
                response.getWriter().write("anonymousAllowed
                executed: false\n");
            }
            try {
                userActivity.noOneAllowed();
                response.getWriter().write("noOneAllowed
                executed: true\n");
            } catch (Exception e) {
                response.getWriter().write("noOneAllowed
                executed: false\n");
            }

        } catch (Exception ex) {
            System.err.println(ex.getMessage());
        }

    }
}
```

To try this code out, you can run these URLs:

- `http://localhost:8080/ch05-authorization/UserAuthorizationServl`
  `et?name=user1`
- `http://localhost:8080/ch05-authorization/UserAuthorizationServl`
  `et?name=user2`
- `http://localhost:8080/ch05-authorization/UserAuthorizationServl`
  `et?name=user3`

The result for `user1`, for example, will be like this:

```
Authentication status: SUCCESS
User: user1
Role "role1" access: true
Role "role2" access: false
Role "role3" access: false
role1Allowed executed: true
role2Allowed executed: false
role2Allowed executed: false
anonymousAllowed executed: true
noOneAllowed executed: false
```

And if you try with a user that doesn't exist, the result will be like this:

```
Authentication status: SEND_FAILURE
User: null
Role "role1" access: false
Role "role2" access: false
Role "role3" access: false
anonymousAllowed executed: true
noOneAllowed executed: false
```

How it works...

Well, we have a lot of things happening here! Let's begin with our `UserActivity` class.

We used the `@RolesAllowed` annotation to define the role that can access each method of the class:

```
@RolesAllowed({Roles.ROLE1})
public void role1Allowed(){
    System.out.println("role1Allowed executed");
}
```

You can add more than one role inside the annotation (it's an array).

We also had two others interesting annotations, @PermitAll and @DenyAll:

- The @PermitAll annotation allows anyone to access the method, even without any authentication.
- The @DenyAll annotation denies everyone access to the method, even authenticated users with the highest privileges.

Then we have what we called executors:

```
@Named
@RunAs(Roles.ROLE1)
public class Role1Executor implements RoleExecutable {

    @Override
    public void run(Executable executable) throws Exception {
        executable.execute();
    }
}
```

We used the @RunAs annotation at the class level, which means that this class inherits all the privileges of the defined role (in this case, "role1"). It means that every single method of this class will have the "role1" privileges.

Now, looking at UserAuthorizationServlet, right at the beginning we have an important object:

```
@Inject
private SecurityContext securityContext;
```

Here, we are asking the server to give us a security context instance so that we can use it for authentication purposes.

Then, if the name parameter is filled, we reach this line:

```
AuthenticationStatus status = securityContext.authenticate(
        request, response, withParams().credential(new
        CallerOnlyCredential(name)));
```

This will ask the Java EE server to process an authentication. That's where our HttpAuthenticationMechanism implementation comes in.

As the preceding code created `CallerOnlyCredential`, our authentication mechanism will be based on it:

```
Credential credential = httpMessageContext.getAuthParameters().
getCredential();
if (!(credential instanceof CallerOnlyCredential)) {
    throw new IllegalStateException("Invalid mechanism");
}

CallerOnlyCredential callerOnlyCredential =
(CallerOnlyCredential) credential;
```

And once we have a credential instance, we can check if the user exists:

```
if (null == callerOnlyCredential.getCaller()) {
    throw new AuthenticationException();
} else switch (callerOnlyCredential.getCaller()) {
    case "user1":
        return httpMessageContext.notifyContainerAboutLogin
        (callerOnlyCredential.getCaller(), new HashSet<>
        (asList(Roles.ROLE1)));
    case "user2":
        return httpMessageContext.notifyContainerAboutLogin
        (callerOnlyCredential.getCaller(), new HashSet<>
        (asList(Roles.ROLE2)));
    case "user3":
        return httpMessageContext.notifyContainerAboutLogin
        (callerOnlyCredential.getCaller(), new HashSet<>
        (asList(Roles.ROLE3)));
    default:
        throw new AuthenticationException();
}
```

So we are saying that `"user1"` has access to `"role1"`, `"user2"` to `"role2"`, and so on.

Once the user role is defined, we are back to the servlet and can choose which environment (executor) will be used:

```
if (request.isUserInRole(Roles.ROLE1)) {
    executable = role1Executor;
} else if (request.isUserInRole(Roles.ROLE2)) {
    executable = role2Executor;
} else if (request.isUserInRole(Roles.ROLE3)) {
    executable = role3Executor;
}
```

And then we try all the methods of the `UserActivity` class. Only the methods allowed for that specific role will be executed; the others will fall into an exception, except for the `@PermitAll` method, which will run anyway, and `@DenyAll`, which will not run anyway.

See also

- Check the full source code of this recipe at `https://github.com/eldermoraes/javaee8-cookbook/tree/master/chapter05/ch05-authorization`.

Protecting data confidentiality and integrity with SSL/TLS

Security also means protecting the transportation of your data, and for this purpose we have the most popular method, which is called the **Secure Sockets Layer** (**SSL**).

Transport Layer Security, or **TLS**, is the newest version of SSL. So, we have SSL 3.0 and TLS 1.0 as the protocols supported by GlassFish 5.0.

This recipe will show you how to enable GlassFish 5.0 to work properly with SSL. All Java EE servers have their own way of doing this.

Getting ready

To enable SSL in GlassFish, you need to configure an HTTP listener for SSL. All you need to do is this:

1. Make sure GlassFish is up and running.
2. Use the `create-ssl` command to create your HTTP listener for SSL.
3. Restart the GlassFish server.

How to do it...

1. To do this task, you need to access the GlassFish remote **command-line interface (CLI)**. You can do it by going to this path:

   ```
   $GLASSFISH_HOME/bin
   ```

2. Once you are there, execute the following command:

   ```
   ./asadmin
   ```

3. When the prompt is ready, you can execute this command:

   ```
   create-ssl --type http-listener --certname cookbookCert http-
   listener-1
   ```

4. Then you can restart the server and your `http-listener-1` will work with SSL. If you want to drop SSL from the listener, just go back to the prompt and execute this command:

   ```
   delete-ssl --type http-listener http-listener-1
   ```

How it works...

With SSL, both the client and the server encrypt data before sending it, and decrypt data upon receiving it. When a browser opens a secured website (using HTTPS), something happens that is called a **handshake**.

In the handshake, the browser asks the server for a session; the server answers by sending a certificate and the public key. The browser validates the certificate and, if it is valid, generates an unique session key, encrypts it with the server public key, and sends it back to the server. Once the server receives the session key, it decrypts it with its private key.

Now, both client and server, and only them, have a copy of the session key and can ensure that the communication is secure.

There's more...

It's strongly recommended that you use a certificate from a **Certification Authority (CA)** instead of a self-created certificate like we did in this recipe.

You can check out `https://letsencrypt.org`, where you can get your free certificate.

The process of using it is the same; you will just change the value in the `--certname` parameter.

See also

- For detailed information about all the security aspects and configuration for GlassFish 5, check out `https://javaee.github.io/glassfish/doc/5.0/security-guide.pdf`.

Using declarative security

When building your application's security features, you can basically use two approaches: **programmatic security** and **declarative security**:

- The programmatic approach is when you define the security policy of your application using code.
- The declarative approach is when you do it by declaring the policies and then applying them accordingly.

This recipe will show you the declarative approach.

Getting ready

Let's start by adding the dependency:

```xml
<dependency>
    <groupId>javax</groupId>
    <artifactId>javaee-api</artifactId>
    <version>8.0</version>
    <scope>provided</scope>
</dependency>
```

How to do it...

1. Let's create a list of roles for our application:

```
public class Roles {
    public static final String ADMIN = "admin";
    public static final String USER = "user";
}
```

2. Then we create a list of tasks that could be performed by only one of the roles, one task that everyone can do, and another task that no one can do:

```
@Stateful
public class UserBean {
    @RolesAllowed({Roles.ADMIN})
    public void adminOperation(){
        System.out.println("adminOperation executed");
    }
    @RolesAllowed({Roles.USER})
    public void userOperation(){
        System.out.println("userOperation executed");
    }

    @PermitAll
    public void everyoneCanDo(){
        System.out.println("everyoneCanDo executed");
    }

    @DenyAll
    public void noneCanDo(){
        System.out.println("noneCanDo executed");
    }
}
```

3. Now we create an environment for both the USER and ADMIN roles to do their stuff:

```
@Named
@RunAs(Roles.USER)
public class UserExecutor implements RoleExecutable {

    @Override
    public void run(Executable executable) throws Exception {
        executable.execute();
    }
}
```

```
@Named
@RunAs(Roles.ADMIN)
public class AdminExecutor implements RoleExecutable {

    @Override
    public void run(Executable executable) throws Exception {
        executable.execute();
    }
}
```

4. Then we implement HttpAuthenticationMechanism:

```
@ApplicationScoped
public class AuthenticationMechanism implements
HttpAuthenticationMechanism {

    @Override
    public AuthenticationStatus validateRequest(HttpServletRequest
    request, HttpServletResponse response, HttpMessageContext
    httpMessageContext)
    throws AuthenticationException {

        if (httpMessageContext.isAuthenticationRequest()) {

            Credential credential =
            httpMessageContext.getAuthParameters().
            getCredential();
            if (!(credential instanceof CallerOnlyCredential)) {
                throw new IllegalStateException("Invalid
                mechanism");
            }

            CallerOnlyCredential callerOnlyCredential =
            (CallerOnlyCredential)
            credential;

            if (null == callerOnlyCredential.getCaller()) {
                throw new AuthenticationException();
            } else switch (callerOnlyCredential.getCaller()) {
                case Roles.ADMIN:
                    return httpMessageContext
                    .notifyContainerAboutLogin
                    (callerOnlyCredential.getCaller(),
                     new HashSet<>
                    (asList(Roles.ADMIN)));
                case Roles.USER:
                    return httpMessageContext
                    .notifyContainerAboutLogin
```

```
                    (callerOnlyCredential.getCaller(),
                    new HashSet<>
                    (asList(Roles.USER)));
                default:
                    throw new AuthenticationException();
            }

        }

        return httpMessageContext.doNothing();
    }

}
```

5. And finally, we create one servlet for each role (USER and ADMIN):

```
@DeclareRoles({Roles.ADMIN, Roles.USER})
@WebServlet(name = "/UserServlet", urlPatterns = {"/UserServlet"})
public class UserServlet extends HttpServlet {

    private static final long serialVersionUID = 1L;

    @Inject
    private SecurityContext securityContext;

    @Inject
    private UserExecutor userExecutor;

    @Inject
    private UserBean userActivity;

    @Override
    public void doGet(HttpServletRequest request,
    HttpServletResponse response) throws ServletException,
    IOException {

        try {
            securityContext.authenticate(
                    request, response, withParams().credential(new
                    CallerOnlyCredential(Roles.USER)));

            response.getWriter().write("Role \"admin\" access: " +
            request.isUserInRole(Roles.ADMIN) + "\n");
            response.getWriter().write("Role \"user\" access: " +
            request.isUserInRole(Roles.USER) + "\n");

            userExecutor.run(() -> {
                try {
```

```
                    userActivity.adminOperation();
                    response.getWriter().write("adminOperation
                    executed: true\n");
                } catch (Exception e) {
                    response.getWriter().write("adminOperation
                    executed: false\n");
                }

                try {
                    userActivity.userOperation();
                    response.getWriter().write("userOperation
                    executed: true\n");
                } catch (Exception e) {
                    response.getWriter().write("userOperation
                    executed: false\n");
                }

            });

            try {
                userActivity.everyoneCanDo();
                response.getWriter().write("everyoneCanDo
                executed: true\n");
            } catch (Exception e) {
                response.getWriter().write("everyoneCanDo
                executed: false\n");
            }

            try {
                userActivity.noneCanDo();
                response.getWriter().write("noneCanDo
                executed: true\n");
            } catch (Exception e) {
                response.getWriter().write("noneCanDo
                executed: false\n");
            }

        } catch (Exception ex) {
            System.err.println(ex.getMessage());
        }

    }
}

@DeclareRoles({Roles.ADMIN, Roles.USER})
@WebServlet(name = "/AdminServlet", urlPatterns =
{"/AdminServlet"})
public class AdminServlet extends HttpServlet {
```

```
private static final long serialVersionUID = 1L;

@Inject
private SecurityContext securityContext;

@Inject
private AdminExecutor adminExecutor;

@Inject
private UserBean userActivity;

@Override
public void doGet(HttpServletRequest request,
HttpServletResponse
response) throws ServletException, IOException {

    try {
        securityContext.authenticate(
                request, response, withParams().credential(new
                CallerOnlyCredential(Roles.ADMIN)));

        response.getWriter().write("Role \"admin\" access: " +
        request.isUserInRole(Roles.ADMIN) + "\n");
        response.getWriter().write("Role \"user\" access: " +
        request.isUserInRole(Roles.USER) + "\n");

        adminExecutor.run(() -> {
            try {
                userActivity.adminOperation();
                response.getWriter().write("adminOperation
                executed: true\n");
            } catch (Exception e) {
                response.getWriter().write("adminOperation
                executed: false\n");
            }

            try {
                userActivity.userOperation();
                response.getWriter().write("userOperation
                executed: true\n");
            } catch (Exception e) {
                response.getWriter().write("userOperation
                executed: false\n");
            }

        });

        try {
```

```
            userActivity.everyoneCanDo();
            response.getWriter().write("everyoneCanDo
            executed: true\n");
        } catch (Exception e) {
            response.getWriter().write("everyoneCanDo
            executed: false\n");
        }

        try {
            userActivity.noneCanDo();
            response.getWriter().write("noneCanDo
            executed: true\n");
        } catch (Exception e) {
            response.getWriter().write("noneCanDo
            executed: false\n");
        }

    } catch (Exception ex) {
        System.err.println(ex.getMessage());
    }

    }
}
```

How it works...

Looking at `UserServlet` (which applies to the `USER` role), we first see the authentication step:

```
securityContext.authenticate(
        request, response, withParams().credential(new
        CallerOnlyCredential(Roles.ADMIN)));
```

For example, we've used the role name as a username because if we look at the `AuthenticationMechanism` class (implementing `HttpAuthenticationMechanism`), we see it doing all the hard work of authenticating and assigning the right role to the user:

```
Credential credential =
httpMessageContext.getAuthParameters()
.getCredential();
if (!(credential instanceof CallerOnlyCredential)) {
    throw new IllegalStateException("Invalid mechanism");
}

CallerOnlyCredential callerOnlyCredential =
(CallerOnlyCredential)
```

```
    credential;

if (null == callerOnlyCredential.getCaller()) {
    throw new AuthenticationException();
} else switch (callerOnlyCredential.getCaller()) {
    case Roles.ADMIN:
        return httpMessageContext.notifyContainerAboutLogin
        (callerOnlyCredential.getCaller(), new HashSet<>
        (asList(Roles.ADMIN)));
    case Roles.USER:
        return httpMessageContext.notifyContainerAboutLogin
        (callerOnlyCredential.getCaller(), new HashSet<>
        (asList(Roles.USER)));
    default:
        throw new AuthenticationException();
}
```

And back to our `UserServlet`, now that the user has the proper role assigned, it is just a matter of what they can and cannot do:

```
userExecutor.run(() -> {
    try {
        userActivity.adminOperation();
        response.getWriter().write("adminOperation
        executed: true\n");
    } catch (Exception e) {
        response.getWriter().write("adminOperation
        executed: false\n");
    }

    try {
        userActivity.userOperation();
        response.getWriter().write("userOperation
        executed: true\n");
    } catch (Exception e) {
        response.getWriter().write("userOperation
        executed:  false\n");
    }

});
```

And also, we try the tasks that everyone and no one can perform:

```
try {
    userActivity.everyoneCanDo();
    response.getWriter().write("everyoneCanDo
    executed: true\n");
} catch (Exception e) {
```

```
        response.getWriter().write("everyoneCanDo
        executed: false\n");
    }

    try {
        userActivity.noneCanDo();
        response.getWriter().write("noneCanDo
        executed: true\n");
    } catch (Exception e) {
        response.getWriter().write("noneCanDo
        executed: false\n");
    }
```

The AdminServlet class goes through exactly the same steps using an AdminExecutor environment, so we will omit it for the sake of space.

To try out this code, just run it on a Java EE 8-compatible server using these URLs:

- http://localhost:8080/ch05-declarative/AdminServlet
- http://localhost:8080/ch05-declarative/UserServlet

The result example for AdminServlet will be like this:

```
Role "admin" access: true
Role "user" access: false
adminOperation executed: true
userOperation executed: false
everyoneCanDo executed: true
noneCanDo executed: false
```

See also

- Check the full source code of this recipe at https://github.com/eldermoraes/ javaee8-cookbook/tree/master/chapter05/ch05-declarative.

Using programmatic security

We've already seen the declarative approach, so now let's see the programmatic approach.

Getting ready

Let's start by adding the dependency:

```xml
<dependency>
    <groupId>javax</groupId>
    <artifactId>javaee-api</artifactId>
    <version>8.0</version>
    <scope>provided</scope>
</dependency>
```

How to do it...

1. Let's first define our roles list:

```java
public class Roles {
    public static final String ADMIN = "admin";
    public static final String USER = "user";
}
```

2. Then, let's define a list of tasks to be done based on the role:

```java
@Stateful
public class UserBean {
    @RolesAllowed({Roles.ADMIN})
    public void adminOperation(){
        System.out.println("adminOperation executed");
    }
    @RolesAllowed({Roles.USER})
    public void userOperation(){
        System.out.println("userOperation executed");
    }

    @PermitAll
    public void everyoneCanDo(){
        System.out.println("everyoneCanDo executed");
    }

}
```

3. Now let's implement the `IndentityStore` interface. Here, we define our policy for validating the user's identity:

```
@ApplicationScoped
public class UserIdentityStore implements IdentityStore {

    @Override
    public CredentialValidationResult validate(Credential
credential) {
        if (credential instanceof UsernamePasswordCredential) {
            return validate((UsernamePasswordCredential)
credential);
        }

        return CredentialValidationResult.NOT_VALIDATED_RESULT;
    }

    public CredentialValidationResult
validate(UsernamePasswordCredential
    usernamePasswordCredential) {

        if (usernamePasswordCredential.
        getCaller().equals(Roles.ADMIN)
                && usernamePasswordCredential.
                getPassword().compareTo("1234"))
        {

            return new CredentialValidationResult(
                    new CallerPrincipal
                    (usernamePasswordCredential.getCaller()),
                    new HashSet<>(Arrays.asList(Roles.ADMIN)));
        } else if (usernamePasswordCredential.
          getCaller().equals(Roles.USER)
                && usernamePasswordCredential.
                getPassword().compareTo("1234"))
        {

            return new CredentialValidationResult(
                    new CallerPrincipal
                    (usernamePasswordCredential.getCaller()),
                    new HashSet<>(Arrays.asList(Roles.USER)));
        }

        return CredentialValidationResult.INVALID_RESULT;
    }

}
```

4. Here, we implement the `HttpAuthenticationMethod` interface:

```
@ApplicationScoped
public class AuthenticationMechanism implements
HttpAuthenticationMechanism {

    @Inject
    private UserIdentityStore identityStore;
    @Override
    public AuthenticationStatus validateRequest(HttpServletRequest
    request,
    HttpServletResponse response, HttpMessageContext
    httpMessageContext)
    throws AuthenticationException {

        if (httpMessageContext.isAuthenticationRequest()) {

            Credential credential =
            httpMessageContext.getAuthParameters()
            .getCredential();
            if (!(credential instanceof
UsernamePasswordCredential)) {
                throw new IllegalStateException("Invalid
                mechanism");
            }

            return httpMessageContext.notifyContainerAboutLogin
            (identityStore.validate(credential));
        }

        return httpMessageContext.doNothing();
    }

}
```

5. And finally, we create the servlet where the user will both authenticate and do their stuff:

```
@DeclareRoles({Roles.ADMIN, Roles.USER})
@WebServlet(name = "/OperationServlet", urlPatterns =
{"/OperationServlet"})
public class OperationServlet extends HttpServlet {

    private static final long serialVersionUID = 1L;

    @Inject
    private SecurityContext securityContext;
```

```java
@Inject
private UserBean userActivity;

@Override
public void doGet(HttpServletRequest request,
HttpServletResponse
response) throws ServletException, IOException {

    String name = request.getParameter("name");
    String password = request.getParameter("password");

    Credential credential = new
UsernamePasswordCredential(name,
    new Password(password));

    AuthenticationStatus status = securityContext.authenticate(
            request, response,
    withParams().credential(credential));

    response.getWriter().write("Role \"admin\" access: " +
    request.isUserInRole(Roles.ADMIN) + "\n");
    response.getWriter().write("Role \"user\" access: " +
    request.isUserInRole(Roles.USER) + "\n");

    if (status.equals(AuthenticationStatus.SUCCESS)) {

        if (request.isUserInRole(Roles.ADMIN)) {
            userActivity.adminOperation();
            response.getWriter().write("adminOperation
            executed: true\n");
        } else if (request.isUserInRole(Roles.USER)) {
            userActivity.userOperation();
            response.getWriter().write("userOperation
            executed: true\n");
        }

        userActivity.everyoneCanDo();
        response.getWriter().write("everyoneCanDo
        executed: true\n");

    } else {
        response.getWriter().write("Authentication failed\n");
    }

    }
}
```

To try out this code, run it in a Java EE 8-compatible server using these URLs:

- `http://localhost:8080/ch05-programmatic/OperationServlet?name=user&password=1234`
- `http://localhost:8080/ch05-programmatic/OperationServlet?name=admin&password=1234`

An example of an `ADMIN` role's result is as follows:

```
Role "admin" access: true
Role "user" access: false
adminOperation executed: true
everyoneCanDo executed: true
```

And if you use a wrong name/password pair, you get this result:

```
Role "admin" access: false
Role "user" access: false
Authentication failed
```

How it works...

Contrary to the declarative approach (see the previous recipe in this chapter), here we are using code to validate the user. We've done it by implementing the `IdentityStore` interface.

For example, even though we've hardcoded the password, you can use the same piece of code to validate the password against a database, LDAP, an external endpoint, and many more:

```
if (usernamePasswordCredential.getCaller().equals(Roles.ADMIN)
        &&
usernamePasswordCredential.getPassword().compareTo("1234"))
{

    return new CredentialValidationResult(
            new CallerPrincipal(usernamePasswordCredential
            .getCaller()),
            new HashSet<>(asList(Roles.ADMIN)));
} else if (usernamePasswordCredential.getCaller()
  .equals(Roles.USER)
        && usernamePasswordCredential.
        getPassword().compareTo("1234"))
{
```

```
return new CredentialValidationResult(
    new CallerPrincipal(usernamePasswordCredential
    .getCaller()),
    new HashSet<>(asList(Roles.USER)));
}

return INVALID_RESULT;
```

Authenticating using `IdentityStore` means just delegating using `HttpAuthenticationMethod`:

```
Credential credential =
httpMessageContext.getAuthParameters().getCredential();
if (!(credential instanceof UsernamePasswordCredential)) {
    throw new IllegalStateException("Invalid mechanism");
}

return httpMessageContext.notifyContainerAboutLogin
(identityStore.validate(credential));
```

And then, `OperationServlet` will just try an authentication:

```
String name = request.getParameter("name");
String password = request.getParameter("password");

Credential credential = new UsernamePasswordCredential(name,
new Password(password));

AuthenticationStatus status = securityContext.authenticate(
    request, response,
    withParams().credential(credential));
```

Based on this, we will define the flow of what will happen next:

```
if (status.equals(AuthenticationStatus.SUCCESS)) {

    if (request.isUserInRole(Roles.ADMIN)) {
        userActivity.adminOperation();
        response.getWriter().write("adminOperation
        executed: true\n");
    } else if (request.isUserInRole(Roles.USER)) {
        userActivity.userOperation();
        response.getWriter().write("userOperation
        executed: true\n");
    }

    userActivity.everyoneCanDo();
    response.getWriter().write("everyoneCanDo executed:
```

```
true\n");

} else {
    response.getWriter().write("Authentication failed\n");
}
```

Pay attention! That is your code defining what each role will do.

See also

- See the full source code for this recipe at `https://github.com/eldermoraes/javaee8-cookbook/tree/master/chapter05/ch05-programmatic`.

6
Reducing the Coding Effort by Relying on Standards

This chapter covers the following recipes:

- Preparing your application to use a connection pool
- Using messaging services for asynchronous communication
- Understanding a servlet's life cycle
- Transaction management

Introduction

One of the most important concepts that you need to know about Java EE is: it is a standard. If you go to the **Java Community Process (JCP)** website, you will find the **Java Specification Request (JSR)** for the Java EE platform (for Version 8 it is JSR 366).

A standard... for what? Well, for an application server! For instance, a Java EE application server.

It means that you can develop your Java EE application knowing it will run in an environment that provides a bunch of resources that you can rely on.

It also means you can easily move from one application server to another, as long as you stick to the Java EE patterns instead of some vendor-specific feature (considered a bad practice). Your application should have the same behavior no matter what Java EE-compatible server you are using.

Oh, yes! Beyond being a standard, Java EE is also a certification. For a Java EE server to be considered compatible, it has to pass through a number of tests to guarantee it implements every single point of the specification (JSR).

This amazing ecosystem allows for less coding of your application and gives you the chance to focus on what really matters to you or to your client. Without a standard environment, you would need to implement your own code for request/response management, queues, connection pooling, and other stuff.

You can definitely do it if you want, but you don't have to. Actually you can even write your own Java EE application server, if you want to.

Having said that let's move on with the chapter! In the following recipes, you are going to learn how to take advantage of some cool features already implemented on your favorite Java EE application server.

Examples will be based on GlassFish 5 but, as I mentioned before, they should have the same behavior for any other compatible implementation.

Preparing your application to use a connection pool

One of the first things we should learn in our life, after feeding, is using a connection pool. Especially when we are talking about databases. This is the case covered here.

Why? Because a connection opened with the database is costly in terms of resources used for it. Even worse, if we look closer at the process of opening a new connection, it uses a lot of CPU resources, for example.

Maybe it won't make much difference if you have two users using a database with a couple of registers in a few tables. But it can start causing trouble if you have dozens of users, or if the database is large and gives you sleepless nights when you have hundreds of users using a huge database.

Actually I, myself, saw in the early days of J2EE 1.3 (the year was 2002), a performance issue being solved by a connection pool in an application used by 20 people. There were a few users, but the database was really big and not so well-designed (the same for the application, I have to say).

But you may say: why does a connection pool help us with this? Because once it is configured, the server will open all the connections you asked for, when it is starting up, and will manage them for you.

The only thing you have to do is to ask: *"Hey, server! Could you lend me a database connection, please?"* and kindly give it back when you are done (which means as quickly as possible).

This recipe will show you how to do it.

Getting ready

First, add the right dependency to your project:

```
<dependency>
    <groupId>javax</groupId>
    <artifactId>javaee-api</artifactId>
    <version>8.0</version>
    <scope>provided</scope>
</dependency>
```

If you still haven't downloaded GlassFish 5 to your development environment, this is the right time to do it.

How to do it...

1. We will begin by configuring our connection pool in GlassFish 5. Once it is up and running, go to this URL:

   ```
   http://localhost:8080
   ```

2. Now click on the **go to the Administration Console** link or if you prefer, go straight to the URL at:

   ```
   http://localhost:4848/
   ```

3. Then follow this path in the left menu:

   Resources | JDBC | JDBC Connection Pools

4. Click on the **New** button. It will open the **New JDBC Connection Pool** page. Fill in the fields as described here:

- **Pool Name:** MysqlPool
- **Resource Type:** javax.sql.DataSource
- **Database Driver Vendor:** MySql

Of course, you can make your own custom choices, but then we will be following different paths!

5. Click on the **Next** button. It will open the second step for our pool creation process.

This new page has three sections: **General Settings, Pool Settings,** and **Transaction and Additional Properties**. For our recipe, we are only dealing with **General Settings** and **Additional Properties**.

6. In the **General Settings** section make sure that **DataSource Classname** has this value selected:

com.mysql.jdbc.jdbc2.optional.MysqlDatasource

7. Now let's move to the **Additional Properties** section. There might be a bunch of properties listed, but we will just fill in a few of them:

- **DatabaseName:** sys
- **ServerName:** localhost
- **User:** root
- **Password:** mysql
- **PortNumber:** 3306

8. Click on the **Finish** button and voilá! Your connection pool is ready... or almost.

You can't access it until you do one more configuration. In the same menu, on the left, following this path:

Resources | JDBC | JDBC Resources

9. Click on the **New** button and then fill in the fields like this:

- **JNDI Name:** jdbc/MysqlPool
- **Pool Name:** MysqlPool

Now you are good to go! Your connection pool is ready to be used. Let's build a simple application to try it:

1. First, we create a class to get a connection from the pool:

```
public class ConnectionPool {

    public static Connection getConnection() throws SQLException,
    NamingException {
        InitialContext ctx = new InitialContext();
        DataSource ds = (DataSource) ctx.lookup("jdbc/MysqlPool");

        return ds.getConnection();
    }
}
```

2. Then, a class that we will use as a representation of the `sys_config` table (MySQL's system table):

```
public class SysConfig {

    private final String variable;
    private final String value;

    public SysConfig(String variable, String value) {
        this.variable = variable;
        this.value = value;
    }

    public String getVariable() {
        return variable;
    }

    public String getValue() {
        return value;
    }
}
```

3. Here we create another class, to create a list based on the data returned from the database:

```
@Stateless
public class SysConfigBean {

    public String getSysConfig() throws SQLException,
    NamingException {
        String sql = "SELECT variable, value FROM sys_config";
```

```
try (Connection conn = ConnectionPool.getConnection();
        PreparedStatement ps = conn.prepareStatement(sql);
        ResultSet rs = ps.executeQuery()
        Jsonb jsonb = JsonbBuilder.create()) {

    List<SysConfig> list = new ArrayList<>();
    while (rs.next()) {
        list.add(new SysConfig(rs.getString("variable"),
        rs.getString("value")));
    }

    Jsonb jsonb = JsonbBuilder.create();
    return jsonb.toJson(list);
    }
  }
}
```

4. And finally a servlet that will try them all:

```
@WebServlet(name = "PoolTestServlet", urlPatterns =
{"/PoolTestServlet"})
public class PoolTestServlet extends HttpServlet {

    @EJB
    private SysConfigBean config;

    @Override
    protected void doGet(HttpServletRequest request,
    HttpServletResponse response)
            throws ServletException, IOException {

        try (PrintWriter writer = response.getWriter()) {
            config = new SysConfigBean();
            writer.write(config.getSysConfig());
        } catch (SQLException | NamingException ex) {
            System.err.println(ex.getMessage());
        }
    }
}
```

To try it just open this URL in your browser:

```
http://localhost:8080/ch06-connectionpooling/PoolTestServlet
```

There's more...

Deciding how many connections your pool will hold, as well as all the other parameters, is an architecture decision made based on a number of factors such as the type of data, database design, application and user behavior, and so on. We could write a whole book about it.

But if you are starting from scratch and/or still don't need much information, consider a number between 10% to 20% of your concurrent users. In other words, if your application has, for instance, 100 concurrent users, you should provide 10 to 20 connections to your pool.

You will know that your connections aren't enough if some methods are taking too much time to get a connection from the pool (it should take no time at all). It means that the server has no available connection at that moment.

So, you need to check if there are some methods taking too long to complete, or even some part in your code that is not closing the connection (consider what gives the connection back to the server). Depending on the issue, it might not be a pooling problem but a design one.

Another important thing for dealing with connection pools is to use the "try-with-resources" statement as we did here:

```
try (Connection conn = ConnectionPool.getConnection();
        PreparedStatement ps = conn.prepareStatement(sql);
        ResultSet rs = ps.executeQuery()) {
```

This will guarantee that these resources will be properly closed once the method is done and also deal with their respective exceptions, also helping you to write less code.

See also

- See this recipe's full source code at: https://github.com/eldermoraes/javaee8-cookbook/tree/master/chapter06/ch06-connectionpooling

Using messaging services for asynchronous communication

The message service, provided in Java EE by the **Java Message Service (JMS)** API, is one of the most important and versatile features provided by Java EE environments.

It uses the Producer-Consumer approach, where one peer (the Producer) puts a message into a queue and another peer (the Consumer) reads the message from there.

Both the Producer and Consumer can be different applications, even using different technologies.

This recipe will show you how to build a messaging service using GlassFish 5. Each Java EE server has its own way to set up the service, so if are using some other implementations, you should take a look at its documentation.

On the other hand, the Java EE code generated here will work on any Java EE 8-compatible implementation. Standard for the win!

Getting ready

First add the proper dependency to your project:

```
<dependency>
    <groupId>javax</groupId>
    <artifactId>javaee-api</artifactId>
    <version>8.0</version>
    <scope>provided</scope>
</dependency>
```

How to do it...

1. We will begin by configuring our messaging service in GlassFish 5. Once the server is up and running, go to this URL:

   ```
   http://localhost:8080
   ```

2. Now click on the **go to the Administration Console** link or if you prefer, go straight to the URL at:

```
http://localhost:4848/
```

Then follow this path in the left menu:

Resources | **JMS Resources** | **Connection Factories**

3. Click on the **New** button. When the page is opened, fill the **General Settings** section fields like this:

- **JNDI Name:** `jms/JmsFactory`
- **Resource Type:** `javax.jms.ConnectionFactory`

We will not touch the **Pool Settings** section here, so just click on the **OK** button to register your new factory.

4. Now follow this path in the left menu:

Resources | **JMS Resources** | **Destination Resources**

5. Click on the **New** button. When the page is opened, fill the section fields like this:

- **JNDI Name:** `jms/JmsQueue`
- **Physical Destination Name:** `JmsQueue`
- **ResourceType:** `javax.jms.Queue`

Click on the **OK** button and you are ready! Now you have a connection factory to access your JMS server and a queue. So let's build an application to use it:

1. First, we create a **message driven bean (MDB)** as a listener for any message dropped into our queue. This is the Consumer:

```java
@MessageDriven(activationConfig = {
    @ActivationConfigProperty(propertyName = "destinationLookup",
    propertyValue = "jms/JmsQueue"),
    @ActivationConfigProperty(propertyName = "destinationType",
    propertyValue = "javax.jms.Queue")
})
public class QueueListener implements MessageListener {

    @Override
    public void onMessage(Message message) {
        TextMessage textMessage = (TextMessage) message;
```

```
        try {
            System.out.print("Got new message on queue: ");
            System.out.println(textMessage.getText());
            System.out.println();
        } catch (JMSException e) {
            System.err.println(e.getMessage());
        }
    }
}
```

2. Now we define the Producer class:

```
@Stateless
public class QueueSender {

    @Resource(mappedName = "jms/JmsFactory")
    private ConnectionFactory jmsFactory;
    @Resource(mappedName = "jms/JmsQueue")
    private Queue jmsQueue;

    public void send() throws JMSException {
        MessageProducer producer;
        TextMessage message;

        try (Connection connection = jmsFactory.createConnection();
            Session session = connection.createSession(false,
            Session.AUTO_ACKNOWLEDGE)) {
            producer = session.createProducer(jmsQueue);
            message = session.createTextMessage();

            String msg = "Now it is " + new Date();
            message.setText(msg);
            System.out.println("Message sent to queue: " + msg);
            producer.send(message);

            producer.close();
        }
    }
}
```

3. And a servlet to access the Producer:

```
@WebServlet(name = "QueueSenderServlet", urlPatterns =
{"/QueueSenderServlet"})
public class QueueSenderServlet extends HttpServlet {
    @Inject
    private QueueSender sender;
```

```
@Override
protected void doGet(HttpServletRequest request,
HttpServletResponse response)
        throws ServletException, IOException {
    try(PrintWriter writer = response.getWriter()){
        sender.send();
        writer.write("Message sent to queue.
        Check the log for details.");
    } catch (JMSException ex) {
        System.err.println(ex.getMessage());
    }
}
}
```

4. Finally, we create a page just to call our servlet:

```html
<html>
    <head>
        <title>JMS recipe</title>
        <meta http-equiv="Content-Type" content="text/html;
         charset=UTF-8">
    </head>
    <body>
        <p>
            <a href="QueueSenderServlet">Send Message to Queue</a>
        </p>
    </body>
</html>
```

Now just deploy and run it. Each time you call QueueSenderServlet you should see something like this on your server log:

```
Info: Message sent to queue: Now it is Tue Dec 19 06:52:17 BRST 2017
Info: Got new message on queue: Now it is Tue Dec 19 06:52:17 BRST 2017
```

How it works...

Thanks to the standards implemented in the Java EE 8 server, our MDB is 100% managed by the container. That's why we could just refer to the queue without looking back:

```
@MessageDriven(activationConfig = {
    @ActivationConfigProperty(propertyName = "destinationLookup",
    propertyValue = "jms/JmsQueue"),
    @ActivationConfigProperty(propertyName = "destinationType",
    propertyValue = "javax.jms.Queue")
})
```

We could have built a Consumer by our own hands, but it would build three times as many code lines and would be synchronous.

We get our container Producer from a session provided by our factory and made for our queue:

```
try (Connection connection = jmsFactory.createConnection();
    Session session = connection.createSession(false,
    Session.AUTO_ACKNOWLEDGE)) {
producer = session.createProducer(jmsQueue);
    ...
}
```

Then all we have to do is to create and send the message:

```
message = session.createTextMessage();

String msg = "Now it is " + new Date();
message.setText(msg);
System.out.println("Message sent to queue: " + msg);
producer.send(message);
```

See also

- You could refer to the full source code for this recipe at: https://github.com/eldermoraes/javaee8-cookbook/tree/master/chapter06/ch06-jms

Understanding a servlet's life cycle

If you are used to creating web applications using Java EE, you probably will have already realized: most of the time it is all about dealing with requests and responses and the most popular way to do it is by using the Servlet API.

This recipe will show you how the server deals with its life cycles and what you should and should not been doing in your code.

Getting ready

First, add the proper dependency to your project:

```xml
<dependency>
    <groupId>javax</groupId>
    <artifactId>javaee-api</artifactId>
    <version>8.0</version>
    <scope>provided</scope>
</dependency>
```

How to do it...

Just write this simple servlet:

```java
@WebServlet(name = "LifecycleServlet",
urlPatterns = {"/LifecycleServlet"})
public class LifecycleServlet extends HttpServlet {

    @Override
    protected void doGet(HttpServletRequest req,
    HttpServletResponse resp) throws ServletException, IOException {
        try(PrintWriter writer = resp.getWriter()){
            writer.write("doGet");
            System.out.println("doGet");
        }
    }
    @Override
    protected void doPost(HttpServletRequest req,
    HttpServletResponse resp) throws ServletException, IOException {
        try(PrintWriter writer = resp.getWriter()){
            writer.write("doPost");
            System.out.println("doPost");
        }
    }
    @Override
    protected void doDelete(HttpServletRequest req,
    HttpServletResponse resp) throws ServletException, IOException {
        try(PrintWriter writer = resp.getWriter()){
            writer.write("doDelete");
            System.out.println("doDelete");
        }
    }
    @Override
    protected void doPut(HttpServletRequest req,
    HttpServletResponse resp) throws ServletException, IOException {
```

```
            try(PrintWriter writer = resp.getWriter()){
                writer.write("doPut");
                System.out.println("doPut");
            }
        }
        @Override
        public void init() throws ServletException {
            System.out.println("init()");
        }

        @Override
        public void destroy() {
            System.out.println("destroy");
        }
    }
```

Once it is deployed to your Java EE server, I suggest you try it using a tool such as SoapUI or similar. It will allow you to send requests using GET, POST, PUT, and DELETE. The browser would only do GET.

If you do it, your system log will look just like this:

```
Info: init(ServletConfig config)
 Info: doGet
 Info: doPost
 Info: doPut
 Info: doDelete
```

And if you undeploy your application it will look as follows:

```
Info:    destroy
```

How it works...

If you pay attention, you will notice that the init log will show only after your servlet is called for the first time. That's when it is really loaded and it is the only time that this method will be called. So if you have some one-shot code for this servlet, that's the place to do it.

Talking about the doGet, doPost, doPut, and doDelete methods, note that they were all automatically called by the server based on the request received. It's possible thanks to another method implemented by the server called service.

You could override the `service` method if you want, but it's a bad practice and should be avoided. Do it only if you know exactly what you are doing, otherwise you could give the wrong destination to some requests. This chapter is about relying on the standards, so why wouldn't you observe them?

Finally, we have the `destroy` method being called when your application is undeployed. This is like the last breath of your servlet. It is also a bad practice to add some code here, as you could prevent some resource from being released, and/or run into some process errors.

See also

- You can refer to the full source code for this recipe at: `https://github.com/eldermoraes/javaee8-cookbook/tree/master/chapter06/ch06-lifecycle`

Transaction management

Transaction management is one of the trickier subjects in computer science. One single wrong line, one unpredicted situation, and your data and/or your user will suffer the consequences.

So it would be nice if we could count on the server to do it for us. And most of the time we can, so let me show you how to do it.

Getting ready

First add the proper dependency to your project:

```
<dependency>
    <groupId>javax</groupId>
    <artifactId>javaee-api</artifactId>
    <version>8.0</version>
    <scope>provided</scope>
</dependency>
```

How to do it...

1. Let's build a bean that will perform all the transactions we need:

```
@Stateful
@TransactionManagement
public class UserBean {
    private ArrayList<Integer> actions;
    @PostConstruct
    public void init(){
        actions = new ArrayList<>();
        System.out.println("UserBean initialized");
    }
    public void add(Integer action){
        actions.add(action);
        System.out.println(action + " added");
    }
    public void remove(Integer action){
        actions.remove(action);
        System.out.println(action + " removed");
    }
    public List getActions(){
        return actions;
    }
    @PreDestroy
    public void destroy(){
        System.out.println("UserBean will be destroyed");
    }
    @Remove
    public void logout(){
        System.out.println("User logout. Resources will be
        released.");
    }
    @AfterBegin
    public void transactionStarted(){
        System.out.println("Transaction started");
    }
    @BeforeCompletion
    public void willBeCommited(){
        System.out.println("Transaction will be commited");
    }
    @AfterCompletion
    public void afterCommit(boolean commited){
        System.out.println("Transaction commited? " + commited);
    }
}
```

2. And a test class to try it:

```
public class UserTest {
    private EJBContainer ejbContainer;
    @EJB
    private UserBean userBean;
    public UserTest() {
    }
    @Before
    public void setUp() throws NamingException {
        ejbContainer = EJBContainer.createEJBContainer();
        ejbContainer.getContext().bind("inject", this);
    }
    @After
    public void tearDown() {
        ejbContainer.close();
    }
    @Test
    public void test(){
        userBean.add(1);
        userBean.add(2);
        userBean.add(3);
        userBean.remove(2);
        int size = userBean.getActions().size();
        userBean.logout();
        Assert.assertEquals(2, size);
    }
}
```

3. If you try this test you should see this output:

```
UserBean initialized
Transaction started
1 added
Transaction will be commited
Transaction commited? true
Transaction started
2 added
Transaction will be commited
Transaction commited? true
Transaction started
3 added
Transaction will be commited
Transaction commited? true
Transaction started
2 removed
Transaction will be commited
Transaction commited? true
```

```
Transaction started
Transaction will be commited
Transaction commited? true
Transaction started
User logout. Resources will be released.
UserBean will be destroyed
Transaction will be commited
Transaction commited? true
```

How it works...

The first thing we did was mark our bean to hold states and have its transactions managed by the server:

```
@Stateful
@TransactionManagement
public class UserBean {
    ...
}
```

What happens then? If you note, no method that deals with adding or removing stuff does any transaction management. But they are still managed:

```
Transaction started
1 added
Transaction will be commited
Transaction commited? true
```

So you have all the transaction intelligence without writing a single line of transaction stuff.

It will transact even when the bean would releases its resources:

```
Transaction started
User logout. Resources will be released.
UserBean will be destroyed
Transaction will be commited
Transaction commited? true
```

See also

- Refer to the full source code for this recipe at: https://github.com/
  eldermoraes/javaee8-cookbook/tree/master/chapter06/ch06-transaction

7
Deploying and Managing Applications on Major Java EE Servers

This chapter covers the following recipes:

- Apache TomEE usage
- GlassFish usage
- WildFly usage

Introduction

One of the most important skills you should have as a Java EE developer is knowing how to work with the most used Java EE application servers in the market.

As we've stated in previous chapters, the standards involved in the Java EE ecosystem allow you to reuse most of the knowledge you already have no matter which server you are using.

However, when we are talking about deployment and some administration tasks, things could be different (and usually are). The differences are not in the way they work, but in the way they are done.

So, in this chapter, we will cover some important and common tasks for Apache TomEE, GlassFish, and WildFly.

Apache TomEE usage

If you have already used Apache Tomcat, you can consider yourself ready to use Apache TomEE. It is based on the Tomcat's core and implements the Java EE specs.

Getting ready

First, you need to download it to your environment. At the time of writing, TomEE has no Java EE 8 compatible version (actually, there is only GlassFish 5). However, the tasks covered here shouldn't change in future versions as they are not attached to the Java EE specs.

To download it, just visit `http://tomee.apache.org/downloads.html`. This recipe in based on version 7.0.2 Plume.

Wherever possible, we will focus on doing tasks using the configuration files.

How to do it...

Refer to the following detailed tasks.

Deploying EAR, WAR, and JAR files

For EAR and WAR files, the deployment folder is:

`$TOMEE_HOME/webapps`

For JAR files, the folder is:

`$TOMEE_HOME/lib`

Creating datasources and a connection pool

To create a datasource and a connection pool to help you use databases in your project, edit the `$TOMEE_HOME/conf/tomee.xml` file.

Inside the `<tomee>` node, insert a child node like this one:

```
<Resource id="MyDataSouceDs" type="javax.sql.DataSource">
    jdbcDriver = org.postgresql.Driver
    jdbcUrl = jdbc:postgresql://[host]:[port]/[database]
    jtaManaged = true
    maxActive = 20
    maxIdle = 20
    minIdle = 0
    userName = user
    password = password
</Resource>
```

The example targets PostgreSQL, so you will need to perform some changes for another database. Of course, you will also need to change the other parameters according to your needs.

Logging setup and rotate

To configure the logging for Apache TomEE, edit the `$TOMEE_HOME/conf/logging.properties` file. The file works with handlers like this:

```
1catalina.org.apache.juli.AsyncFileHandler.level = FINE
1catalina.org.apache.juli.AsyncFileHandler.directory =
${catalina.base}/logs
1catalina.org.apache.juli.AsyncFileHandler.prefix = catalina.
```

So, you can define the logging level, directory, and prefix according to your needs.

If you need to configure log rotation, just add these lines to your handler:

```
1catalina.org.apache.juli.AsyncFileHandler.limit = 1024
1catalina.org.apache.juli.AsyncFileHandler.count = 10
```

In this example, we are defining this file to rotate on every 1024 kilobytes (1 MB) and keep the last 10 files on our disk.

Starting and stopping

To start the Apache TomEE, just execute this script:

```
$TOMEE_HOME/bin/startup.sh
```

To stop it, execute the following script:

```
$TOMEE_HOME/bin/shutdown.sh
```

Session clustering

If you want to build a cluster using Apache TomEE nodes, you need to edit the `$TOMEE_HOME/conf/server.xml` file. Then, find this line:

```
<Engine name="Catalina" defaultHost="localhost">
```

Insert a child node, like this:

```
<Cluster
  className="org.apache.catalina.ha.tcp.SimpleTcpCluster"
          channelSendOptions="8">

    <Manager
    className="org.apache.catalina.ha.session
          .DeltaManager"
          expireSessionsOnShutdown="false"
          notifyListenersOnReplication="true"/>

    <Channel
     className="org.apache.catalina.tribes.group
     .GroupChannel">
     <Membership
     className="org.apache.catalina
    .tribes.membership .McastService"
          address="228.0.0.4"
          port="45564"
          frequency="500"
          dropTime="3000"/>
    <Receiver className="org.apache.catalina.tribes
    .transport.nio.NioReceiver"
          address="auto"
          port="4000"
          autoBind="100"
          selectorTimeout="5000"
          maxThreads="6"/>

    <Sender className="org.apache.catalina.tribes
    .transport.ReplicationTransmitter">
      <Transport className="org.apache.catalina.tribes
      .transport.nio.PooledParallelSender"/>
    </Sender>
```

```
    <Interceptor className="org.apache.catalina.tribes
    .group.interceptors.TcpFailureDetector"/>
    <Interceptor className="org.apache.catalina.tribes
    .group.interceptors.MessageDispatchInterceptor"/>
</Channel>

<Valve className="org.apache.catalina
.ha.tcp.ReplicationValve"
        filter=""/>
<Valve className="org.apache.catalina
.ha.session.JvmRouteBinderValve"/>

<Deployer className="org.apache.catalina
.ha.deploy.FarmWarDeployer"
        tempDir="/tmp/war-temp/"
        deployDir="/tmp/war-deploy/"
        watchDir="/tmp/war-listen/"
        watchEnabled="false"/>

<ClusterListener className="org.apache.catalina
.ha.session.ClusterSessionListener"/>
</Cluster>
```

This block will set up your server to run in a dynamic discovery cluster. What this means is that every server that runs in the same network using this configuration will become a new member in the cluster and so will share the alive sessions.

All these parameters are so important, so I really recommend you to keep all of them unless you are absolutely sure of what you are doing.

There's more...

The best way to set up a Java EE cluster today is using containers (specially Docker containers). So, I'd recommend that you have a look at Chapter 11, *Rising to the Cloud – Java EE, Containers, and Cloud Computing*. If you mix the content of that chapter with the content of this one, you will have a powerful environment for your application.

To allow your application to share its session with all the nodes in the cluster, you need to edit the web.xml file, find the web-app node, and insert this:

```
<distributable/>
```

Without it, your session clustering will not work. You also need to keep all objects that you are holding in the session as serializable.

See also

- For more information about Apache TomEE visit `http://tomee.apache.org/`

GlassFish usage

The great thing about GlassFish is that it is the **Reference Implementation (RI)**. So, whenever you have a new version of Java EE, being a developer, you already have the respective GlassFish version to try it.

Getting ready

First, you need to download it to your environment. At the time of writing, GlassFish 5 is the only Java EE 8 server that has been released.

To download it, just visit `https://javaee.github.io/glassfish/download`. This recipe in based on version 5 (Java EE 8 compatible).

Wherever possible, we will focus on doing the tasks using the configuration files.

How to do it...

Refer to the following detailed tasks.

Deploying EAR, WAR, and JAR files

For EAR and WAR files, the deployment folder is:

`$GLASSFISH_HOME/glassfish/domains/[domain_name]/autodeploy`

Usually `domain_name` is `domain1`, unless you've changed it in the installation process.

For JAR files, the folder is:

`$GLASSFISH_HOME/glassfish/lib`

Creating datasources and a connection pool

To create a datasource and a connection pool to help you use databases in your project, edit the `$GLASSFISH_HOME/glassfish/domains/[domain_name]/config/domain.xml` file. Inside the `<resources>` node, insert a child node like this one:

```
<jdbc-connection-pool
  pool-resize-quantity="4"
  max-pool-size="64"
  max-wait-time-in-millis="120000"
  driver-classname="com.mysql.jdbc.Driver"
  datasource-classname="com.mysql.jdbc.jdbc2.optional
  .MysqlDataSource"
  steady-pool-size="16"
  name="MysqlPool"
  idle-timeout-in-seconds="600"
  res-type="javax.sql.DataSource">
    <property name="databaseName" value="database"></property>
    <property name="serverName" value="[host]"></property>
    <property name="user" value="user"></property>
    <property name="password" value="password"></property>
    <property name="portNumber" value="3306"></property>
</jdbc-connection-pool>
<jdbc-resource pool-name="MySqlDs" jndi-name="jdbc/MySqlDs">
</jdbc-resource>
```

Then, look for this node:

```
<server config-ref="server-config" name="server">
```

Add this child to it:

```
<resource-ref ref="jdbc/MySqlDs"></resource-ref>
```

The example targets MySQL, so you will need to perform some changes for another database. Of course, you will also need to change the other parameters according to your needs.

Logging setup and rotate

To configure logging for GlassFish, edit the `$GLASSFISH_HOME/glassfish/domains/domain1/config/logging.properties` file:

The file works with handlers like this:

```
handlers=java.util.logging.ConsoleHandler
handlerServices=com.sun.enterprise.server.logging.GFFileHandler
java.util.logging.ConsoleHandler.formatter=com.sun.enterprise.server.loggin
g.UniformLogFormatter
com.sun.enterprise.server.logging.GFFileHandler.formatter=com.sun.enterpris
e.server.logging.ODLLogFormatter
com.sun.enterprise.server.logging.GFFileHandler.file=${com.sun.aas.instance
Root}/logs/server.log
com.sun.enterprise.server.logging.GFFileHandler.rotationTimelimitInMinutes=
0
com.sun.enterprise.server.logging.GFFileHandler.flushFrequency=1
java.util.logging.FileHandler.limit=50000
com.sun.enterprise.server.logging.GFFileHandler.logtoConsole=false
com.sun.enterprise.server.logging.GFFileHandler.rotationLimitInBytes=200000
0
com.sun.enterprise.server.logging.GFFileHandler.excludeFields=
com.sun.enterprise.server.logging.GFFileHandler.multiLineMode=true
com.sun.enterprise.server.logging.SyslogHandler.useSystemLogging=false
java.util.logging.FileHandler.count=1
com.sun.enterprise.server.logging.GFFileHandler.retainErrorsStasticsForHour
s=0
log4j.logger.org.hibernate.validator.util.Version=warn
com.sun.enterprise.server.logging.GFFileHandler.maxHistoryFiles=0
com.sun.enterprise.server.logging.GFFileHandler.rotationOnDateChange=false
java.util.logging.FileHandler.pattern=%h/java%u.log
java.util.logging.FileHandler.formatter=java.util.logging.XMLFormatter
```

So, you can define the logging level, directory, format, and more according to your needs.

If you need to configure log rotation, you have to focus on these lines:

```
com.sun.enterprise.server.logging.GFFileHandler
.rotationTimelimitInMinutes=0
com.sun.enterprise.server.logging.GFFileHandler
.rotationLimitInBytes=2000000
com.sun.enterprise.server.logging.GFFileHandler
.maxHistoryFiles=0
com.sun.enterprise.server.logging.GFFileHandler
.rotationOnDateChange=false
```

In this example, we are defining this file to rotate on every 2000 kilobytes (2 MB) and will not rotate on date change. There's no limit for history files.

Starting and stopping

To start GlassFish, just execute this script:

```
$GLASSFISH_HOME/bin/asadmin start-domain --verbose
```

To stop it, excecute the following script:

```
$GLASSFISH_HOME/bin/asadmin stop-domain
```

Session clustering

Building a cluster using GlassFish is a little tricky and involves using both command line and the admin panel, but it is completely doable! Let's check it out.

First, you need two or more instances (called nodes) up and running. You can do it in any way you like—each one running in a different machine, using virtual machines or containers (my favorite option). Either way you choose, the way of getting the cluster up is the same:

1. So, get your first node and open its admin panel:

   ```
   https://[hostname]:4848
   ```

2. Click on the **Clusters** option in the left menu and then click on the **New** button. Name the cluster `myCluster` and click on the **OK** button.

3. Select your cluster from the list. In the opened page, select the **Instances** option in the tab and then click on **New**. Name the instance `node1` and click on **OK**.

4. Now, go the **General** tab and click on the **Start Cluster** button. Voilá! Your cluster is up and running with your first node.

5. Now, go to the second machine (VM, container, other server, or any server) with GlassFish already installed and run this command:

   ```
   $GLASSFISH_HOME/bin/asadmin --host [hostname_node1] --port 4848
   create-local-instance --cluster myCluster node2
   ```

   This will set the second machine as a member of the cluster. If you refresh the **Cluster** page on the first machine, you will see the new member (`node2`).

6. You will notice that `node2` has stopped. Click on it and in the new page click on the **Node** link (it will usually show the hostname of `node2`).

7. In the opened page, change the **Type** value to SSH. Some new fields will show up in a SSH section.

8. Change **SSH User Authentication** to SSH Password and fill the **SSH User Password** field with the proper password.

9. Click on the **Save** button. If you run some SSH error (usually connection refused), set the **Force** option to **Enabled,** and click on **Save** button again.

10. Go back to the command line on the machine hosting node2 and run this command:

```
$GLASSFISH_HOME/glassfish/lib/nadmin start-local-instance --node
[node2_hostname] --sync normal node2
```

If everything went well, your node2 should be up and running and you should now have a real cluster. You can repeat these steps how ever many times you need to add new nodes to your cluster.

There's more...

A common issue for this clustering with GlassFish arises when you don't have the SSH service running in your nodes; as there are tons of options of them for many operating systems, we won't cover each one of them here.

The best way to set up a Java EE cluster today is using containers (specially Docker containers). So, I'd recommend that you have a look at Chapter 11, *Rising to the Cloud – Java EE, Containers, and Cloud Computing*. If you mix that content with this, you will have a powerful environment for your application.

To allow your application to share its session with all the nodes in the cluster, you need to edit the web.xml file, find the web-app node, and insert this:

```
<distributable/>
```

Without it, your session clustering will not work. You need also to keep all objects that you are holding in the session as serializable.

Finally, there's a commercial version of GlassFish, which is Payara Server. If you are looking for support and other commercial perks, you should take a look at it.

See also

- For more information about GlassFish, visit `https://javaee.github.io/glassfish/`.

WildFly usage

WildFly is another great Java EE implementation. It was known as **JBoss AS**, but changed its name some years ago (although we still have the JBoss EAP as the *enterprise-production ready* version). As its administration and use are slightly different from Apache TomEE and GlassFish, it's worth having a proper look at it.

Getting ready

First, you need to download it to your environment. At the time of writing, WildFly has no Java EE 8-compatible version (actually there is only GlassFish 5). However, the tasks covered here shouldn't change in a future version, as they are not attached to the Java EE specs. To download it, just visit `http://wildfly.org/downloads/`.

This recipe in based on version 11.0.0.Final (Java EE7 Full and Web Distribution).

Wherever possible, we will focus on doing the tasks using the configuration files.

How to do it...

Refer to the following detailed tasks.

Deploying EAR, WAR, and JAR files

For EAR and WAR files, the deployment folder is:

`$WILDFLY_HOME/standalone/deployments`

For JAR files (like JDBC connections, for example), WildFly creates a flexible folder structure. So, the best way to distribute them is using its UI, as we will show in the connection pool topic (the next one).

Creating datasources and a connection pool

Take the following steps to create your datasources and connection pool:

1. To create a datasource and a connection pool to help you use databases in your project, start WildFly and visit the following URL:

   ```
   http://localhost:9990/
   ```

2. Click on **Deployments** and then click on the **Add** button. In the opened page, select **Upload a new deployment** and click on the **Next** button. In the opened page, select the proper JDBC connector (we will use MySQL for this recipe) and click on **Next**.
3. Verify the information in the opened page and click on **Finish**.
4. Now that your JDBC connector is available in the server, you can go ahead and create your datasource. Go to **Home** in the administration panel and click on the **Configuration** option.
5. In the opened page, follow this path:

   Subsystems | Datasources | Non-XA | Datasource | Add

6. In the opened window select **MySQL Datasource** and click on **Next**. Then, fill the fields like this:

     - **Name:** MySqlDS
     - **JNDI Name:** java:/MySqlDS

7. Click on **Next**. In the next page, click on **Detected Driver**, select the proper MySQL connector (the one you just uploaded) and click on **Next**.
8. The last step is to fill the connection settings fields, like this:

   - **Connection URL:** jdbc:mysql://localhost:3306/sys
   - **Username:** root
   - **Password:** mysql

9. Click on the **Next** button, review the information, and click on **Finish**. Your newly created connection will appear in the datasources list. You can click on the dropdown list and select **Test** to check whether everything is working well.

Logging setup and rotate

To configure the logging for WildFly, edit the
`$WILDFLY_HOME/standalone/configuration/standalone.xml` file.

To customize the logging properties, find the `<profile>` node and then find `<subsystem xmlns='urn:jboss:domain:logging:3.0'>` inside it.

It is based on handles like this:

```
<console-handler name="CONSOLE">
        <level name="INFO"/>
        <formatter>
            <named-formatter name="COLOR-PATTERN"/>
        </formatter>
</console-handler>
<periodic-rotating-file-handler name="FILE"
 autoflush="true">
        <formatter>
            <named-formatter name="PATTERN"/>
        </formatter>
        <file relative-to="jboss.server.log.dir"
         path="server.log"/>
        <suffix value=".yyyy-MM-dd"/>
        <append value="true"/>
</periodic-rotating-file-handler>
<logger category="com.arjuna">
        <level name="WARN"/>
</logger>
<logger category="org.jboss.as.config">
        <level name="DEBUG"/>
</logger>
<logger category="sun.rmi">
        <level name="WARN"/>
</logger>
<root-logger>
        <level name="INFO"/>
        <handlers>
            <handler name="CONSOLE"/>
            <handler name="FILE"/>
        </handlers>
</root-logger>
<formatter name="PATTERN">
        <pattern-formatter pattern=
        "%d{yyyy-MM-dd HH:mm:ss,SSS} %-5p [%c] (%t) %s%e%n"/>
</formatter>
<formatter name="COLOR-PATTERN">
```

```
                <pattern-formatter pattern="%K{level}%d
                {HH:mm:ss,SSS} %-5p [%c] (%t) %s%e%n"/>
        </formatter>
```

By default, it will rotate daily:

```
<periodic-rotating-file-handler name="FILE"
 autoflush="true">
     <formatter>
         <named-formatter name="PATTERN"/>
     </formatter>
     <file relative-to="jboss.server.log.dir"
      path="server.log"/>
     <suffix value=".yyyy-MM-dd"/>
     <append value="true"/>
</periodic-rotating-file-handler>
```

If you want it to rotate based on the size, you should remove the preceding handler and then insert this one:

```
<size-rotating-file-handler name="FILE" autoflush="true">
     <formatter>
         <pattern-formatter pattern="%d{yyyy-MM-dd
         HH:mm:ss,SSS} %-5p [%c] (%t) %s%e%n"/>
     </formatter>
     <file relative-to="jboss.server.log.dir"
     path="server.log"/>
     <rotate-size value="2m"/>
     <max-backup-index value="5"/>
     <append value="true"/>
</size-rotating-file-handler>
```

In this case, the log will rotate when the file reaches 2 MB and will keep a history of five files in the backup.

Starting and stopping

To start GlassFish, just execute this script:

```
$WILDFLY_HOME/bin/standalone.sh
```

To stop it, execute this script:

```
$WILDFLY_HOME/bin/jboss-cli.sh --connect command=:shutdown
```

Session clustering

If you go to the `$WILDFLY_HOME/standalone/configuration` folder, you will see these files:

- `standalone.xml`
- `standalone-ha.xml`
- `standalone-full.xml`
- `standalone-full-ha.xml`

`standalone.xml` is the default, with all default configuration. To build a cluster, we need to use the `standalone-ha.xml` file (`ha` comes from **high availability**), so rename it to end it as `standalone.xml`.

Then, you start the server. You should not do the following:

```
$WILDFLY_HOME/bin/standalone.sh
```

Instead, you should do this:

```
$WILDFLY_HOME/bin/standalone.sh -b 0.0.0.0 -bmanagement 0.0.0.0
```

You should now do the same in whatever other nodes (machines, VMs, containers, and so on) that you want to get into the cluster. Of course, they need to be in the same network.

There's more...

The best way to set up a Java EE cluster today is using containers (specially Docker containers). So, I'd recommend that you have a look at the `Chapter 11`, *Rising to the Cloud – Java EE, Containers, and Cloud Computing* chapter. If you mix that content with this, you will have a powerful environment for your application.

To allow your application to share its session with all nodes in the cluster, you need to edit the `web.xml` file, find the `web-app` node, and insert this:

```
<distributable/>
```

Without it, your session clustering will not work.

See also

- For more information about WildFly, visit `http://wildfly.org/`

8
Building Lightweight Solutions Using Microservices

This chapter covers the following recipes:

- Building microservices from a monolith
- Building decoupled services
- Building an automated pipeline for microservices

Introduction

Microservices are really one of the top buzzwords nowadays. It's easy to understand why: in a growing software industry where the amount of services, data, and users increases crazily, we really need a way to build and deliver faster, decoupled, and scalable solutions.

Why are microservices good? Why use them?

Actually, with growing demand, the need to deal with each module separately has increased. For example, in your customer application, maybe user information needs to be scaled in a different way from the address information.

In the monolith paradigm, you need to deal with it atomically: you build a cluster for the whole application or you scale up (or down) your entire host. The problem with this approach is that you can't focus your effort and resources on a specific feature, module, or function: you are always guided by what is needed at that moment.

In the microservice approach, you do it separately. Then you can not only scale (up or down) one single unit in your application, but you can also separate your data for each service (which you should do), separate technology (best tool for the best work), and more.

Other than scale technology, microservices are made to scale people. With a bigger application, bigger architecture, and bigger databases, also come bigger teams. And if you build your team like a monolith application, you are probably getting likely results.

So, as the application is split into a few (or a lot of) modules, you can also define cross-functional teams to take care of each module. This means that each team can have its own programmer, designer, database administrator, system administrator, network specialist, manager, and so on. Each team has responsibility over the module it is dealing with.

It brings agility to the process of thinking about and delivering software, and then maintaining and evolving it.

In this chapter, there are some recipes to help you get started with microservices or go deeper into your ongoing project.

Building microservices from a monolith

One common question that I have already heard dozens of times is, *"how do I break down my monolith into microservices?"*, or, *"how do I migrate from a monolith approach to microservices?"*

Well, that's what this recipe is all about.

Getting ready

For both monolith and microservice projects, we will use the same dependency:

```
<dependency>
    <groupId>javax</groupId>
    <artifactId>javaee-api</artifactId>
    <version>8.0</version>
    <scope>provided</scope>
</dependency>
```

How to do it...

Let's begin by building a monolith to split into microservices.

Building a monolith

First, we need the entities that will represent the data kept by the application.

Here is the User entity:

```
@Entity
public class User implements Serializable {

    private static final long serialVersionUID = 1L;

    @Id
    @GeneratedValue(strategy = GenerationType.AUTO)
    private Long id;
    @Column
    private String name;
    @Column
    private String email;

    public User(){
    }

    public User(String name, String email) {
        this.name = name;
        this.email = email;
    }

    public Long getId() {
        return id;
    }

    public void setId(Long id) {
        this.id = id;
    }
    public String getName() {
        return name;
    }

    public void setName(String name) {
        this.name = name;
    }

    public String getEmail() {
        return email;
    }

    public void setEmail(String email) {
```

```
        this.email = email;
    }
}
```

Here is the `UserAddress` entity:

```java
@Entity
public class UserAddress implements Serializable {

    private static final long serialVersionUID = 1L;

    @Id
    @GeneratedValue(strategy = GenerationType.AUTO)
    private Long id;

    @Column
    @ManyToOne
    private User user;
    @Column
    private String street;
    @Column
    private String number;
    @Column
    private String city;
    @Column
    private String zip;
    public UserAddress(){
    }
    public UserAddress(User user, String street, String number,
                       String city, String zip) {
        this.user = user;
        this.street = street;
        this.number = number;
        this.city = city;
        this.zip = zip;
    }

    public Long getId() {
        return id;
    }

    public void setId(Long id) {
        this.id = id;
    }

    public User getUser() {
        return user;
    }
```

```
    public void setUser(User user) {
        this.user = user;
    }

    public String getStreet() {
        return street;
    }

    public void setStreet(String street) {
        this.street = street;
    }

    public String getNumber() {
        return number;
    }

    public void setNumber(String number) {
        this.number = number;
    }

    public String getCity() {
        return city;
    }

    public void setCity(String city) {
        this.city = city;
    }

    public String getZip() {
        return zip;
    }

    public void setZip(String zip) {
        this.zip = zip;
    }
}
```

Now we define one bean to deal with the transaction over each entity.

Here is the UserBean class:

```
@Stateless
public class UserBean {

    @PersistenceContext
    private EntityManager em;

    public void add(User user) {
```

```
        em.persist(user);
    }

    public void remove(User user) {
        em.remove(user);
    }

    public void update(User user) {
        em.merge(user);
    }

    public User findById(Long id) {
        return em.find(User.class, id);
    }

    public List<User> get() {
        CriteriaBuilder cb = em.getCriteriaBuilder();
        CriteriaQuery<User> cq = cb.createQuery(User.class);
        Root<User> pet = cq.from(User.class);
        cq.select(pet);
        TypedQuery<User> q = em.createQuery(cq);
        return q.getResultList();
    }
}
```

Here is the `UserAddressBean` class:

```
@Stateless
public class UserAddressBean {

    @PersistenceContext
    private EntityManager em;
    public void add(UserAddress address){
        em.persist(address);
    }
    public void remove(UserAddress address){
        em.remove(address);
    }
    public void update(UserAddress address){
        em.merge(address);
    }
    public UserAddress findById(Long id){
        return em.find(UserAddress.class, id);
    }
    public List<UserAddress> get() {
        CriteriaBuilder cb = em.getCriteriaBuilder();
        CriteriaQuery<UserAddress> cq = cb.createQuery(UserAddress.class);
        Root<UserAddress> pet = cq.from(UserAddress.class);
```

```
        cq.select(pet);
        TypedQuery<UserAddress> q = em.createQuery(cq);
        return q.getResultList();
    }
}
```

Finally, we build two services to perform the communication between the client and the beans.

Here is the UserService class:

```
@Path("userService")
public class UserService {
    @EJB
    private UserBean userBean;
    @GET
    @Path("findById/{id}")
    @Consumes(MediaType.APPLICATION_JSON)
    @Produces(MediaType.APPLICATION_JSON)
    public Response findById(@PathParam("id") Long id){
        return Response.ok(userBean.findById(id)).build();
    }
    @GET
    @Path("get")
    @Consumes(MediaType.APPLICATION_JSON)
    @Produces(MediaType.APPLICATION_JSON)
    public Response get(){
        return Response.ok(userBean.get()).build();
    }
    @POST
    @Path("add")
    @Consumes(MediaType.APPLICATION_JSON)
    @Produces(MediaType.APPLICATION_JSON)
    public Response add(User user){
        userBean.add(user);
        return Response.accepted().build();
    }
    @DELETE
    @Path("remove/{id}")
    @Consumes(MediaType.APPLICATION_JSON)
    @Produces(MediaType.APPLICATION_JSON)
    public Response remove(@PathParam("id") Long id){
        userBean.remove(userBean.findById(id));
        return Response.accepted().build();
    }
}
```

Here is the `UserAddressService` class:

```
@Path("userAddressService")
public class UserAddressService {
    @EJB
    private UserAddressBean userAddressBean;
    @GET
    @Path("findById/{id}")
    @Consumes(MediaType.APPLICATION_JSON)
    @Produces(MediaType.APPLICATION_JSON)
    public Response findById(@PathParam("id") Long id){
        return Response.ok(userAddressBean.findById(id)).build();
    }
    @GET
    @Path("get")
    @Consumes(MediaType.APPLICATION_JSON)
    @Produces(MediaType.APPLICATION_JSON)
    public Response get(){
        return Response.ok(userAddressBean.get()).build();
    }
    @POST
    @Path("add")
    @Consumes(MediaType.APPLICATION_JSON)
    @Produces(MediaType.APPLICATION_JSON)
    public Response add(UserAddress address){
        userAddressBean.add(address);
        return Response.accepted().build();
    }
    @DELETE
    @Path("remove/{id}")
    @Consumes(MediaType.APPLICATION_JSON)
    @Produces(MediaType.APPLICATION_JSON)
    public Response remove(@PathParam("id") Long id){
        userAddressBean.remove(userAddressBean.findById(id));
        return Response.accepted().build();
    }
}
```

Now let's break it down!

Building microservices from the monolith

Our monolith deals with `User` and `UserAddress`. So we will break it down into three microservices:

- A user microservice
- A user address microservice
- A gateway microservice

A gateway service is an API between the application client and the services. Using it allows you to simplify this communication, also giving you the freedom of doing whatever you like with your services without breaking the API contracts (or at least minimizing it).

The user microservice

The `User` entity, `UserBean`, and `UserService` will remain exactly as they are in the monolith. Only now they will be delivered as a separated unit of deployment.

The user address microservice

The `UserAddress` classes will suffer just a single change from the monolith version, but keep their original APIs (that is great from the point of view of the client).

Here is the `UserAddress` entity:

```
@Entity
public class UserAddress implements Serializable {

    private static final long serialVersionUID = 1L;

    @Id
    @GeneratedValue(strategy = GenerationType.AUTO)
    private Long id;

    @Column
    private Long idUser;
    @Column
    private String street;
    @Column
    private String number;
    @Column
    private String city;
    @Column
    private String zip;
```

```
public UserAddress(){
}
public UserAddress(Long user, String street, String number,
                   String city, String zip) {
    this.idUser = user;
    this.street = street;
    this.number = number;
    this.city = city;
    this.zip = zip;
}

public Long getId() {
    return id;
}

public void setId(Long id) {
    this.id = id;
}

public Long getIdUser() {
    return idUser;
}

public void setIdUser(Long user) {
    this.idUser = user;
}

public String getStreet() {
    return street;
}

public void setStreet(String street) {
    this.street = street;
}

public String getNumber() {
    return number;
}

public void setNumber(String number) {
    this.number = number;
}

public String getCity() {
    return city;
}

public void setCity(String city) {
```

```
            this.city = city;
        }

    public String getZip() {
        return zip;
    }

    public void setZip(String zip) {
        this.zip = zip;
    }
}
```

Note that User is no longer a property/field in the UserAddress entity, but only a number (idUser). We will get into more details about it in the following section.

The gateway microservice

First, we create a class that helps us deal with the responses:

```
public class GatewayResponse {

    private String response;
    private String from;

    public String getResponse() {
        return response;
    }

    public void setResponse(String response) {
        this.response = response;
    }

    public String getFrom() {
        return from;
    }

    public void setFrom(String from) {
        this.from = from;
    }
}
```

Then, we create our gateway service:

```
@Consumes(MediaType.APPLICATION_JSON)
@Path("gatewayResource")
@RequestScoped
public class GatewayResource {
```

```java
    private final String hostURI = "http://localhost:8080/";
    private Client client;
    private WebTarget targetUser;
    private WebTarget targetAddress;

    @PostConstruct
    public void init() {
        client = ClientBuilder.newClient();
        targetUser = client.target(hostURI +
        "ch08-micro_x_mono-micro-user/");
        targetAddress = client.target(hostURI +
        "ch08-micro_x_mono-micro-address/");
    }

    @PreDestroy
    public void destroy(){
        client.close();
    }

    @GET
    @Path("getUsers")
    @Produces(MediaType.APPLICATION_JSON)
    public Response getUsers() {
        WebTarget service =
        targetUser.path("webresources/userService/get");

        Response response;
        try {
            response = service.request().get();
        } catch (ProcessingException e) {
            return Response.status(408).build();
        }

        GatewayResponse gatewayResponse = new GatewayResponse();
        gatewayResponse.setResponse(response.readEntity(String.class));
        gatewayResponse.setFrom(targetUser.getUri().toString());

        return Response.ok(gatewayResponse).build();
    }

    @POST
    @Path("addAddress")
    @Produces(MediaType.APPLICATION_JSON)
    public Response addAddress(UserAddress address) {
        WebTarget service =
        targetAddress.path("webresources/userAddressService/add");

        Response response;
```

```
try {
    response = service.request().post(Entity.json(address));
} catch (ProcessingException e) {
    return Response.status(408).build();
}

return Response.fromResponse(response).build();
    }

}
```

As we receive the UserAddress entity in the gateway, we have to have a version of it in the gateway project too. For brevity, we will omit the code, as it is the same as in the UserAddress project.

How it works...

Let's understand how things work here.

The monolith

The monolith application couldn't be simpler: just a project with two services using two beans to manage two entities. If you want to understand what is happening there regarding JAX-RS, CDI, and/or JPA, check the relevant recipes earlier in this book.

The microservices

So we split the monolith into three projects (microservices): the user service, the user address service, and the gateway service.

The user service classes remained unchanged after the migration from the monolith version. So there's nothing to comment on.

The UserAddress class had to be changed to become a microservice. The first change was made on the entity.

Here is the monolith version:

```
@Entity
public class UserAddress implements Serializable {

    ...
```

```
@Column
@ManyToOne
private User user;
...
public UserAddress(User user, String street, String number,
                   String city, String zip) {
    this.user = user;
    this.street = street;
    this.number = number;
    this.city = city;
    this.zip = zip;
}


...

public User getUser() {
    return user;
}

public void setUser(User user) {
    this.user = user;
}


...

}
```

Here is the microservice version:

```
@Entity
public class UserAddress implements Serializable {

    ...

    @Column
    private Long idUser;
    ...
    public UserAddress(Long user, String street, String number,
                       String city, String zip) {
        this.idUser = user;
        this.street = street;
        this.number = number;
        this.city = city;
        this.zip = zip;
    }

    public Long getIdUser() {
        return idUser;
```

```
    }

    public void setIdUser(Long user) {
        this.idUser = user;
    }

    ...


}
```

Note that in the monolith version, `user` was an instance of the `User` entity:

```
private User user;
```

In the microservice version, it became a number:

```
private Long idUser;
```

This happened for two main reasons:

1. In the monolith, we have the two tables in the same database (`User` and `UserAddress`), and they both have physical and logical relationships (foreign key). So it makes sense to also keep the relationship between both the objects.
2. The microservice should have its own database, completely independent from the other services. So we choose to keep only the user ID, as it is enough to load the address properly anytime the client needs.

This change also resulted in a change in the constructor.

Here is the monolith version:

```
public UserAddress(User user, String street, String number,
                   String city, String zip)
```

Here is the microservice version:

```
public UserAddress(Long user, String street, String number,
                   String city, String zip)
```

This could lead to a change of contract with the client regarding the change of the constructor signature. But thanks to the way it was built, it wasn't necessary.

Here is the monolith version:

```
public Response add(UserAddress address)
```

Here is the microservice version:

```
public Response add(UserAddress address)
```

Even if the method is changed, it could easily be solved with `@Path` annotation, or if we really need to change the client, it would be only the method name and not the parameters (which used to be more painful).

Finally, we have the gateway service, which is our implementation of the API gateway design pattern. Basically it is the one single point to access the other services.

The nice thing about it is that your client doesn't need to care about whether the other services changed the URL, the signature, or even whether they are available. The gateway will take care of them.

The bad part is that it is also on a single point of failure. Or, in other words, without the gateway, all services are unreachable. But you can deal with it using a cluster, for example.

There's more...

Though Java EE is perfect for microservices, there are other options using the same bases and that may be a little lighter in some scenarios.

One of them is KumuluzEE (`https://ee.kumuluz.com/`). It's based on Java EE and has many microservice *must-have* features, such as service discovery. It won a Duke Choice Awards prize, which is huge!

The other one is Payara Micro (`https://www.payara.fish/payara_micro`). Payara is the company that owns a commercial implementation of GlassFish, the Payara Server, and from the Payara Server, they created the Payara Fish. The cool thing about it is that it is just a 60 MB JAR file that you start using the command line and boom! Your microservice is running.

Finally, the awesome thing about these two projects is that they are aligned with the Eclipse MicroProfile project (`http://microprofile.io/`). MicroProfile is defining the path and the standards for microservices in the Java EE ecosystem right now, so it is worth following.

One last note about the code covered in this recipe: it would be nice in a real-world solution to use a DTO to separate the database representation from the service one.

See also

The full source code of this recipe can be found in the following repositories:

- **Monolith**: https://github.com/eldermoraes/javaee8-cookbook/tree/master/chapter08/ch08-micro_x_mono-mono
- **User microservice**: https://github.com/eldermoraes/javaee8-cookbook/tree/master/chapter08/ch08-micro_x_mono-micro-user
- **UserAddress microservice**: https://github.com/eldermoraes/javaee8-cookbook/tree/master/chapter08/ch08-micro_x_mono-micro-address
- **Gateway microservice**: https://github.com/eldermoraes/javaee8-cookbook/tree/master/chapter08/ch08-micro_x_mono-micro-gateway

Building decoupled services

Maybe you have, at least heard something about building decoupled things in the software world: decoupled classes, decoupled modules, and also decoupled services.

But what does it mean for a software unit being decoupled from another?

In a practical way, two things are coupled when any changes made to one of them requires you to also change the other one. For example, if you have a method that returns a String and changes it to return a Double, all the methods calling that one are required to be changed.

There are levels of coupling. For example, you could have all your classes and methods very well designed for loose coupling, but they are all written in Java. If you change one of them to .NET and would like to keep all of them together (in the same deployment package), you need to change all the other ones to the new language.

Another thing to mention about coupling is how much one unit *knows* about the other one. They are tightly coupled when they know a lot about each other and they are the opposite, loosely coupled, if they know a little or almost nothing about each other. This point of view is related mostly to the behavior of two (or more) parts.

The last way to look at coupling is in terms of a contract. If changing the contract breaks the clients, they are tightly coupled. If not, they are loosely coupled. That's why the best way to promote loose coupling is using interfaces. As they create contracts for its implementers, using them for communication between classes promotes loose coupling.

Well... what about services? In our case, microservices.

One service is loosely coupled from another one when changing it does not require changing the other. You can think about both in terms of behavior or contract.

This is especially important when talking about microservices, because you can have dozens, hundreds, or even thousands of them in your application and if changing one of them requires you to change the others, you could just ruin you entire application.

This recipe will show you how to avoid tight coupling in your microservices, from the first line of code, so you can avoid refactoring in the future (at least for this reason).

Getting ready

Let's start by adding our Java EE 8 dependency:

```
<dependency>
    <groupId>javax</groupId>
    <artifactId>javaee-api</artifactId>
    <version>8.0</version>
    <scope>provided</scope>
</dependency>
```

How to do it...

1. First, we create a User POJO:

```
public class User implements Serializable{

    private String name;
    private String email;

    public String getName() {
        return name;
    }

    public void setName(String name) {
        this.name = name;
    }

    public String getEmail() {
        return email;
    }
```

```
        public void setEmail(String email) {
            this.email = email;
        }
    }
```

2. Then we create a class with two methods (endpoints) for returning `User`:

```
@Path("userService")
public class UserService {
    @GET
    @Path("getUserCoupled/{name}/{email}")
    @Produces(MediaType.APPLICATION_JSON)
    public Response getUserCoupled(
            @PathParam("name") String name,
            @PathParam("email") String email){
        //GET USER CODE
        return Response.ok().build();
    }
    @GET
    @Path("getUserDecoupled")
    @Produces(MediaType.APPLICATION_JSON)
    public Response getUserDecoupled(@HeaderParam("User")
    User user){
        //GET USER CODE
        return Response.ok().build();
    }
}
```

3. Finally, we create another service (another project) to consume `UserService`:

```
@Path("doSomethingService")
public class DoSomethingService {
    private final String hostURI = "http://localhost:8080/";
    private Client client;
    private WebTarget target;

    @PostConstruct
    public void init() {
        client = ClientBuilder.newClient();
        target = client.target(hostURI + "ch08-decoupled-user/");
    }
    @Path("doSomethingCoupled")
    @Produces(MediaType.APPLICATION_JSON)
    public Response doSomethingCoupled(String name, String email){
        WebTarget service =
        target.path("webresources/userService/getUserCoupled");
        service.queryParam("name", name);
        service.queryParam("email", email);
```

```
                    Response response;
                    try {
                        response = service.request().get();
                    } catch (ProcessingException e) {
                        return Response.status(408).build();
                    }

                    return
                    Response.ok(response.readEntity(String.class)).build();
            }
            @Path("doSomethingDecoupled")
            @Produces(MediaType.APPLICATION_JSON)
            public Response doSomethingDecoupled(User user){
                WebTarget service =
                target.path("webresources/userService/getUserDecoupled");

                    Response response;
                    try {
                        response = service.request().header("User",
                        Entity.json(user)).get();
                    } catch (ProcessingException e) {
                        return Response.status(408).build();
                    }

                    return
                    Response.ok(response.readEntity(String.class)).build();
            }
    }
```

How it works...

As you may have already noticed, we created two situations in this code: one clearly coupled (getUserCoupled) and another decoupled (getUserDecoupled):

```
    public Response getUserCoupled(
            @PathParam("name") String name,
            @PathParam("email") String email)
```

Why is this a coupled method and thus a coupled service? Because it is highly attached to the method signature. Imagine it is a search service and "name" and "email" are filters. Now imagine that sometime in the future you need to add another filter. One more parameter in the signature.

OK, you could keep the two methods alive at the same time, so that you wouldn't break the client and have to change the clients. How many are there? Mobile, services, web pages, and many more. All those need to be changed to support the new feature.

Now look at this:

```
public Response getUserDecoupled(@HeaderParam("User") User user)
```

In this `User` search method, what if you need to add a new parameter to the filter? OK, go ahead and add it! No changes in the contract, all clients are happy.

If your `User` POJO starts with only two properties and ends with a hundred after a year, no problem. Your service contract is left untouched and even your clients, who are not using the new fields, are still working. Sweet!

The result of coupled/decoupled services can be seen in the calling service:

```
public Response doSomethingCoupled(String name, String email){
    WebTarget service =
    target.path("webresources/userService/getUserCoupled");
    service.queryParam("name", name);
    service.queryParam("email", email);


    . . .

}
```

The calling service is totally coupled to the called one: it has to *know* the called service properties' names and needs to add/update each time it changes.

Now look at this:

```
public Response doSomethingDecoupled(User user){
    WebTarget service =
    target.path("webresources/userService/getUserDecoupled");

    Response response;
    try {
        response = service.request().header("User",
        Entity.json(user)).get();
        . . .
}
```

In this case, you only need to refer to the one and only service parameter (`"User"`) and it will never change, no matter how the `User` POJO is changed.

See also

See the full source code at the following links:

- **UserService**: `https://github.com/eldermoraes/javaee8-cookbook/tree/master/chapter08/ch08-decoupled-user`
- **DoSomethingService**: `https://github.com/eldermoraes/javaee8-cookbook/tree/master/chapter08/ch08-decoupled-dosomethingwithuser`

Building an automated pipeline for microservices

Maybe you are wondering, *"why is there an automation recipe in a Java EE 8 book?"*, or even, *"is there any specification under Java EE 8 that defines a pipeline automation?"*

The answer to the second question is *no*. At least no at this very moment. The answer to the first one I'll explain here.

Many times in conferences I am asked the question, *"how do I migrate my monolith to microservices?"* It comes in some variations, but at the end of the day the question is the same.

People want to do it for different reasons:

- They want to keep up with the trend
- They want to work with something that looks like a new fashion
- They want to scale an application
- They want to be able to use different stacks under the same solution
- They want to look cool

Any of these reasons are OK and you can justify your migration to microservices with any of them, if you want. I would question the real motivation of some of them, but...

Instead of giving them advice, tips, guidelines, or any other tech talk, I usually ask a simple question: *"Do you already have an automated pipeline for your monolith?"*

Most of the time, the answer is a disappointed *"no"*, followed by a curious, *"why?"*.

Well the answer is simple: if you don't automate the pipeline you, monolith, one single package, and sometimes you have problems with it, then what makes you think that it will be easier when you have dozens, hundreds, or even thousands of deployment files?

Let me be more specific:

- Do you build your deployment artifact manually? Using an IDE or something?
- Do you deploy it manually?
- Did you ever have problems with the deployment for any reason such as errors, missing artifacts, or anything else?
- Did you ever have problems due to the lack of tests?

If you answered *yes* to at least one of these questions and don't have an automated pipeline, imagine these problems multiplied by... again, dozens, hundreds, or thousands.

Some people don't even write unit tests. Imagine those hidden errors going to production in a countless amount of artifacts called microservices. Your microservices project will probably fail even before going live.

So yes, you need to automate as many things as possible in your pipeline before even thinking of microservices. This is the only way to prevent the problems from spreading out.

There are three maturity stages for an automation pipeline:

1. **Continuous integration (CI)**: Basically, this ensures that your new code will be merged into the main branch (for example, the `master` branch) as soon as possible. It is based on the fact that the less code you merge, the fewer errors you add to it. It is reached mostly by running unit tests during build time.
2. **Continuous delivery**: This is one step further from CI, where you guarantee your artifact will be ready to be deployed just by a click of a button. This usually requires an artifact repository for your binaries and a tool to manage it. When using continuous delivery, you decide when you will do the deployment, but the best practice is to do it as soon as possible to avoid adding a lot of new code in production in just one shot.
3. **Continuous deployment (CD)**: This is the last, *state-of-the-art* part of automation. In CD, there's no human interaction since the code is committed until it is deployed in production. The only thing that would prevent an artifact from being deployed is an error in any of the pipeline stages. All the major success cases of microservices worldwide use CD in their projects, doing hundreds or even thousands of deployments daily.

This recipe will show you how you can go from zero (no automation at all) to three (CD) in any Java EE project. It's little a conceptual recipe, but with also some code.

Don't argue against concepts; they are the key to your career as a Java EE developer.

"Going microservices" is a huge thing and means lots of things both in your application and organization. Some people even say that microservices are all about scaling people, and not technology.

Here we will, of course, keep on the tech side of things.

Getting ready

Being a lot of things, microservices will also bring a lot of tools with them. This recipe doesn't intend to go deep into the setup of each tool, but shows you how it will work in a microservices-automated pipeline.

The tools chosen here are not the only option for the roles they perform. They are only my favorites for those roles.

Preparing the application

To prepare your application—your microservices—for an automation, you will need:

- **Apache Maven**: This is mainly used to build the stage and it will also help you with many activities surrounding it. It manages the dependencies, runs unit tests, and many more.
- **JUnit**: This is used to write unit tests that will be executed at the build stage.
- **Git**: For the sake of the most sacred things you can imagine, use some version control for your source code. Here, I'll base it on GitHub.

Preparing the environment

To prepare the environment of your pipeline, you will need:

- **Sonatype Nexus**: This is a binary repository. In other words, when you build your artifact, it will be stored in Nexus and be ready to be deployed wherever you need/want.

- **Jenkins**: I used to say that Jenkins is an automator for everything. Actually I've worked in a project where we used it to build an automated pipeline (continuous delivery) for about 70 applications, with completely different technologies (languages, databases, operation systems, and so on). You will use it basically for building and deploying.

How to do it...

You will be guided to reach each one of the three automation maturity stages: continuous integration, continuous delivery, and continuous deployment.

Continuous integration

Here, you need to make your new code go to the main branch as soon as possible. You will achieve it by using:

- Git
- Maven
- JUnit

So, you will guarantee that your code is building properly and that the tests are planned and executed successfully.

Git

I'll not get too deeply into how to use Git and its commands, as it's not the focus of this book. If you are completely new to the Git world, get started by looking at this cheat sheet:

```
https://education.github.com/git-cheat-sheet-education.pdf
```

Maven

Maven is one of the most powerful tools I've ever seen, and thus has a bunch of features embedded. If you are new to it, check out this reference:

```
https://maven.apache.org/guides/MavenQuickReferenceCard.pdf
```

The most important file in a Maven-based project is the `pom.xml` (**POM** stands for **Project Object Model**). For example, when you create a new Java EE 8 project, it should look like this:

```xml
<?xml version="1.0" encoding="UTF-8"?>
<project xmlns="http://maven.apache.org/POM/4.0.0"
xmlns:xsi="http://www.w3.org/2001/XMLSchema-instance"
xsi:schemaLocation="http://maven.apache.org/POM/4.0.0
http://maven.apache.org/xsd/maven-4.0.0.xsd">
    <modelVersion>4.0.0</modelVersion>

    <groupId>com.eldermoraes</groupId>
    <artifactId>javaee8-project-template</artifactId>
    <version>1.0</version>
    <packaging>war</packaging>

    <name>javaee8-project-template</name>

    <properties>
        <endorsed.dir>${project.build.directory}/endorsed</endorsed.dir>
        <project.build.sourceEncoding>UTF-8</project.build.sourceEncoding>
    </properties>
    <dependencies>
        <dependency>
            <groupId>javax</groupId>
            <artifactId>javaee-api</artifactId>
            <version>8.0</version>
            <scope>provided</scope>
        </dependency>
    </dependencies>

    <build>
        <plugins>
            <plugin>
                <groupId>org.apache.maven.plugins</groupId>
                <artifactId>maven-compiler-plugin</artifactId>
                <version>3.1</version>
                <configuration>
                    <source>1.8</source>
                    <target>1.8</target>
                    <compilerArguments>
                        <endorseddirs>${endorsed.dir}</endorseddirs>
                    </compilerArguments>
                </configuration>
            </plugin>
            <plugin>
                <groupId>org.apache.maven.plugins</groupId>
```

```
        <artifactId>maven-war-plugin</artifactId>
        <version>2.3</version>
        <configuration>
            <failOnMissingWebXml>false</failOnMissingWebXml>
        </configuration>
    </plugin>
  </plugins>
</build>

</project>
```

Then your project is ready for building using Maven like this (running in the same folder where pom.xml is located):

mvn

JUnit

You will use JUnit to run your unit tests. Let's check it.

Here is a class to be tested:

```
public class JUnitExample {
    @Size (min = 6, max = 10,message = "Name should be between 6 and 10
            characters")
    private String name;

    public String getName() {
        return name;
    }

    public void setName(String name) {
        this.name = name;
    }
}
```

Here is a testing class:

```
public class JUnitTest {
    private static Validator VALIDATOR;
    @BeforeClass
    public static void setUpClass() {
        VALIDATOR =
Validation.buildDefaultValidatorFactory().getValidator();
    }

    @Test
```

```
    public void smallName(){
        JUnitExample junit = new JUnitExample();
        junit.setName("Name");
        Set<ConstraintViolation<JUnitExample>> cv =
        VALIDATOR.validate(junit);
        assertFalse(cv.isEmpty());
    }
    @Test
    public void validName(){
        JUnitExample junit = new JUnitExample();
        junit.setName("Valid Name");
        Set<ConstraintViolation<JUnitExample>> cv =
        VALIDATOR.validate(junit);
        assertTrue(cv.isEmpty());
    }

    @Test
    public void invalidName(){
        JUnitExample junit = new JUnitExample();
        junit.setName("Invalid Name");
        Set<ConstraintViolation<JUnitExample>> cv =
        VALIDATOR.validate(junit);
        assertFalse(cv.isEmpty());
    }
}
```

Whenever you run the building process for this project, the preceding test will be executed and will ensure that those conditions are still valid.

Now you are ready for continuous integration. Just make sure to merge your new and working code into the main branch as soon as possible. Now let's move on to continuous delivery.

Continuous delivery

Now that you are a committer machine, let's go to the next level and make your application ready to deploy whenever you want.

First, you'll need your just-built artifact to be available in a proper repository. This is when we use Sonatype Nexus.

I won't go into the setup details in this book. One easy way to do it is by using Docker containers. You can see more information about it at, https://hub.docker.com/r/sonatype/nexus/.

Once your Nexus is available, you need to go to the `pom.xml` file and add this configuration:

```
<distributionManagement>
    <repository>
        <id>Releases</id>
        <name>Project</name>
        <url>[NEXUS_URL]/nexus/content/repositories/releases/</url>
    </repository>
</distributionManagement>
```

Now instead of building, just use the following:

mvn

You'll do so like this:

mvn deploy

So once your artifact is built, Maven will upload it to Sonatype Nexus. Now it is properly stored for future deployment.

Now you are almost ready to dance to the automation song. Let's bring Jenkins to the party.

As mentioned for Nexus, I will not get into the details about setting up Jenkins. I also recommend you do it using Docker. See the following link for details:

`https://hub.docker.com/_/jenkins/`

If you have absolutely no idea on how to use Jenkins, please refer to this official guide:

`https://jenkins.io/user-handbook.pdf`

Once your Jenkins is up and running, you'll create two jobs:

1. **Your-Project-Build**: This job will be used to build your project from the source code.
2. **Your-Project-Deploy**: This job will be used to deploy your artifact after being built and stored in Nexus.

You will configure the first one to download the source code of your project and build it using Maven. The second will download it from Nexus and deploy to the application server.

Remember that the deployment process involves some steps in most cases:

1. Stop the application server.
2. Remove the previous version.
3. Download the new version from Nexus.
4. Deploy the new version.
5. Start the application server.

So you'd probably create a shell script to be executed by Jenkins. Remember, we are automating, so no manual processes.

Downloading the artifact can be a little tricky, so maybe you could use something like this in your shell script:

```
wget --user=username --password=password
"[NEXUS_URL]/nexus/service/local/artifact/maven/content?g=<group>&a=<artifa
ct>
&v=<version>&r=releases"
```

If everything goes fine until this point, then you'll have two buttons: one for building and another for deploying. You are ready and set to build with no need to use any IDE to deploy, and no need to touch the application server.

Now you are sure that both processes (build and deploy) will be executed exactly the same way every time. You can now plan them to be executed in a shorter period of time.

Well, now we will move to the next and best step: continuous deployment.

Continuous deployment

To move from delivery to deployment is a matter of maturity—you need a reliable process that ensures only the working code is going into production.

You already have your code running unit tests on every build. Actually, you didn't forget to write unit tests, right?

On every success, your built artifact is properly stored and you manage the right versioning for your application.

You have mastered the deployment process for your application, dealing properly with any condition that might occur. Your application server is never going down again without your knowledge and you achieved it with the help of just two buttons! Build and deploy. You rock!

If you are at this point, your next move shouldn't be a big deal. You only need to automate the two jobs so you don't need to hit the button anymore.

In the build job, you'll set it to be executed whenever Jenkins finds any changes in the source code repository (check the documentation if you don't know how to do it).

Once it is done, there is just one last configuration: make the build step on the build job call another job—the deploy job. So any time the build is executed successfully, the deploy is also executed right away.

Cheers! You've made it.

There's more...

Of course, you will not only perform unit tests or API tests. You also need to test your UI, if you have one.

I'd recommend to do it using the Selenium Webdriver. You can find more information here, `http://www.seleniumhq.org/docs/03_webdriver.jsp`.

In this case, you would probably want to deploy your application to a QA environment, run the UI tests, and then go into production if everything is fine. So it's just a matter of adding some new jobs to your pipeline, now you know how to do it.

See also

- The source code of the JUnit example can be found at, `https://github.com/eldermoraes/javaee8-cookbook/tree/master/chapter08/ch08-automation`.

Using Multithreading on Enterprise Context

This chapter covers the following recipes:

- Building asynchronous tasks with returning results
- Using transactions with asynchronous tasks
- Checking the status of asynchronous tasks
- Building managed threads with returning results
- Scheduling asynchronous tasks with returning results
- Using injected proxies for asynchronous tasks

Introduction

Threading is a common issue in most software projects, no matter which language or other technology is involved. When talking about enterprise applications, things become even more important, and sometimes harder.

A single mistake in some thread can affect the whole system, or even the whole infrastructure. Think about some resources that are never released, memory consumption that never stops increasing, and so on.

The Java EE environment has some great features for dealing with these and plenty of other challenges, and this chapter will show you some of them.

Building asynchronous tasks with returning results

One of the first challenges you will face if you have never worked with asynchronous tasks is: how on Earth do you return results from an asynchronous task if you don't know when the execution will end?

Well, this recipe show you how. `AsyncResponse` for the win!

Getting ready

Let's first add our Java EE 8 dependency:

```
<dependency>
    <groupId>javax</groupId>
    <artifactId>javaee-api</artifactId>
    <version>8.0</version>
    <scope>provided</scope>
</dependency>
```

How to do it...

1. First, we create a `User` POJO:

    ```
    package com.eldermoraes.ch09.async.result;

    /**
     *
     * @author eldermoraes
     */
    public class User {

        private Long id;
        private String name;

        public Long getId() {
            return id;
        }

        public void setId(Long id) {
            this.id = id;
        }
    ```

```
public String getName() {
    return name;
}

public void setName(String name) {
    this.name = name;
}
public User(Long id, String name) {
    this.id = id;
    this.name = name;
}
@Override
public String toString() {
    return "User{" + "id=" + id + ", name="
                    + name + '}';
}
}
```

2. Then we create `UserService` to emulate a *remote* slow endpoint:

```
@Stateless
@Path("userService")
public class UserService {
    @GET
    public Response userService(){
        try {
            TimeUnit.SECONDS.sleep(5);
            long id = new Date().getTime();
            return Response.ok(new User(id, "User " + id)).build();
        } catch (InterruptedException ex) {
            return
            Response.status(Response.Status.INTERNAL_SERVER_ERROR)
            .entity(ex).build();
        }
    }
}
```

3. Now we create an asynchronous client that will reach that endpoint and get the result:

```
@Stateless
public class AsyncResultClient {

    private Client client;
    private WebTarget target;

    @PostConstruct
    public void init() {
```

```
            client = ClientBuilder.newBuilder()
                    .readTimeout(10, TimeUnit.SECONDS)
                    .connectTimeout(10, TimeUnit.SECONDS)
                    .build();
            target = client.target("http://localhost:8080/
                    ch09-async-result/userService");
        }

        @PreDestroy
        public void destroy(){
            client.close();
        }
        public CompletionStage<Response> getResult(){
            return
            target.request(MediaType.APPLICATION_JSON).rx().get();
        }
    }
```

4. And finally, we create a service (endpoint) that will use the client to write the result in the response:

```
@Stateless
@Path("asyncService")
public class AsyncService {

    @Inject
    private AsyncResultClient client;

    @GET
    public void asyncService(@Suspended AsyncResponse response)
    {
        try{
            client.getResult().thenApply(this::readResponse)
            .thenAccept(response::resume);
        } catch(Exception e){
            response.resume(Response.status(Response.Status.
            INTERNAL_SERVER_ERROR).entity(e).build());
        }
    }

    private String readResponse(Response response) {
        return response.readEntity(String.class);
    }
}
```

To run this example, just deploy it in GlassFish 5 and open this URL in your browser:

```
http://localhost:8080/ch09-async-result/asyncService
```

How it works...

First, our remote endpoint is creating `User` and converting it to a response entity:

```
return Response.ok(new User(id, "User " + id)).build();
```

So, with no effort at all, your `User` is now a JSON object.

Now let's take a look at the key method in `AsyncResultClient`:

```
public CompletionStage<Response> getResult(){
    return target.request(MediaType.APPLICATION_JSON).rx().get();
}
```

The `rx()` method is a part of the Reactive Client API introduced in Java EE 8. We'll discuss reactive in more detail in the next chapter. It basically returns `CompletionStageInvoker`, which will allow you to get `CompletionStage<Response>` (the returning value for this method).

In other words, this is an asynchronous/non-blocking code that gets results from the remote endpoint.

Note that we use the `@Stateless` annotation with this client so that we can inject it into our main endpoint:

```
@Inject
private AsyncResultClient client;
```

Here's our asynchronous method for writing a response:

```
@GET
public void asyncService(@Suspended AsyncResponse response) {
    client.getResult().thenApply(this::readResponse)
    .thenAccept(response::resume);
}
```

Note that it's a `void` method. It doesn't return anything because it will return the result to a callback.

The @Suspended annotation combined with AsyncResponse will make the response resume once the processing is done, and this happens because we are using the beautiful, one-line, Java 8-style code:

```
client.getResult().thenApply(this::readResponse)
.thenAccept(response::resume);
```

Before going into the details, let's just clarify our local readResponse method:

```
private String readResponse(Response response) {
    return response.readEntity(String.class);
}
```

It just reads the User entity embedded in Response and transforms it to a String object (a JSON string).

Another way that this one-line code could be written is like this:

```
client.getResult()
        .thenApply(r -> readResponse(r))
        .thenAccept(s -> response.resume(s));
```

But the first way is more concise, less verbose, and more fun!

The key is the resume method from the AsyncReponse object. It will write the response to the callback and return it to whoever asked it.

See also

- The full source code of this recipe is at https://github.com/eldermoraes/javaee8-cookbook/tree/master/chapter09/ch09-async-result.

Using transactions with asynchronous tasks

Using asynchronous tasks could be already a challenge: what if you need to add some spice and add a transaction to it?

Usually, a transaction means something like *code blocking*. Isn't it awkward to combine two opposing concepts? Well, it's not! They can work together nicely, as this recipe will show you.

Getting ready

Let's first add our Java EE 8 dependency:

```
<dependency>
    <groupId>javax</groupId>
    <artifactId>javaee-api</artifactId>
    <version>8.0</version>
    <scope>provided</scope>
</dependency>
```

How to do it...

1. Let's first create a User POJO:

```
public class User {

    private Long id;
    private String name;

    public Long getId() {
        return id;
    }

    public void setId(Long id) {
        this.id = id;
    }

    public String getName() {
        return name;
    }

    public void setName(String name) {
        this.name = name;
    }
    public User(Long id, String name) {
        this.id = id;
        this.name = name;
    }
    @Override
    public String toString() {
        return "User{" + "id=" + id + ",
                    name=" + name + '}';
    }
}
```

2. And here is a slow bean that will return `User`:

```
@Stateless
public class UserBean {
    public User getUser(){
        try {
            TimeUnit.SECONDS.sleep(5);
            long id = new Date().getTime();
            return new User(id, "User " + id);
        } catch (InterruptedException ex) {
            System.err.println(ex.getMessage());
            long id = new Date().getTime();
            return new User(id, "Error " + id);
        }
    }
}
```

3. Now we create a task to be executed that will return `User` using some transaction stuff:

```
public class AsyncTask implements Callable<User> {

    private UserTransaction userTransaction;
    private UserBean userBean;

    @Override
    public User call() throws Exception {
        performLookups();
        try {
            userTransaction.begin();
            User user = userBean.getUser();
            userTransaction.commit();
            return user;
        } catch (IllegalStateException | SecurityException |
            HeuristicMixedException | HeuristicRollbackException |
            NotSupportedException | RollbackException |
            SystemException e) {
            userTransaction.rollback();
            return null;
        }
    }

    private void performLookups() throws NamingException{
        userBean = CDI.current().select(UserBean.class).get();
        userTransaction = CDI.current()
        .select(UserTransaction.class).get();
    }
```

}

4. And finally, here is the service endpoint that will use the task to write the result to a response:

```
@Path("asyncService")
@RequestScoped
public class AsyncService {
    private AsyncTask asyncTask;
    @Resource(name = "LocalManagedExecutorService")
    private ManagedExecutorService executor;
    @PostConstruct
    public void init(){
        asyncTask = new AsyncTask();
    }
    @GET
    public void asyncService(@Suspended AsyncResponse response){
        Future<User> result = executor.submit(asyncTask);
        while(!result.isDone()){
            try {
                TimeUnit.SECONDS.sleep(1);
            } catch (InterruptedException ex) {
                System.err.println(ex.getMessage());
            }
        }
        try {
            response.resume(Response.ok(result.get()).build());
        } catch (InterruptedException | ExecutionException ex) {
            System.err.println(ex.getMessage());
            response.resume(Response.status(Response
            .Status.INTERNAL_SERVER_ERROR)
            .entity(ex.getMessage()).build());
        }
    }
}
```

To try this code, just deploy it to GlassFish 5 and open this URL:

```
http://localhost:8080/ch09-async-transaction/asyncService
```

How it works...

The magic happens in the `AsyncTask` class, where we will first take a look at the `performLookups` method:

```
private void performLookups() throws NamingException{
    Context ctx = new InitialContext();
    userTransaction = (UserTransaction)
    ctx.lookup("java:comp/UserTransaction");
    userBean = (UserBean) ctx.lookup("java:global/
    ch09-async-transaction/UserBean");
}
```

It will give you the instances of both `UserTransaction` and `UserBean` from the application server. Then you can relax and rely on the things already instantiated for you.

As our task implements a `Callabe<V>` object that it needs to implement the `call()` method:

```
@Override
public User call() throws Exception {
    performLookups();
    try {
        userTransaction.begin();
        User user = userBean.getUser();
        userTransaction.commit();
        return user;
    } catch (IllegalStateException | SecurityException |
            HeuristicMixedException | HeuristicRollbackException
            | NotSupportedException | RollbackException |
            SystemException e) {
        userTransaction.rollback();
        return null;
    }
}
```

You can see `Callable` as a `Runnable` interface that returns a result.

Our transaction code lives here:

```
        userTransaction.begin();
        User user = userBean.getUser();
        userTransaction.commit();
```

And if anything goes wrong, we have the following:

```
} catch (IllegalStateException | SecurityException |
    HeuristicMixedException | HeuristicRollbackException
    | NotSupportedException | RollbackException |
    SystemException e) {
    userTransaction.rollback();
    return null;
}
```

Now we will look at `AsyncService`. First, we have some declarations:

```
private AsyncTask asyncTask;
@Resource(name = "LocalManagedExecutorService")
private ManagedExecutorService executor;
@PostConstruct
public void init(){
    asyncTask = new AsyncTask();
}
```

 We are asking the container to give us an instance from `ManagedExecutorService`, which It is responsible for executing the task in the enterprise context.

Then we call an `init()` method, and the bean is constructed (`@PostConstruct`). This instantiates the task.

Now we have our task execution:

```
@GET
public void asyncService(@Suspended AsyncResponse response){
    Future<User> result = executor.submit(asyncTask);
    while(!result.isDone()){
        try {
            TimeUnit.SECONDS.sleep(1);
        } catch (InterruptedException ex) {
            System.err.println(ex.getMessage());
        }
    }
    try {
        response.resume(Response.ok(result.get()).build());
    } catch (InterruptedException | ExecutionException ex) {
        System.err.println(ex.getMessage());
        response.resume(Response.status(Response.
        Status.INTERNAL_SERVER_ERROR)
        .entity(ex.getMessage()).build());
```

```
        }
    }
```

Note that the executor returns `Future<User>`:

```
Future<User> result = executor.submit(asyncTask);
```

This means this task will be executed asynchronously. Then we check its execution status until it's done:

```
while(!result.isDone()){
    try {
        TimeUnit.SECONDS.sleep(1);
    } catch (InterruptedException ex) {
        System.err.println(ex.getMessage());
    }
}
```

And once it's done, we write it down to the asynchronous response:

```
response.resume(Response.ok(result.get()).build());
```

See also

- The full source code of this recipe is at `https://github.com/eldermoraes/javaee8-cookbook/tree/master/chapter09/ch09-async-transaction`.

Checking the status of asynchronous tasks

Beyond executing asynchronous tasks, which opens up a lot of possibilities, sometimes it is useful and necessary to get the status of those tasks.

For example, you could use it as a check the time elapsed on each task stage. You should also think about logging and monitoring.

This recipe will show you an easy way to do this.

Getting ready

Let's first add our Java EE 8 dependency:

```xml
<dependency>
    <groupId>javax</groupId>
    <artifactId>javaee-api</artifactId>
    <version>8.0</version>
    <scope>provided</scope>
</dependency>
```

How to do it...

1. Let's first create a User POJO:

```java
public class User {

    private Long id;
    private String name;

    public Long getId() {
        return id;
    }

    public void setId(Long id) {
        this.id = id;
    }

    public String getName() {
        return name;
    }

    public void setName(String name) {
        this.name = name;
    }
    public User(Long id, String name) {
        this.id = id;
        this.name = name;
    }
    @Override
    public String toString() {
        return "User{" + "id=" + id + ",
        name=" + name + '}';
    }
}
```

2. Then we create a slow bean for returning `User`:

```
public class UserBean {
    public User getUser(){
        try {
            TimeUnit.SECONDS.sleep(5);
            long id = new Date().getTime();
            return new User(id, "User " + id);
        } catch (InterruptedException ex) {
            long id = new Date().getTime();
            return new User(id, "Error " + id);
        }
    }
}
```

3. Now we create a managed task so we can monitor it:

```
@Stateless
public class AsyncTask implements Callable<User>,
ManagedTaskListener {

    private final long instantiationMili = new Date().getTime();
    private static final Logger LOG = Logger.getAnonymousLogger();
    @Override
    public User call() throws Exception {
        return new UserBean().getUser();
    }

    @Override
    public void taskSubmitted(Future<?> future,
    ManagedExecutorService mes, Object o) {
        long mili = new Date().getTime();
        LOG.log(Level.INFO, "taskSubmitted: {0} -
        Miliseconds since instantiation: {1}",
        new Object[]{future, mili - instantiationMili});
    }

    @Override
    public void taskAborted(Future<?> future,
    ManagedExecutorService mes, Object o, Throwable thrwbl)
    {
        long mili = new Date().getTime();
        LOG.log(Level.INFO, "taskAborted: {0} -
        Miliseconds since instantiation: {1}",
        new Object[]{future, mili - instantiationMili});
    }

    @Override
```

```
public void taskDone(Future<?> future,
ManagedExecutorService mes, Object o,
Throwable thrwbl) {
    long mili = new Date().getTime();
    LOG.log(Level.INFO, "taskDone: {0} -
    Miliseconds since instantiation: {1}",
    new Object[]{future, mili - instantiationMili});
}

@Override
public void taskStarting(Future<?> future,
ManagedExecutorService mes, Object o) {
    long mili = new Date().getTime();
    LOG.log(Level.INFO, "taskStarting: {0} -
    Miliseconds since instantiation: {1}",
    new Object[]{future, mili - instantiationMili});
}

}
```

4. And finally, we create a service endpoint to execute our task and return its results:

```
@Stateless
@Path("asyncService")
public class AsyncService {

    @Resource
    private ManagedExecutorService executor;

    @GET
    public void asyncService(@Suspended AsyncResponse response) {
        int i = 0;

        List<User> usersFound = new ArrayList<>();
        while (i < 4) {
            Future<User> result = executor.submit(new AsyncTask());

            while (!result.isDone()) {
                try {
                    TimeUnit.SECONDS.sleep(1);
                } catch (InterruptedException ex) {
                    System.err.println(ex.getMessage());
                }
            }

            try {
```

```
                            usersFound.add(result.get());
                    } catch (InterruptedException | ExecutionException ex)
        {
                            System.err.println(ex.getMessage());
                    }

                    i++;
            }

            response.resume(Response.ok(usersFound).build());
        }

    }
```

To try this code, just deploy it to GlassFish 5 and open this URL:

```
http://localhost:8080/ch09-task-status/asyncService
```

How it works...

If you have been through the last recipe, you will already be familiar with the Callable task, so I won't give you more details about it here. But now, we are implementing our task using both the Callable and ManagedTaskListener interfaces. The second one gives us all the methods for checking the task's status:

```
@Override
public void taskSubmitted(Future<?> future,
ManagedExecutorService mes, Object o) {
    long mili = new Date().getTime();
    LOG.log(Level.INFO, "taskSubmitted: {0} -
    Miliseconds since instantiation: {1}",
    new Object[]{future, mili - instantiationMili});
}

@Override
public void taskAborted(Future<?> future,
ManagedExecutorService mes, Object o, Throwable thrwbl) {
    long mili = new Date().getTime();
    LOG.log(Level.INFO, "taskAborted: {0} -
    Miliseconds since instantiation: {1}",
    new Object[]{future, mili - instantiationMili});
}

@Override
public void taskDone(Future<?> future,
```

```
ManagedExecutorService mes, Object o, Throwable thrwbl) {
    long mili = new Date().getTime();
    LOG.log(Level.INFO, "taskDone: {0} -
    Miliseconds since instantiation: {1}",
    new Object[]{future, mili - instantiationMili});
}

@Override
public void taskStarting(Future<?> future,
ManagedExecutorService mes, Object o) {
    long mili = new Date().getTime();
    LOG.log(Level.INFO, "taskStarting: {0} -
    Miliseconds since instantiation: {1}",
    new Object[]{future, mili - instantiationMili});
}
```

The best part is that you don't need to call any of them—ManagedExecutorService (explained next) will do it for you.

Finally, we have AsyncService. The first declaration is for our executor:

```
@Resource
private ManagedExecutorService executor;
```

In the service itself, we are getting four users from our asynchronous task:

```
List<User> usersFound = new ArrayList<>();
while (i < 4) {
    Future<User> result = executor.submit(new AsyncTask());

    while (!result.isDone()) {
        try {
            TimeUnit.SECONDS.sleep(1);
        } catch (InterruptedException ex) {
            System.err.println(ex.getMessage());
        }
    }

    try {
        usersFound.add(result.get());
    } catch (InterruptedException | ExecutionException ex) {
        System.err.println(ex.getMessage());
    }

    i++;
}
```

Once it's done, it's written to the asynchronous response:

```
response.resume(Response.ok(usersFound).build());
```

Now, if you look at your server log output, there are messages from the ManagedTaskListener interface.

See also

- See the full source code of this recipe at https://github.com/eldermoraes/ javaee8-cookbook/tree/master/chapter09/ch09-task-status.

Building managed threads with returning results

Sometimes you need to improve the way you look at the threads you are using; maybe to improve your logging features, maybe to manage their priorities. It would be nice if you could also get the results back from them. This recipe will show you how to do it.

Getting ready

Let's first add our Java EE 8 dependency:

```
<dependency>
    <groupId>javax</groupId>
    <artifactId>javaee-api</artifactId>
    <version>8.0</version>
    <scope>provided</scope>
</dependency>
```

How to do it...

1. Let's first create a User POJO:

```
public class User {

    private Long id;
```

```
        private String name;

        public Long getId() {
            return id;
        }

        public void setId(Long id) {
            this.id = id;
        }

        public String getName() {
            return name;
        }

        public void setName(String name) {
            this.name = name;
        }
        public User(Long id, String name) {
            this.id = id;
            this.name = name;
        }
        @Override
        public String toString() {
            return "User{" + "id=" + id + ",
        name=" + name + '}';
        }
    }
```

2. And then, we create a slow bean to return `User`:

```
@Stateless
public class UserBean {
    @GET
    public User getUser(){
        try {
            TimeUnit.SECONDS.sleep(5);
            long id = new Date().getTime();
            return new User(id, "User " + id);
        } catch (InterruptedException ex) {
            long id = new Date().getTime();
            return new User(id, "Error " + id);
        }
    }
}
```

3. And finally, we create an endpoint to get the result from the task:

```
@Stateless
@Path("asyncService")
public class AsyncService {

    @Inject
    private UserBean userBean;

    @Resource(name = "LocalManagedThreadFactory")
    private ManagedThreadFactory factory;

    @GET
    public void asyncService(@Suspended AsyncResponse
    response) {
        Thread thread = factory.newThread(() -> {
            response.resume(Response.ok(userBean
            .getUser()).build());
        });
        thread.setName("Managed Async Task");
        thread.setPriority(Thread.MIN_PRIORITY);
        thread.start();
    }

}
```

To try this code, just deploy it to GlassFish 5 and open this URL:

```
http://localhost:8080/ch09-managed-thread/asyncService
```

How it works...

The only way you should use threads in an enterprise context, and if you really want to use it, is when the application server creates the thread. So here, we are kindly asking the container to do it using `factory`:

```
@Resource(name = "LocalManagedThreadFactory")
private ManagedThreadFactory factory;
```

Using some functional-style code, we create our thread:

```
Thread thread = factory.newThread(() -> {
    response.resume(Response.ok(userBean.getUser()).build());
});
```

Now, moving to the managed stuff, we can set the name and priority of the just-created thread:

```
thread.setName("Managed Async Task");
thread.setPriority(Thread.MIN_PRIORITY);
```

And don't forget to ask the container to start it:

```
thread.start();
```

See also

- See the full source code of this recipe at `https://github.com/eldermoraes/javaee8-cookbook/tree/master/chapter09/ch09-managed-thread`.

Scheduling asynchronous tasks with returning results

Using tasks means also being able to define when they should be executed. This recipe is all about this topic, and also about getting the returning results whenever they return.

Getting ready

Let's first add our Java EE 8 dependency:

```
<dependency>
    <groupId>javax</groupId>
    <artifactId>javaee-api</artifactId>
    <version>8.0</version>
    <scope>provided</scope>
</dependency>
```

How to do it...

1. Let's first create a `User` POJO:

```java
public class User {

    private Long id;
    private String name;

    public Long getId() {
        return id;
    }

    public void setId(Long id) {
        this.id = id;
    }

    public String getName() {
        return name;
    }

    public void setName(String name) {
        this.name = name;
    }
    public User(Long id, String name) {
        this.id = id;
        this.name = name;
    }
    @Override
    public String toString() {
        return "User{" + "id=" + id + ",
    name=" + name + '}';
    }
}
```

2. And then, we create a slow bean to return `User`:

```java
public class UserBean {
    public User getUser(){
        try {
            TimeUnit.SECONDS.sleep(5);
            long id = new Date().getTime();
            return new User(id, "User " + id);
        } catch (InterruptedException ex) {
            long id = new Date().getTime();
            return new User(id, "Error " + id);
        }
    }
```

```
        }
    }
```

3. Now we create a simple `Callable` task to communicate with the bean:

```java
public class AsyncTask implements Callable<User> {

    private final UserBean userBean =
    CDI.current().select(UserBean.class).get();

    @Override
    public User call() throws Exception {
        return userBean.getUser();
    }
}
```

4. And finally, we create our service to schedule and write the task's result in the response:

```java
@Stateless
@Path("asyncService")
public class AsyncService {

    @Resource(name = "LocalManagedScheduledExecutorService")
    private ManagedScheduledExecutorService executor;

    @GET
    public void asyncService(@Suspended AsyncResponse response) {

        ScheduledFuture<User> result = executor.schedule
        (new AsyncTask(), 5, TimeUnit.SECONDS);

        while (!result.isDone()) {
            try {
                TimeUnit.SECONDS.sleep(1);
            } catch (InterruptedException ex) {
                System.err.println(ex.getMessage());
            }
        }

        try {
            response.resume(Response.ok(result.get()).build());
        } catch (InterruptedException | ExecutionException ex) {
            System.err.println(ex.getMessage());
            response.resume(Response.status(Response.Status
            .INTERNAL_SERVER_ERROR).entity(ex.getMessage())
            .build());
        }
```

```
        }

    }
```

To try this code, just deploy it to GlassFish 5 and open this URL:

```
http://localhost:8080/ch09-scheduled-task/asyncService
```

How it works...

All the magic relies on the `AsyncService` class, so we will focus on that.

First, we ask the server an instance of an executor:

```
@Resource(name = "LocalManagedScheduledExecutorService")
private ManagedScheduledExecutorService executor;
```

But it is not just any executor—it's an executor that's specific to scheduling:

```
ScheduledFuture<User> result = executor.schedule(new AsyncTask(),
5, TimeUnit.SECONDS);
```

So, we are scheduling our task to be executed in five seconds. Note that we are also not using a regular `Future`, but `ScheduledFuture`.

The rest is a usual task execution:

```
while (!result.isDone()) {
    try {
        TimeUnit.SECONDS.sleep(1);
    } catch (InterruptedException ex) {
        System.err.println(ex.getMessage());
    }
}
```

And this is how we write the results to the response:

```
response.resume(Response.ok(result.get()).build());
```

See also

- See the full source code of this recipe at `https://github.com/eldermoraes/javaee8-cookbook/tree/master/chapter09/ch09-scheduled-task`.

Using injected proxies for asynchronous tasks

When using tasks, you could also create your own executor. If you have very specific needs, it could be really handy.

This recipe will show you how to create a proxy executor that can be injected and used in the whole context of your application.

Getting ready

Let's first add our Java EE 8 dependency:

```
<dependency>
    <groupId>javax</groupId>
    <artifactId>javaee-api</artifactId>
    <version>8.0</version>
    <scope>provided</scope>
</dependency>
```

How to do it...

1. First, we create a User POJO:

```
public class User implements Serializable{

    private Long id;
    private String name;

    public Long getId() {
        return id;
    }

    public void setId(Long id) {
        this.id = id;
    }

    public String getName() {
        return name;
    }

    public void setName(String name) {
```

```
            this.name = name;
        }
        public User(Long id, String name) {
            this.id = id;
            this.name = name;
        }
        @Override
        public String toString() {
            return "User{" + "id=" + id + ",
            name=" + name + '}';
        }
    }
```

2. Then we create a slow bean to return `User`:

```
public class UserBean {
    public User getUser(){
        try {
            TimeUnit.SECONDS.sleep(5);
            long id = new Date().getTime();
            return new User(id, "User " + id);
        } catch (InterruptedException ex) {
            long id = new Date().getTime();
            return new User(id, "Error " + id);
        }
    }
}
```

3. Now we create a simple `Callable` task to communicate with the slow bean:

```
@Stateless
public class AsyncTask implements Callable<User>{

    @Override
    public User call() throws Exception {
        return new UserBean().getUser();
    }

}
```

4. Here, we call our proxy:

```
@Singleton
public class ExecutorProxy {

    @Resource(name = "LocalManagedThreadFactory")
    private ManagedThreadFactory factory;
```

```
@Resource(name = "LocalContextService")
private ContextService context;

private ExecutorService executor;

@PostConstruct
public void init(){
    executor = new ThreadPoolExecutor(1, 5, 10,
    TimeUnit.SECONDS, new ArrayBlockingQueue<>(5),
    factory);
}
public Future<User> submit(Callable<User> task){
    Callable<User> ctxProxy =
    context.createContextualProxy(task, Callable.class);
    return executor.submit(ctxProxy);
}
}
```

5. And finally, we create the endpoint that will use the proxy:

```
@Stateless
@Path("asyncService")
public class AsyncService {

    @Inject
    private ExecutorProxy executor;

    @GET
    public void asyncService(@Suspended AsyncResponse response)
    {
        Future<User> result = executor.submit(new AsyncTask());
        response.resume(Response.ok(result).build());
    }

}
```

To try this code, just deploy it to GlassFish 5 and open this URL:

```
http://localhost:8080/ch09-proxy-task/asyncService
```

How it works...

The magic really happens here in the `ExecutorProxy` task. First note that we are defining it as follows:

```
@Singleton
```

We are making sure to have one and only one instance of it in the context.

Now note that even though we are creating our own executor, we are still relying on the application server context for it:

```
@Resource(name = "LocalManagedThreadFactory")
private ManagedThreadFactory factory;

@Resource(name = "LocalContextService")
private ContextService context;
```

This guarantees that you don't violate any context rules and ruin your application for good.

Then we create a pool for executing threads:

```
private ExecutorService executor;

@PostConstruct
public void init(){
    executor = new ThreadPoolExecutor(1, 5, 10,
    TimeUnit.SECONDS, new ArrayBlockingQueue<>(5), factory);
}
```

And finally, we create the method for sending tasks to the executing queue:

```
public Future<User> submit(Callable<User> task){
    Callable<User> ctxProxy = context.createContextualProxy(task,
    Callable.class);
    return executor.submit(ctxProxy);
}
```

Now our proxy is ready to be injected:

```
@Inject
private ExecutorProxy executor;
```

It is also ready to be called and to return results:

```
@GET
public void asyncService(@Suspended AsyncResponse response) {
    Future<User> result = executor.submit(new AsyncTask());
    response.resume(Response.ok(result).build());
}
```

See also

- See the full source code of this recipe at `https://github.com/eldermoraes/ javaee8-cookbook/tree/master/chapter09/ch09-proxy-task`.

10
Using Event-Driven Programming to Build Reactive Applications

This chapter covers the following recipes:

- Building reactive applications using asynchronous servlets
- Building reactive applications using events and observers
- Building reactive applications using websockets
- Building reactive applications using message-driven beans
- Building reactive applications using JAX-RS
- Building reactive applications using asynchronous session beans
- Using lambdas and `CompletableFuture` to improve reactive applications

Introduction

Reactive development became a trending topic in many developers conferences, meetups, blog posts, and other countless content sources (both online and offline).

But what is a reactive application? Well, there's a official definition of it contained in something called **The Reactive Manifesto** (please refer to `https://www.reactivemanifesto.org` for more details).

In short, according to the manifesto, reactive systems are:

- **Responsive**: The system responds in a timely manner if at all possible
- **Resilient**: The system stays responsive in the face of failure

- **Elastic**: The system stays responsive under varying workloads
- **Message driven**: Reactive systems rely on asynchronous message-passing to establish a boundary between components that ensures loose coupling, isolation, and location transparency

So, this chapter will show you how to use Java EE 8 features to meet one or more of those reactive system requirements.

Building reactive applications using asynchronous servlets

Servlets are probably one of most well-known Java EE technologies (perhaps even the most known). Actually, servlets existed even before J2EE became a real specification.

This recipe will show you how to use servlets asynchronously.

Getting ready

Let's first add our Java EE 8 dependency:

```
<dependency>
    <groupId>javax</groupId>
    <artifactId>javaee-api</artifactId>
    <version>8.0</version>
    <scope>provided</scope>
</dependency>
```

How to do it...

1. First, we create a User POJO:

```
public class User implements Serializable{

    private Long id;
    private String name;
    public User(long id, String name){
        this.id = id;
        this.name = name;
    }
```

```
public Long getId() {
    return id;
}

public void setId(Long id) {
    this.id = id;
}

public String getName() {
    return name;
}

public void setName(String name) {
    this.name = name;
}
}
```

2. Then, create a slow `UserBean` to return a `User`:

```
@Stateless
public class UserBean {
    public User getUser(){
        long id = new Date().getTime();

        try {
            TimeUnit.SECONDS.sleep(5);
            return new User(id, "User " + id);
        } catch (InterruptedException ex) {
            System.err.println(ex.getMessage());
            return new User(id, "Error " + id);
        }
    }
}
```

3. And finally, create our asynchronous servlet:

```
@WebServlet(name = "UserServlet", urlPatterns = {"/UserServlet"},
asyncSupported = true)
public class UserServlet extends HttpServlet {

    @Inject
    private UserBean userBean;
    private final Jsonb jsonb = JsonbBuilder.create();
    @Override
    protected void doGet(HttpServletRequest req,
    HttpServletResponse resp) throws ServletException,
    IOException {
        AsyncContext ctx = req.startAsync();
```

```
        ctx.start(() -> {
            try (PrintWriter writer =
            ctx.getResponse().getWriter()){
                writer.write(jsonb.toJson(userBean.getUser()));
            } catch (IOException ex) {
                System.err.println(ex.getMessage());
            }
            ctx.complete();
        });
    }

    @Override
    public void destroy() {
        try {
            jsonb.close();
        } catch (Exception ex) {
            System.err.println(ex.getMessage());
        }
    }

}
```

How it works...

From the all important things here, we should start with a simple annotation:

```
asyncSupported = true
```

This will tell the application server that this very servlet supports asynchronous features. By the way, you will need this in the whole servlet chain (including filters, if there are any), otherwise application server will not work.

As the servlets are instantiated by the server, we can inject other context members on it, such as our stateless bean:

```
@Inject
private UserBean userBean;
```

The main servlet method holds the actual request and response references, and the request will give us the context reference to the async API:

```
AsyncContext ctx = req.startAsync();
```

Then, you can execute your previous blocking function in a non-blocking way:

```
ctx.start(() -> {
    ...
    ctx.complete();
});
```

See also

- The full source code of this recipe is at https://github.com/eldermoraes/javaee8-cookbook/tree/master/chapter10/ch10-async-servlet.

Building reactive applications using events and observers

Events and observers are a great way to write code in a reactive way without thinking too much about it, thanks to the great work done by the CDI specification.

This recipe will show you how easy is to use it to improve the user experience of your application.

Getting ready

Let's first add our Java EE 8 dependency:

```
<dependency>
    <groupId>javax</groupId>
    <artifactId>javaee-api</artifactId>
    <version>8.0</version>
    <scope>provided</scope>
</dependency>
```

How to do it...

1. Let's first create a `User` POJO:

```java
public class User implements Serializable{

    private Long id;
    private String name;
    public User(long id, String name){
        this.id = id;
        this.name = name;
    }

    public Long getId() {
        return id;
    }

    public void setId(Long id) {
        this.id = id;
    }

    public String getName() {
        return name;
    }

    public void setName(String name) {
        this.name = name;
    }
}
```

2. And then, let's create a REST endpoint with event and observer features:

```java
@Stateless
@Path("asyncService")
public class AsyncService {
    @Inject
    private Event<User> event;
    private AsyncResponse response;
    @GET
    public void asyncService(@Suspended AsyncResponse response){
        long id = new Date().getTime();
        this.response = response;
        event.fireAsync(new User(id, "User " + id));
    }
```

```
public void onFireEvent(@ObservesAsync User user){
    response.resume(Response.ok(user).build());
}
}
```

How it works...

First, we ask the application server to create a `Event` source for the `User` POJO:

```
@Inject
private Event<User> event;
```

This means that it will listen to any events fired against any `User` object. So what we need to do is create a method to deal with it:

```
public void onFireEvent(@ObservesAsync User user){
    response.resume(Response.ok(user).build());
}
```

So now this method is the proper listener. The `@ObserversAsync` annotation guarantees it. So once an async event is fired, it will do whatever we asked (or coded).

Then, we created a simple asynchronous endpoint to fire it:

```
@GET
public void asyncService(@Suspended AsyncResponse response){
    long id = new Date().getTime();
    this.response = response;
    event.fireAsync(new User(id, "User " + id));
}
```

See also

- The full source code of this recipe is at `https://github.com/eldermoraes/javaee8-cookbook/tree/master/chapter10/ch10-event-observer`.

Building reactive applications using websockets

Websockets are a great way to create decoupled communication channels for your applications. Doing it asynchronously is even better and cooler for non-blocking features.

This recipe will show how to do it.

Getting ready

Let's first add our Java EE 8 dependency:

```xml
<dependency>
    <groupId>javax</groupId>
    <artifactId>javaee-api</artifactId>
    <version>8.0</version>
    <scope>provided</scope>
</dependency>
```

How to do it...

1. The first thing we need is our server endpoint:

```java
@Singleton
@ServerEndpoint(value = "/asyncServer")
public class AsyncServer {
    private final List<Session> peers =
Collections.synchronizedList(new ArrayList<>());
    @OnOpen
    public void onOpen(Session peer){
        peers.add(peer);
    }
    @OnClose
    public void onClose(Session peer){
        peers.remove(peer);
    }
    @OnError
    public void onError(Throwable t){
        System.err.println(t.getMessage());
    }
    @OnMessage
    public void onMessage(String message, Session peer){
```

```
        peers.stream().filter((p) ->
        (p.isOpen())).forEachOrdered((p) -> {
            p.getAsyncRemote().sendText(message +
            " - Total peers: " + peers.size());
        });
    }
}
```

2. Then, we need a client to communicate with the server:

```
@ClientEndpoint
public class AsyncClient {

    private final String asyncServer = "ws://localhost:8080
    /ch10-async-websocket/asyncServer";

    private Session session;
    private final AsyncResponse response;

    public AsyncClient(AsyncResponse response) {
        this.response = response;
    }

    public void connect() {
        WebSocketContainer container =
        ContainerProvider.getWebSocketContainer();
        try {
            container.connectToServer(this, new URI(asyncServer));
        } catch (URISyntaxException | DeploymentException |
          IOException ex) {
            System.err.println(ex.getMessage());
        }

    }

    @OnOpen
    public void onOpen(Session session) {
        this.session = session;
    }

    @OnMessage
    public void onMessage(String message, Session session) {
        response.resume(message);
    }

    public void send(String message) {
        session.getAsyncRemote().sendText(message);
    }
```

```
        public void close(){
            try {
                session.close();
            } catch (IOException ex) {
                System.err.println(ex.getMessage());
            }
        }
    }
```

3. And finally, we need a simple REST endpoint to talk to the client:

```
@Stateless
@Path("asyncService")
public class AsyncService {
    @GET
    public void asyncService(@Suspended AsyncResponse response){
        AsyncClient client = new AsyncClient(response);
        client.connect();
        client.send("Message from client " + new Date().getTime());
        client.close();
    }
}
```

How it works...

The first important thing in our server is this annotation:

```
@Singleton
```

Of course, we must ensure that we have one and only one instance of the server endpoint. This will ensure that all peers are managed under the same umbrella.

Let's move on to talk about peers:

```
private final List<Session> peers = Collections.synchronizedList
(new ArrayList<>());
```

The list holding them is a synchronized list. This is important because you will add/remove peers while iterating on the list, so things could be messed up if you don't protect it.

All the default websocket methods are managed by the application server:

```
@OnOpen
public void onOpen(Session peer){
    peers.add(peer);
}
@OnClose
public void onClose(Session peer){
    peers.remove(peer);
}
@OnError
public void onError(Throwable t){
    System.err.println(t.getMessage());
}
@OnMessage
public void onMessage(String message, Session peer){
    peers.stream().filter((p) -> (p.isOpen())).forEachOrdered((p) ->
    {
        p.getAsyncRemote().sendText(message + " - Total peers: "
        + peers.size());
    });
}
```

Also, let's give a special mention to the code on our `onMessage` method:

```
@OnMessage
public void onMessage(String message, Session peer){
    peers.stream().filter((p) -> (p.isOpen())).forEachOrdered((p)
    -> {
        p.getAsyncRemote().sendText(message + " - Total peers: "
        + peers.size());
    });
}
```

We are sending a message to the peer only if it is open.

Now looking to our client, we have a reference to the server URI:

```
private final String asyncServer = "ws://localhost:8080/
ch10-async-websocket/asyncServer";
```

Note that the protocol is `ws`, specific to websocket communication.

Then, we have a method to open the connection with the server endpoint:

```
public void connect() {
    WebSocketContainer container =
    ContainerProvider.getWebSocketContainer();
    try {
        container.connectToServer(this, new URI(asyncServer));
    } catch (URISyntaxException | DeploymentException | IOException ex) {
        System.err.println(ex.getMessage());
    }
}
```

And once we have the message confirmation from the server, we can do something about it:

```
@OnMessage
public void onMessage(String message, Session session) {
    response.resume(message);
}
```

This response will appear on the endpoint that is calling the client:

```
@GET
public void asyncService(@Suspended AsyncResponse response){
    AsyncClient client = new AsyncClient(response);
    client.connect();
    client.send("Message from client " + new Date().getTime());
}
```

We are passing the reference to the client so the client can use it to write the message on it.

See also

- The full source code of this recipe is at `https://github.com/eldermoraes/javaee8-cookbook/tree/master/chapter10/ch10-async-websocket`.

Building reactive applications using message-driven beans

The Java Messaging Service is one of the oldest Java EE APIs, and it's been reactive since day one: just read the manifesto linked in the introduction of this chapter.

This recipe will show you how to use message-driven beans, or MDBs, to deliver and consume asynchronous messages with just a few annotations.

Getting ready

Let's first add our Java EE 8 dependency:

```
<dependency>
    <groupId>javax</groupId>
    <artifactId>javaee-api</artifactId>
    <version>8.0</version>
    <scope>provided</scope>
</dependency>
```

To check the details about queue setup in GlassFish 5, please refer to the recipe *Using Messaging Services for Asynchronous Communication* at Chapter 5, *Security of Enterprise Architecture*.

How to do it...

1. First, we create a User POJO:

```
public class User implements Serializable{

    private Long id;
    private String name;
    public User(long id, String name){
        this.id = id;
        this.name = name;
    }

    public Long getId() {
        return id;
    }

    public void setId(Long id) {
        this.id = id;
    }

    public String getName() {
        return name;
    }
```

```
        public void setName(String name) {
            this.name = name;
        }
    }
```

2. Then, we create a message sender:

```
@Stateless
public class Sender {
    @Inject
    private JMSContext context;
    @Resource(lookup = "jms/JmsQueue")
    private Destination queue;
    public void send(User user){
        context.createProducer()
                .setDeliveryMode(DeliveryMode.PERSISTENT)
                .setDisableMessageID(true)
                .setDisableMessageTimestamp(true)
                .send(queue, user);
    }
}
```

3. Now, we create a message consumer. This is our MDB:

```
@MessageDriven(activationConfig = {
    @ActivationConfigProperty(propertyName = "destinationLookup",
    propertyValue = "jms/JmsQueue"),
    @ActivationConfigProperty(propertyName = "destinationType",
    propertyValue = "javax.jms.Queue")
})
public class Consumer implements MessageListener{

    @Override
    public void onMessage(Message msg) {
        try {
            User user = msg.getBody(User.class);
            System.out.println("User: " + user);
        } catch (JMSException ex) {
            System.err.println(ex.getMessage());
        }
    }
}
```

4. And finally, we create an endpoint, just to send a mock user to the queue:

```
@Stateless
@Path("mdbService")
public class MDBService {
    @Inject
    private Sender sender;
    public void mdbService(@Suspended AsyncResponse response){
        long id = new Date().getTime();
        sender.send(new User(id, "User " + id));
        response.resume("Message sent to the queue");
    }
}
```

How it works...

We start by asking the application server a JMS context instance:

```
@Inject
private JMSContext context;
```

We also send a reference to the queue we want to work with:

```
@Resource(lookup = "jms/JmsQueue")
private Destination queue;
```

Then, using the context, we create a producer to send the message to the queue:

```
context.createProducer()
        .setDeliveryMode(DeliveryMode.PERSISTENT)
        .setDisableMessageID(true)
        .setDisableMessageTimestamp(true)
        .send(queue, user);
```

Pay attention to these three methods:

- setDeliveryMode: This method can be PERSISTENT or NON_PERSISTENT. If using PERSISTENT, the server will take special care of the message and not lose it.

- setDisableMessageID: This one is used for creating MessageID, which increases the server effort to create and deliver the message and also increases its size. This property (true or false) gives a hint to the server that you are not going to need/use it, so it can improve the process.

- `setDisableMessageTimestamp`: This is the same as for `setDisableMessageID`.

Also, note that we are sending a `User` instance to the queue. So you can easily send object instances, not only text messages, as long as they implement the serializable interface.

The MDB itself, or our message consumer, is basically a few annotations and an interface implementation.

Here is its annotation:

```
@MessageDriven(activationConfig = {
    @ActivationConfigProperty(propertyName = "destinationLookup",
    propertyValue = "jms/JmsQueue"),
    @ActivationConfigProperty(propertyName = "destinationType",
    propertyValue = "javax.jms.Queue")
})
```

Here, we are using two properties: one to define which queue we are looking up (`destinationLookup`) and another to define that it is really the queue type we are using (`destinationType`).

Here is the implementation:

```
@Override
public void onMessage(Message msg) {
    try {
        User user = msg.getBody(User.class);
        System.out.println("User: " + user);
    } catch (JMSException ex) {
        System.err.println(ex.getMessage());
    }
}
```

Note that it is easy to get the `User` instance from the message's body:

```
User user = msg.getBody(User.class);
```

No heavy lifting at all.

And the endpoint used to send the message couldn't be simpler. We inject the `Sender` (which is a stateless bean):

```
@Inject
private Sender sender;
```

Then, we call an asynchronous method:

```
public void mdbService(@Suspended AsyncResponse response){
    long id = new Date().getTime();
    sender.send(new User(id, "User " + id));
    response.resume("Message sent to the queue");
}
```

See also

- See the full source code of this recipe at https://github.com/eldermoraes/
  javaee8-cookbook/tree/master/chapter10/ch10-mdb.

Building reactive applications using JAX-RS

The JAX-RS API also has some great features for event-driven programming. This recipe will show you can use an async invoker from the request to write responses through callbacks.

Getting ready

Let's first add our Java EE 8 dependency:

```
<dependency>
    <groupId>javax</groupId>
    <artifactId>javaee-api</artifactId>
    <version>8.0</version>
    <scope>provided</scope>
</dependency>
```

How to do it...

1. First, we create a User POJO:

```
public class User implements Serializable{

    private Long id;
    private String name;
    public User(long id, String name){
```

```
            this.id = id;
            this.name = name;
    }

    public Long getId() {
        return id;
    }

    public void setId(Long id) {
        this.id = id;
    }

    public String getName() {
        return name;
    }

    public void setName(String name) {
        this.name = name;
    }
}
```

2. Here, we define `UserBean`, which will act as a remote endpoint:

```
@Stateless
@Path("remoteUser")
public class UserBean {

    @GET
    public Response remoteUser() {
        long id = new Date().getTime();
        try {
            TimeUnit.SECONDS.sleep(5);
            return Response.ok(new User(id, "User " + id))
            .build();
        } catch (InterruptedException ex) {
            System.err.println(ex.getMessage());
            return Response.ok(new User(id, "Error " + id))
            .build();
        }
    }

}
```

3. Then finally, we define a local endpoint that will consume the remote one:

```
@Stateless
@Path("asyncService")
public class AsyncService {
    private Client client;
    private WebTarget target;

    @PostConstruct
    public void init() {
        client = ClientBuilder.newBuilder()
                .readTimeout(10, TimeUnit.SECONDS)
                .connectTimeout(10, TimeUnit.SECONDS)
                .build();
        target = client.target("http://localhost:8080/
        ch10-async-jaxrs/remoteUser");
    }

    @PreDestroy
    public void destroy(){
        client.close();
    }
    @GET
    public void asyncService(@Suspended AsyncResponse response){
        target.request().async().get(new
        InvocationCallback<Response>() {
            @Override
            public void completed(Response rspns) {
                response.resume(rspns);
            }

            @Override
            public void failed(Throwable thrwbl) {
                response.resume(Response.status(Response.Status.
                INTERNAL_SERVER_ERROR).entity(thrwbl.getMessage())
                .build());
            }
        });
    }
}
```

How it works...

We start the bean by creating the communication with the remote endpoint right in the bean instantiation. Doing this will avoid the overhead of doing it later while the invocation is happening:

```
private Client client;
private WebTarget target;

@PostConstruct
public void init() {
    client = ClientBuilder.newBuilder()
            .readTimeout(10, TimeUnit.SECONDS)
            .connectTimeout(10, TimeUnit.SECONDS)
            .build();
    target = client.target("http://localhost:8080/
    ch10-async-jaxrs/remoteUser");
}
```

Then, we created an anonymous InvocationCallback implementation within our async invoker:

```
target.request().async().get(new InvocationCallback<Response>()
{
    @Override
    public void completed(Response rspns) {
        response.resume(rspns);
    }

    @Override
    public void failed(Throwable thrwbl) {
        System.err.println(thrwbl.getMessage());
    }
});
```

That way, we can rely on the `completed` and `failed` events and deal with them properly.

See also

- See the full source code of this recipe at `https://github.com/eldermoraes/javaee8-cookbook/tree/master/chapter10/ch10-async-jaxrs`.

Building reactive applications using asynchronous session beans

Session beans can also become reactive and event driven just by using annotations. This recipe will show you how to do it.

Getting ready

Let's first add our Java EE 8 dependency:

```
<dependency>
    <groupId>javax</groupId>
    <artifactId>javaee-api</artifactId>
    <version>8.0</version>
    <scope>provided</scope>
</dependency>
```

How to do it...

1. First, we create a `User` POJO:

```
public class User implements Serializable{

    private Long id;
    private String name;
    public User(long id, String name){
        this.id = id;
        this.name = name;
    }

    public Long getId() {
```

```
            return id;
    }

    public void setId(Long id) {
        this.id = id;
    }

    public String getName() {
        return name;
    }

    public void setName(String name) {
        this.name = name;
    }
}
```

2. Then, we create our asynchronous session bean:

```
@Stateless
public class UserBean {
    @Asynchronous
    public Future<User> getUser(){
        long id = new Date().getTime();
        User user = new User(id, "User " + id);
        return new AsyncResult(user);
    }
    @Asynchronous
    public void doSomeSlowStuff(User user){
        try {
            TimeUnit.SECONDS.sleep(5);
        } catch (InterruptedException ex) {
            System.err.println(ex.getMessage());
        }
    }
}
```

3. And finally, we create the endpoint that will call the bean:

```
@Stateless
@Path("asyncService")
public class AsyncService {
    @Inject
    private UserBean userBean;
    @GET
    public void asyncService(@Suspended AsyncResponse response){
        try {
            Future<User> result = userBean.getUser();
            while(!result.isDone()){
```

```
        try {
            TimeUnit.SECONDS.sleep(1);
        } catch (InterruptedException ex) {
            System.err.println(ex.getMessage());
        }
    }
    response.resume(Response.ok(result.get()).build());
} catch (InterruptedException | ExecutionException ex) {
    System.err.println(ex.getMessage());
}
}
}
```

How it works...

Let's first check the `getUser` method from the session bean:

```
@Asynchronous
public Future<User> getUser(){
    long id = new Date().getTime();
    User user = new User(id, "User " + id);
    return new AsyncResult(user);
}
```

Once we user the `@Asynchronous` annotation, we have to turn its returning value to a `Future` instance of something (in our case, `User`).

We also created a `void` method to show you how to create a non-blocking code with session beans:

```
@Asynchronous
public void doSomeSlowStuff(User user){
    try {
        TimeUnit.SECONDS.sleep(5);
    } catch (InterruptedException ex) {
        System.err.println(ex.getMessage());
    }
}
```

And finally, we created our calling endpoint:

```
@GET
public void asyncService(@Suspended AsyncResponse response){
    try {
        Future<User> result = userBean.getUser();
        while(!result.isDone()){
            try {
                TimeUnit.SECONDS.sleep(1);
            } catch (InterruptedException ex) {
                System.err.println(ex.getMessage());
            }
        }
        response.resume(Response.ok(result.get()).build());
    } catch (InterruptedException | ExecutionException ex) {
        System.err.println(ex.getMessage());
    }
}
```

As `getUser` returns `Future`, we can work with an async status check. Once it is done, we write the results in the response (also asynchronous).

See also

- See the full source code of this recipe at `https://github.com/eldermoraes/ javaee8-cookbook/tree/master/chapter10/ch10-async-bean`.

Using lambdas and CompletableFuture to improve reactive applications

The Java language always had the reputation of being a verbose language. But since the advent of lambdas, this issue has improved a lot.

We can use lambdas and also bring `CompletableFuture` to the party to improve not only the coding, but also the behavior of reactive applications. This recipe will show you how.

Getting ready

Let's first add our Java EE 8 dependency:

```xml
<dependency>
    <groupId>javax</groupId>
    <artifactId>javaee-api</artifactId>
    <version>8.0</version>
    <scope>provided</scope>
</dependency>
```

How to do it...

1. First, we create a `User` POJO:

```java
public class User implements Serializable{

    private Long id;
    private String name;
    public User(long id, String name){
        this.id = id;
        this.name = name;
    }

    public Long getId() {
        return id;
    }

    public void setId(Long id) {
        this.id = id;
    }

    public String getName() {
        return name;
    }

    public void setName(String name) {
        this.name = name;
    }
}
```

2. Then, we call `UserBean` to return a `User` instance:

```java
@Stateless
public class UserBean {

    public User getUser() {
        long id = new Date().getTime();
        try {
            TimeUnit.SECONDS.sleep(5);
            return new User(id, "User " + id);
        } catch (InterruptedException ex) {
            System.err.println(ex.getMessage());
            return new User(id, "Error " + id);
        }
    }

}
```

3. And finally, we create an async endpoint to call the bean:

```java
@Stateless
@Path("asyncService")
public class AsyncService {

    @Inject
    private UserBean userBean;

    @GET
    public void asyncService(@Suspended AsyncResponse response)
    {
        CompletableFuture
                .supplyAsync(() -> userBean.getUser())
                .thenAcceptAsync((u) -> {
                    response.resume(Response.ok(u).build());
                }).exceptionally((t) -> {
                    response.resume(Response.status
                    (Response.Status.
                    INTERNAL_SERVER_ERROR).entity(t.getMessage())
                    .build());
                    return null;
                });
    }
}
```

How it works...

We are using basically two `CompletableFuture` methods:

- `supplyAsync`: This will start an async call to whatever you put inside of it. We put in a lambda call.
- `thenAcceptAsync`: Once the async process is done, the returning value will come here. Thanks to lambdas, we can call this returning value as `u` (and could be whatever we want). Then, we use it to write it down to the asynchronous response.

See also

- See the full source code of this recipe at `https://github.com/eldermoraes/javaee8-cookbook/tree/master/chapter10/ch10-completable-future`.

11
Rising to the Cloud – Java EE, Containers, and Cloud Computing

This chapter covers the following recipes:

- Building Java EE containers using Docker
- Using Oracle Cloud for container orchestration in the cloud
- Using Jelastic for container orchestration in the cloud
- Using OpenShift for container orchestration in the cloud
- Using AWS for container orchestration in the cloud

Introduction

There are two things that have happened in the computer industry that have changed it for good—**cloud computing** and **containers**. Cloud computing came first and changed the way to look at infrastructure, the way to consume software, and the way to grow many businesses. Now, computation is a commodity.

Containers change and are changing the way we build and deliver software. They are also the essential glue for DevOps and the way to take CI/CD to another level.

Put them together and you will have one of the most powerful environments in IT. But can Java EE take advantage of it? Of course! If an application server is an abstraction of Java EE applications, containers are an abstraction of the server, and once you have them built in a standard such as Docker, you have the power to use such tools to manage an application server.

This chapter will show you how to put your Java EE application inside a container and how to deliver this container with some of the best providers we have today.

Building Java EE containers using Docker

Since day one, Java EE has been based on containers. If you doubt it, just have a look at this diagram:

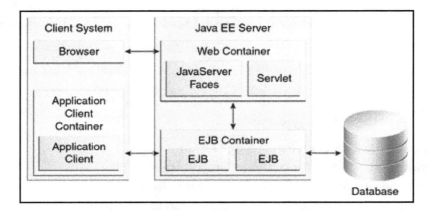

Java EE architecture: https://docs.oracle.com/javaee/6/tutorial/doc/bnacj.html

It belongs to Oracle's official documentation for Java EE 6 and, actually, has been much the same architecture since the times of Sun.

If you pay attention, you will notice that there are different containers: a web container, an EJB container, and an application client container. In this architecture, it means that the applications developed with those APIs will rely on many features and services provided by the container.

When we take the Java EE application server and put it inside a Docker container, we are doing the same thing— it is relying on some of the features and services provided by the Docker environment.

This recipe will show you how to deliver a Java EE application in a container bundle, which is called an **appliance**.

Getting ready

First, of course, you need the Docker platform installed in your environment. There are plenty of options, so I suggest you go the following link and get more details:

`https://docs.docker.com/install/`

And if you are not familiar with Docker commands, I recommend you have a look at this beautiful cheat sheet:

`https://zeroturnaround.com/rebellabs/docker-commands-and-best-practices-cheat-sheet/`

You'll also need to create an account at Docker Hub so you can store your own images. Check it out: `https://hub.docker.com/`.

It's free for public images.

How to do it...

To build your Java EE container, you'll first need a Docker image. To build it, you'll need a Dockerfile such as this:

```
FROM openjdk:8-jdk

ENV GLASSFISH_HOME /usr/local/glassfish
ENV PATH ${GLASSFISH_HOME}/bin:$PATH
ENV GLASSFISH_PKG latest-glassfish.zip
ENV GLASSFISH_URL
https://download.oracle.com/glassfish/5.0/nightly/latest-glassfish.zip

RUN mkdir -p ${GLASSFISH_HOME}

WORKDIR ${GLASSFISH_HOME}

RUN set -x \
  && curl -fSL ${GLASSFISH_URL} -o ${GLASSFISH_PKG} \
    && unzip -o $GLASSFISH_PKG \
    && rm -f $GLASSFISH_PKG \
  && mv glassfish5/* ${GLASSFISH_HOME} \
  && rm -Rf glassfish5

RUN addgroup glassfish_grp \
    && adduser --system glassfish \
    && usermod -G glassfish_grp glassfish \
```

```
        && chown -R glassfish:glassfish_grp ${GLASSFISH_HOME} \
        && chmod -R 777 ${GLASSFISH_HOME}

COPY docker-entrypoint.sh /
RUN chmod +x /docker-entrypoint.sh

USER glassfish

ENTRYPOINT ["/docker-entrypoint.sh"]

EXPOSE 4848 8080 8181
CMD ["asadmin", "start-domain", "-v"]
```

This image will be our base image from which we will construct other images in this chapter. Now we need to build it:

```
docker build -t eldermoraes/gf-javaee-jdk8 .
```

Go ahead and push it to your Docker Registry at Docker Hub:

```
docker push eldermoraes/gf-javaee-jdk8
```

Now you can create another image by customizing the previous one, and then put your app on it:

```
FROM eldermoraes/gf-javaee-jdk8

ENV DEPLOYMENT_DIR ${GLASSFISH_HOME}/glassfish/domains/domain1/autodeploy/

COPY app.war ${DEPLOYMENT_DIR}
```

In the same folder, we have a Java EE application file (`app.war`) that will be deployed inside the container. Check the *See also* section to download all the files.

Once you save your Dockerfile, you can build your image:

```
docker build -t eldermoraes/gf-javaee-cookbook .
```

Now you can create the container:

```
docker run -d --name gf-javaee-cookbook \
    -h gf-javaee-cookbook \
    -p 80:8080 \
    -p 4848:4848 \
    -p 8686:8686 \
    -p 8009:8009 \
    -p 8181:8181 \
    eldermoraes/gf-javaee-cookbook
```

Wait a few seconds and open this URL in your browser:

```
http://localhost/app
```

How it works...

Let's understand our first Dockerfile:

```
FROM openjdk:8-jdk
```

This FROM keyword will ask Docker to pull the openjdk:8-jdk image, but what does it mean?

It means that there's a registry somewhere where your Docker will find prebuilt images. If there's no image registry in your local environment, it will search for it in Docker Hub, the official and public Docker registry in the cloud.

And when you say that you are using a pre-built image, it means that you don't need to build, in our case, the whole Linux container from scratch. There's already a template that you can rely on:

```
ENV GLASSFISH_HOME /usr/local/glassfish
ENV PATH ${GLASSFISH_HOME}/bin:$PATH
ENV GLASSFISH_PKG latest-glassfish.zip
ENV GLASSFISH_URL
https://download.oracle.com/glassfish/5.0/nightly/latest-glassfish.zip

RUN mkdir -p ${GLASSFISH_HOME}

WORKDIR ${GLASSFISH_HOME}
```

Here are just some environment variables to help with the coding.

```
RUN set -x \
  && curl -fSL ${GLASSFISH_URL} -o ${GLASSFISH_PKG} \
    && unzip -o $GLASSFISH_PKG \
    && rm -f $GLASSFISH_PKG \
  && mv glassfish5/* ${GLASSFISH_HOME} \
  && rm -Rf glassfish5
```

The RUN clause in Dockerfiles execute some bash commands inside the container when it has been created. Basically, what is happening here is that GlassFish is being downloaded and then prepared in the container:

```
RUN addgroup glassfish_grp \
```

```
&& adduser --system glassfish \
&& usermod -G glassfish_grp glassfish \
&& chown -R glassfish:glassfish_grp ${GLASSFISH_HOME} \
&& chmod -R 777 ${GLASSFISH_HOME}
```

For safety, we define the user that will hold the permissions for GlassFish files and processes:

```
COPY docker-entrypoint.sh /
RUN chmod +x /docker-entrypoint.sh
```

Here we are including a bash script inside the container to perform some GlassFish administrative tasks:

```
#!/bin/bash

if [[ -z $ADMIN_PASSWORD ]]; then
  ADMIN_PASSWORD=$(date| md5sum | fold -w 8 | head -n 1)
  echo "#########GENERATED ADMIN PASSWORD: $ADMIN_PASSWORD
  ##########"
fi

echo "AS_ADMIN_PASSWORD=" > /tmp/glassfishpwd
echo "AS_ADMIN_NEWPASSWORD=${ADMIN_PASSWORD}" >> /tmp/glassfishpwd

asadmin --user=admin --passwordfile=/tmp/glassfishpwd change-admin-password
--domain_name domain1
asadmin start-domain

echo "AS_ADMIN_PASSWORD=${ADMIN_PASSWORD}" > /tmp/glassfishpwd

asadmin --user=admin --passwordfile=/tmp/glassfishpwd enable-secure-admin
asadmin --user=admin stop-domain
rm /tmp/glassfishpwd

exec "$@"
```

After copying the bash file into the container, we go to the final block:

```
USER glassfish

ENTRYPOINT ["/docker-entrypoint.sh"]

EXPOSE 4848 8080 8181
CMD ["asadmin", "start-domain", "-v"]
```

The USER clause defines the user that will be used from this point in the file. It's great because from there, all the tasks will be done by the glassfish user.

The ENTRYPOINT clause will execute the docker-entrypoint.sh script.

The EXPOSE clause will define the ports that will be available for containers that use this image.

And finally, the CMD clause will call the GlassFish script that will initialize the container.

Now let's understand our second Dockerfile:

```
FROM eldermoraes/gf-javaee-jdk8
```

We need to take into account the same considerations about the prebuilt image, but now the image was made by you. Congratulations!

```
ENV DEPLOYMENT_DIR ${GLASSFISH_HOME}/glassfish/domains/domain1/autodeploy/
```

Here, we are building an environment variable to help with the deployment. It's done in the same way as for Linux systems:

```
COPY app.war ${DEPLOYMENT_DIR}
```

This COPY command will literally copy the app.war file to the folder defined in the DEPLOYMENT_DIR environment variable.

From here, you are ready to build an image and create a container. The image builder is self-explanatory:

```
docker build -t eldermoraes/gf-javaee-cookbook .
```

Let's check the docker run command:

```
docker run -d --name gf-javaee-cookbook \
    -h gf-javaee-cookbook \
    -p 80:8080 \
    -p 4848:4848 \
    -p 8686:8686 \
    -p 8009:8009 \
    -p 8181:8181 \
    eldermoraes/gf-javaee-cookbook
```

If we break it down, this is what the various elements of the command mean:

- `-h`: Defines the host name of the container.
- `-p`: Defines which ports will be exposed and how it will be done. It is useful, for example, when more than one container is using the same port by default—you just use them differently.
- `eldermoraes/gf-javaee-cookbook`: The reference to the image you just built.

See also

- The source code and files used in this recipe are at `https://github.com/eldermoraes/javaee8-cookbook/tree/master/chapter11/ch11-docker`.

Using Oracle Cloud for container orchestration in the cloud

The best way to use containers in the cloud is by using a provider. Why? Because they can provide a good infrastructure and a nice service for a small price.

This recipe will show you how to get the container created in the first recipe of this chapter and deliver it using Oracle Cloud.

Getting ready

If you don't have an account with Oracle Cloud you can register for a trial at `https://cloud.oracle.com/tryit`.

That's all you need, beyond having created the Docker image in the first recipe of this chapter.

How to do it...

1. After logging in to the platform, you will see this dashboard:

Oracle Cloud dashboard

2. Scroll down the page until you find **Oracle Cloud Infrastructure - Container Service** and click on it:

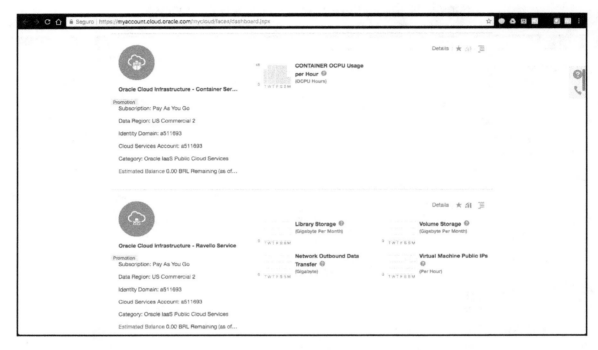

Container Service Access

3. On the main page of the container service (the following screenshot), click on the **My Services URL** link :

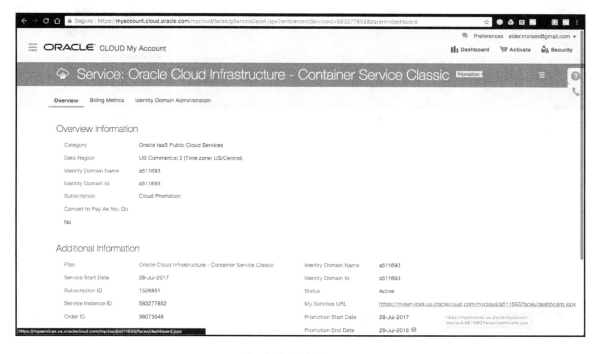

Container Service Overview page

4. You will get to the **Cloud Services** dashboard. Click on **Container Classic**:

Cloud Services Dashboard

5. On the page that opens, click on the **Open Service Console** button:

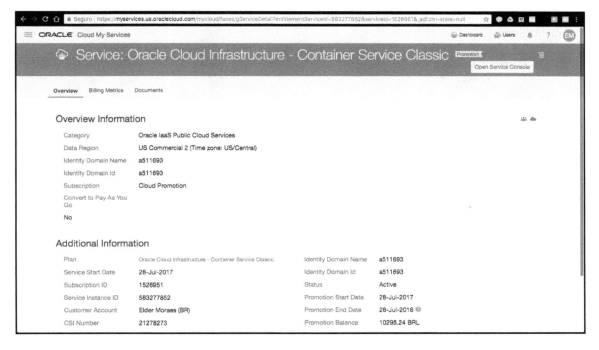

Service Console Access

6. On the next page, click on the **Create Instance** button:

Container Cloud Service welcome page

7. Fill in the form like this:

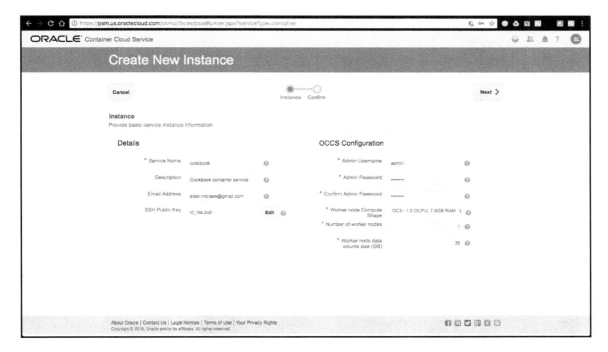

Fields for instance creation

In the **SSH Public Key** field, you need to set a valid public key that has a private pair. Without it, you will not be able to log in to the service using SSH.

Click on **Next**.

8. On the page that opens, confirm your data and click on the **Create** button:

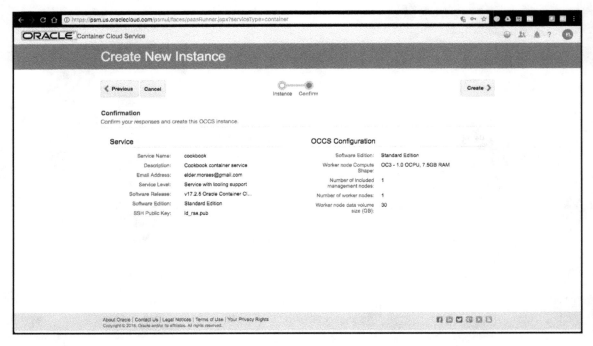

Data confirmation

9. Then you'll be back to the main page while the service is created (note the
   Creating service... label):

New service being created

10. Once the service is created, click on the **Options** button and click on **Container Console**:

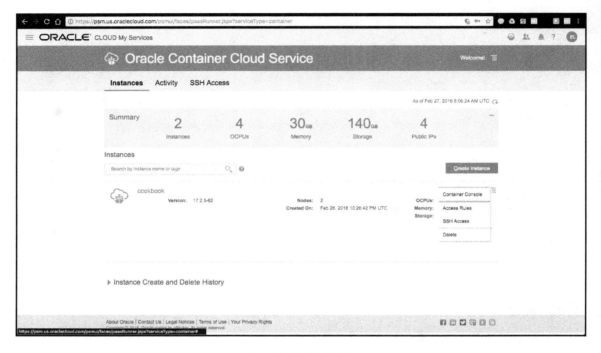

Access to the Container Console

You are now in the dashboard of the service you have just created:

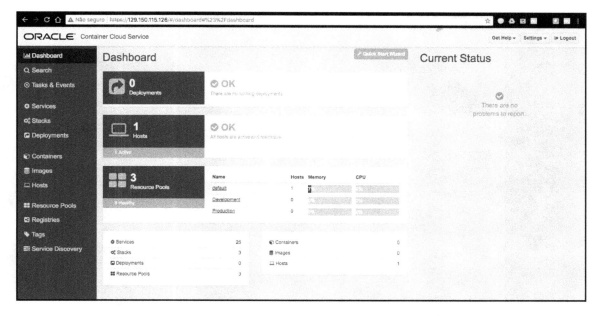

Container Cloud Service dashboard

11. Click on **Services** (left side) and then **New Service** (right side):

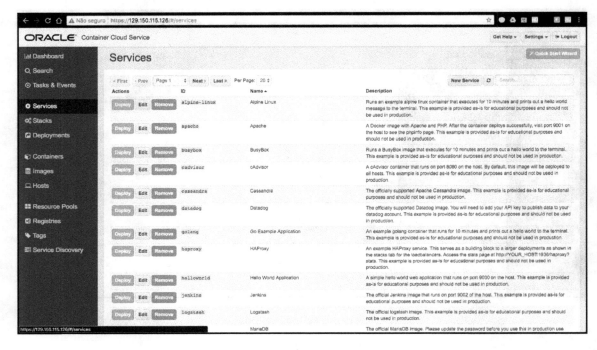

Services page

12. In the popup, give a name to the service (the **Service Name** field), and in the **Image** field you need to fill in the details of the pre-built image:

Fields for service creation

13. In the **Available Options** field, check the **Ports** option. It will open
the **Ports** section under **Environment Variables**. Click on the **Add** button and fill
in the form in the popup like this:

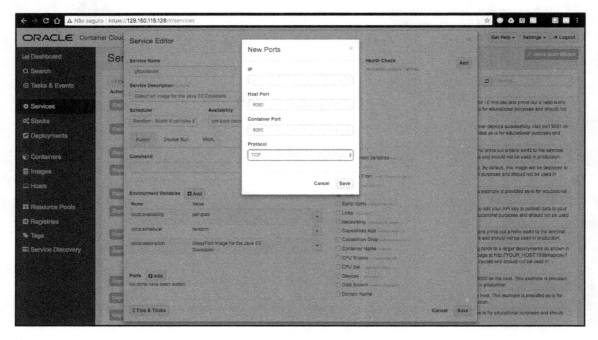

Ports forwarding

14. Now your service is on this list. Click on its **Deploy** button:

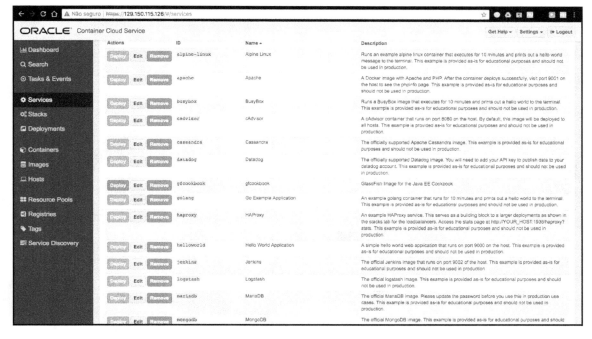

Services list

15. In the popup, fill in the form as shown in the screenshot and click on **Deploy**:

Popup for service deployment

16. Now, just wait a moment until your new service is up and running:

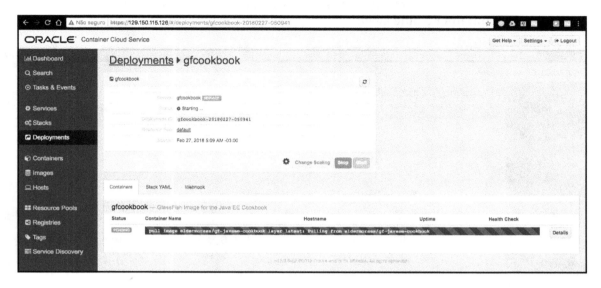

Ongoing deployment

17. Once your deployment is done, it will become green and you will have information about the container you have created. Click on the link under the **Container Name** label:

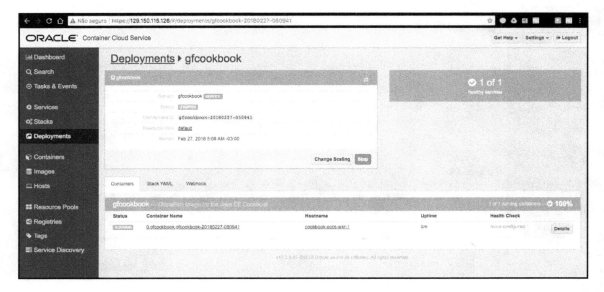

Deployment done

You now will see details about your container:

Container details

18. Click on the tab labeled **Environment Variables** and find a variable called **OCCS_HOSTIPS**. On the same line there's an IP in the **public_ip** label. Copy it:

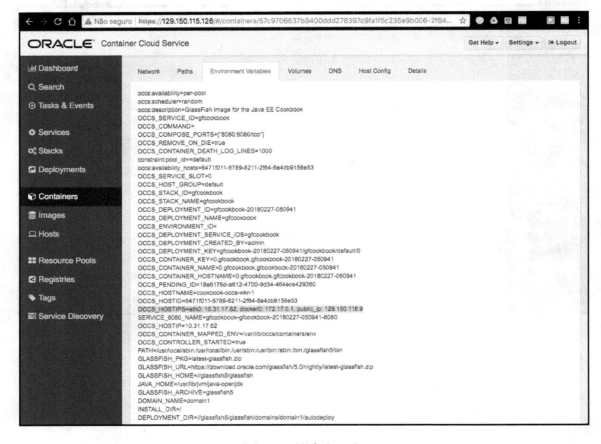

Environment variable for the container

Use it to navigate to `http://[public_ip]:8080/app`:

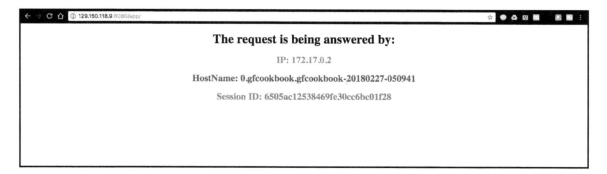

Test page for our application

If you can see the preceding image, you've made it! Now your container is orchestrated in the cloud using Oracle Cloud.

How it works...

The reason why it's so simple is that you are using a platform that was designed to make it simple. So, all the heavy lifting that you'd have to do in your own infrastructure is done by the platform.

There's more...

The reason why you should use a provider to orchestrate your containers in the cloud is not only because of the ease of creating services, but also because the platform will take care of keeping it up and running.

So, if your container goes wrong and needs to be stopped, restarted, or even killed and recreated, the platform will do it automatically.

Using Jelastic for container orchestration in the cloud

The best way to use containers in the cloud is by using a provider. Why? Because they can provide you a good infrastructure and a nice service for a small price.

This recipe will show you how to get the container created in the first recipe of this chapter and deliver it using Jelastic.

Getting ready

If you don't have an account with Jelastic, you can sign for a free trial at `https://jelastic.com/`.

How to do it...

1. After logging into the platform you will get to this main page:

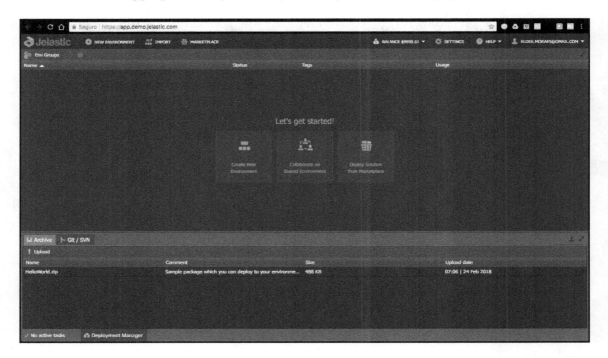

Jelastic main page

2. First things first. Click on the **Settings** button (top right). It will open the **Account settings** section (bottom left):

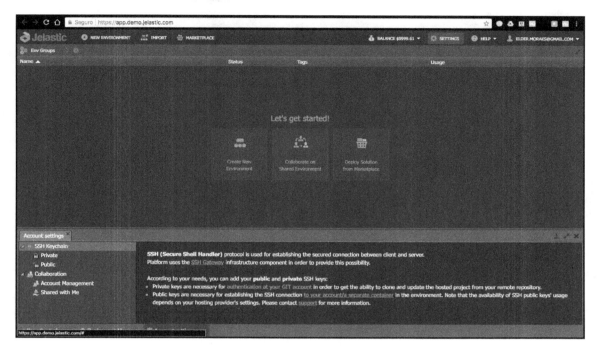

Account settings

3. Click on **Public** inside **SSH Keychain** and upload your public SSH key:

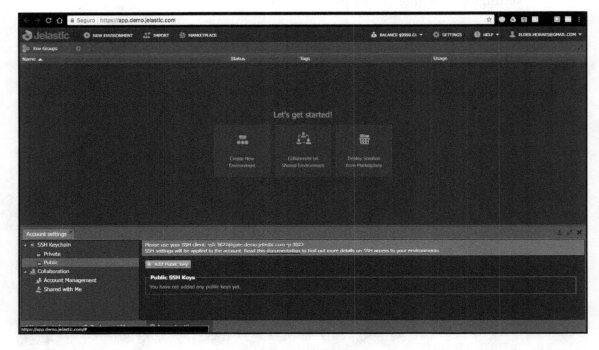

SSH Public Key information

4. Make sure your SSH key is really uploaded, otherwise you will not be able to log into the platform using SSH:

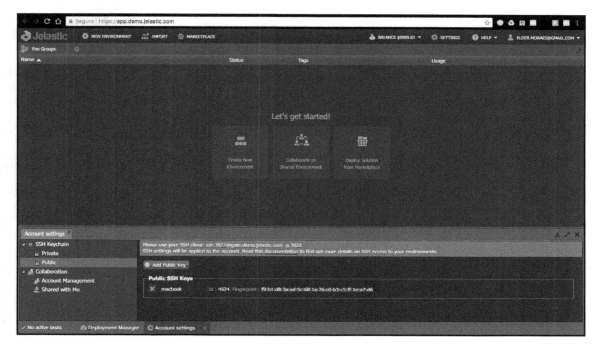

SSH confirmation

5. At the top of the page, click on the **Marketplace** button. Go on to the **Other** section and select **Docker Engine CE**. Click on **Install**:

Marketplace popup

6. Give this environment a name and click on **Install**:

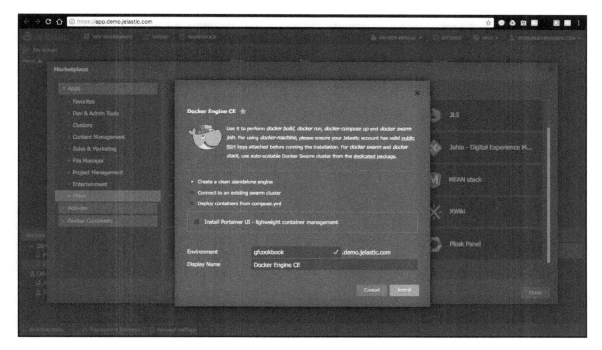

Docker Engine CE configuration popup

Wait until it's done:

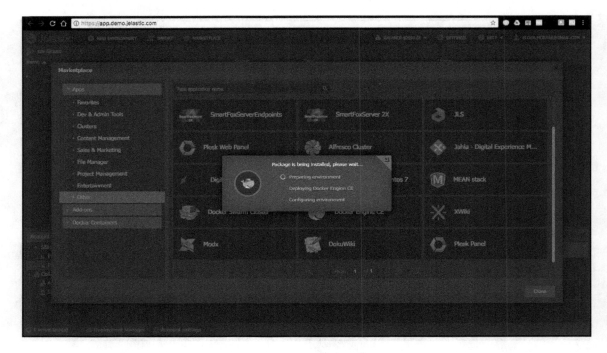

Installation status

7. Once it's finished, it will show a popup with the command you'll have to use to log in to the platform. Copy it:

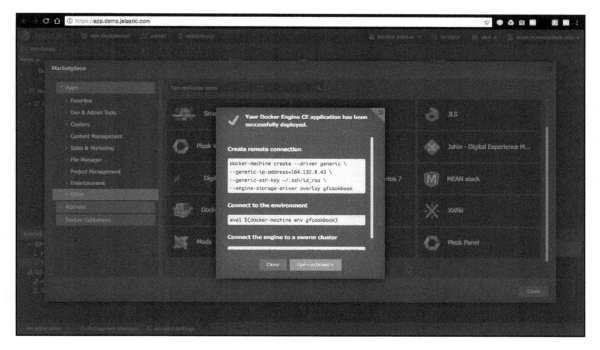

Install confirmation and commands for connection

8. Open a Terminal in your machine and paste the copied command:

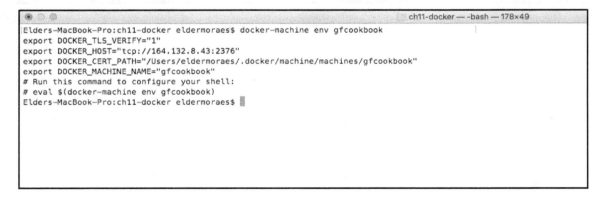

```
ch11-docker — -bash — 178×49
Elders-MacBook-Pro:ch11-docker eldermoraes$ docker-machine create --driver generic \
> --generic-ip-address=164.132.8.43 \
> --generic-ssh-key ~/.ssh/id_rsa \
> --engine-storage-driver overlay gfcookbook
Creating CA: /Users/eldermoraes/.docker/machine/certs/ca.pem
Creating client certificate: /Users/eldermoraes/.docker/machine/certs/cert.pem
Running pre-create checks...
Creating machine...
(gfcookbook) Importing SSH key...
Waiting for machine to be running, this may take a few minutes...
Detecting operating system of created instance...
Waiting for SSH to be available...
Detecting the provisioner...
Provisioning with centos...
Copying certs to the local machine directory...
Copying certs to the remote machine...
Setting Docker configuration on the remote daemon...
Checking connection to Docker...
Docker is up and running!
To see how to connect your Docker Client to the Docker Engine running on this virtual machine, run: docker-machine env gfcookbook
Elders-MacBook-Pro:ch11-docker eldermoraes$
```

Command execution on terminal

At the end of the output of the console window, there is the command:

docker-machine env [environment-name]

The output will be like this:

```
ch11-docker — -bash — 178×49
Elders-MacBook-Pro:ch11-docker eldermoraes$ docker-machine env gfcookbook
export DOCKER_TLS_VERIFY="1"
export DOCKER_HOST="tcp://164.132.8.43:2376"
export DOCKER_CERT_PATH="/Users/eldermoraes/.docker/machine/machines/gfcookbook"
export DOCKER_MACHINE_NAME="gfcookbook"
# Run this command to configure your shell:
# eval $(docker-machine env gfcookbook)
Elders-MacBook-Pro:ch11-docker eldermoraes$
```

Environment variables output

9. Now, you can just run your command to create a container:

```
docker run -d --name gf-javaee-cookbook \
    -h gf-javaee-cookbook \
    -p 80:8080 \
    -p 4848:4848 \
    -p 8686:8686 \
    -p 8009:8009 \
    -p 8181:8181 \
    eldermoraes/gf-javaee-cookbook
```

Check the output:

Container log output

It's quite the same as if you were running in your own local machine, but you are actually running on the Jelastic platform.

Now, if you go back to the main page you will see your environment up and running:

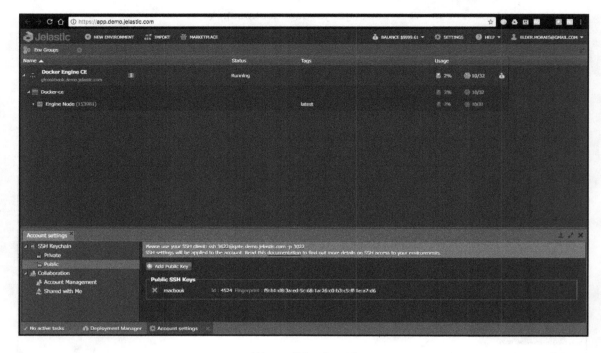

Main page with the node created

Under the **Docker Engine CE** label there's the URL of your environment. Just click on it and add /app to the end:

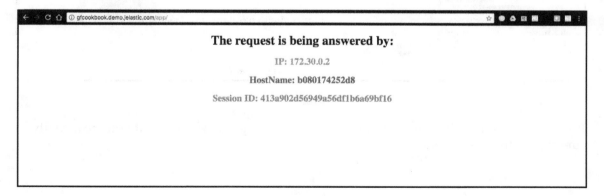

Test page for our application

If you can see this page, congratulations! Your application is deployed on Jelastic.

How it works...

The reason why it's so simple is because you are using a platform that's designed to make it simple. So all the heavy lifting that you'd need to do it in your own infrastructure is done by the platform.

There's more...

The reason why you should use a provider to orchestrate your containers in the cloud is not only regarding the ease of creating services, but also because the platform will take care of keeping it up and running.

So if your container goes wrong and needs to be stopped, restarted, or even killed and recreated, the platform will do it automatically.

Using OpenShift for container orchestration in the cloud

The best way to use containers in the cloud is by using a provider. Why? Because they can provide you a good infrastructure and a nice service for a small price.

This recipe will show you how to get the container created in the first recipe of this chapter and deliver it using OpenShift.

Getting ready

If you don't have an account with OpenShift you can sign up for a free trial. Visit `https://www.openshift.com/` and click on **Sign up for free**.

How to do it...

1. After logging in to the platform, you will see this main page:

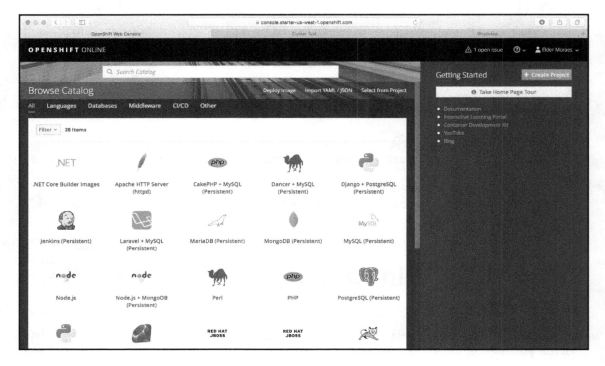

Openshift main page

2. Click on the **Create Project** button and fill in the blanks. Click on **Create**:

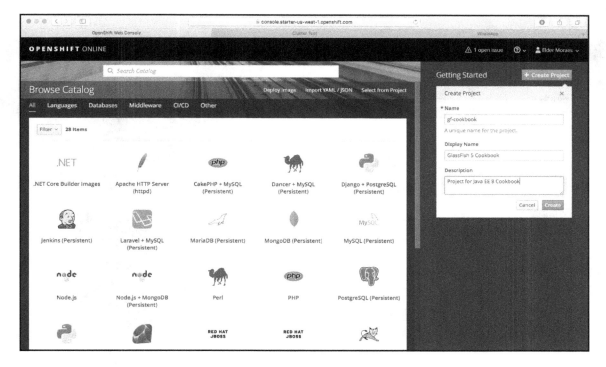

Filling fields for a new project

3. Once your project is created, click on it:

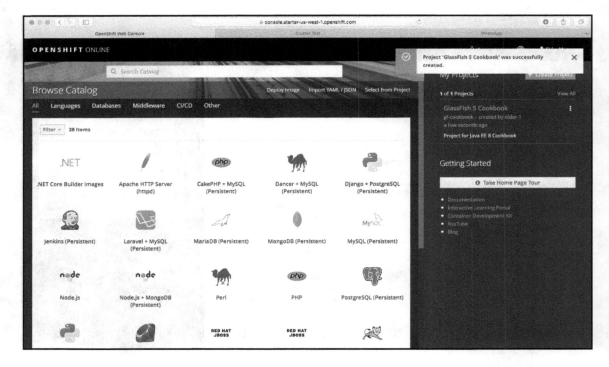

Access for the new project

4. On the opened page, click on **Add to Project** (top right) and then **Deploy Image**:

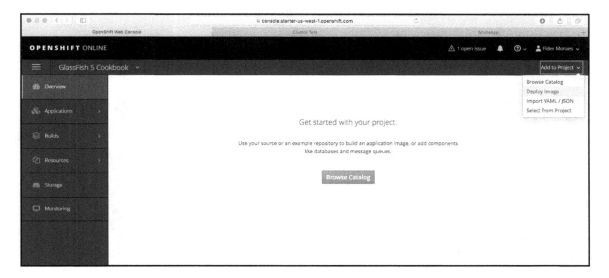

Project main page

5. In the popup select **Image Name**, fill in the form with our pre-built image
(`eldermoraes/gf-javaee-cookbook`) and click on the Search icon.

You will see a warning like this:

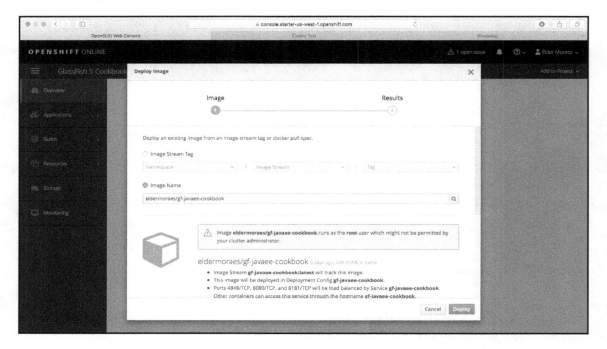

Image deployment popup

Let me save you time: don't deploy it, because it will not work. The OpenShift platform demands that your container should run with a user other than `root`. So we need to build another image for it.

Fortunately, it's quite simple. The new Dockerfile is like this:

```
FROM eldermoraes/gf-javaee-jdk8

ENV DEPLOYMENT_DIR
${GLASSFISH_HOME}/glassfish/domains/domain1/autodeploy/

COPY app.war ${DEPLOYMENT_DIR}

USER root

RUN chown -R glassfish:glassfish_grp ${DEPLOYMENT_DIR}/app.war \
    && chmod -R 777 ${DEPLOYMENT_DIR}/app.war

USER glassfish
```

6. Then you build a new image based on this Dockerfile:

```
docker build -t eldermoraes/gf-javaee-cookbook-os .
```

7. Then push this new image to the Docker Hub:

```
docker push eldermoraes/gf-javaee-cookbook-os
```

Now you are good to go:

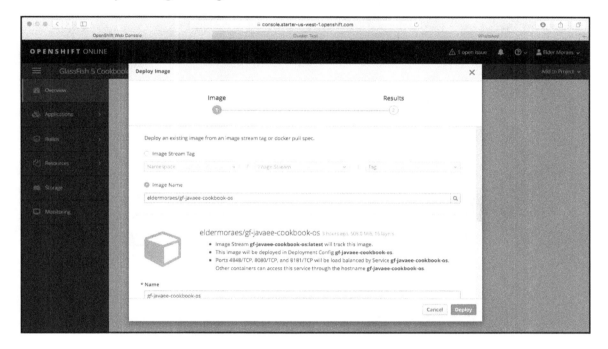

Image deployment popup

8. There are no warnings, so go ahead and click on **Deploy**. In the page that opens, click on the **Continue to the project overview** label:

Image deployment confirmation

9. Watch the following page until the pod icon is blue. When it's ready, click on the **Create Route** link:

Monitoring the pod creation

10. In the popup, fill in the **Path** field with /app and in **Target Port** choose **8080 -> 8080 (TCP)**:

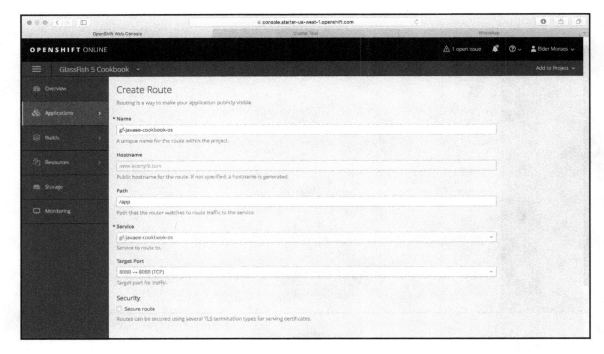

Route creation

11. Click on **Create** and wait:

Route confirmation

12. Once it's done, click on the **Overview** menu (top left). In the same row as the application name, there's a URL pointing to your container:

Test page for our application

If you can see the page, congratulations! Your application is now orchestrated at OpenShift.

How it works...

The reason why it's so simple is because you are using a platform that's designed to make it simple. So all the heavy lifting that you'd need to do it in your own infrastructure is done by the platform.

The change we've made to make the application run in the OpenShift is quite simple:

```
USER root

RUN chown -R glassfish:glassfish_grp ${DEPLOYMENT_DIR}/app.war \
    && chmod -R 777 ${DEPLOYMENT_DIR}/app.war

USER glassfish
```

First, we use the `root` user to change the permissions of `app.war`. Then the main point is to specify to use the `glassfish` user. This feature tells Docker that the internal process will be owned by the `glassfish` user, and not by `root`.

There's more...

The reason why you should use a provider to orchestrate your containers in the cloud is not only based on the ease of creating services, but also because the platform will take care of keeping it up and running.

So, if your container goes wrong and needs to be stopped, restarted, or even killed and recreated, the platform will do it automatically.

See also

- See the full source code for this recipe at `https://github.com/eldermoraes/javaee8-cookbook/tree/master/chapter11/ch11-openshift`.

Using AWS for container orchestration in the cloud

The best way to use containers in the cloud is by using a provider. Why? Because they can provide you with a good infrastructure and a nice service for a small price.

This recipe will show you how to get the container created in the first recipe of this chapter and deliver it using **Amazon Web Services (AWS)**.

Getting ready

If you don't have an account with AWS, register for a free trial at `https://aws.amazon.com/free/start-your-free-trial/`.

How to do it...

1. Once you log in to the platform, you will get to this main page:

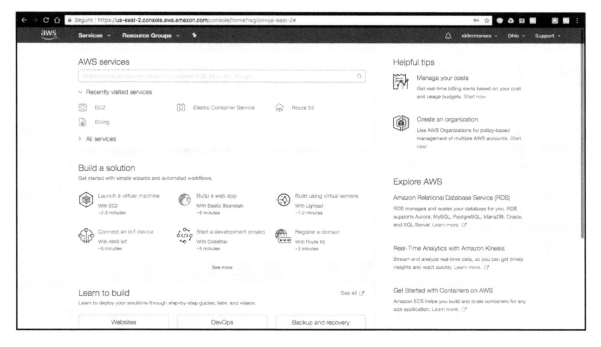

AWS main page

2. Click on the **Services** menu (top left) and then **Elastic Container Service** (under the **Compute** menu):

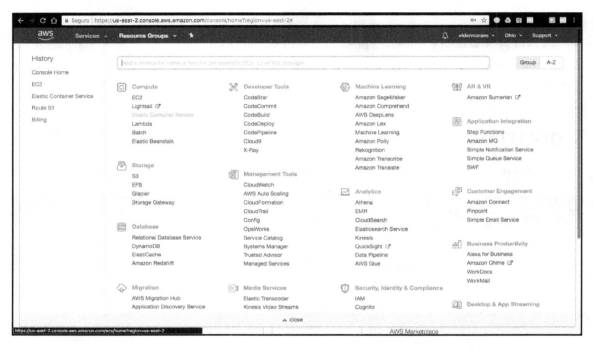

Services list

3. On the page that opens, click on **Get started**:

Getting started page for ECS

4. Check only the **Deploy a sample application onto an Amazon ECS Cluster** option. Then click on **Continue**:

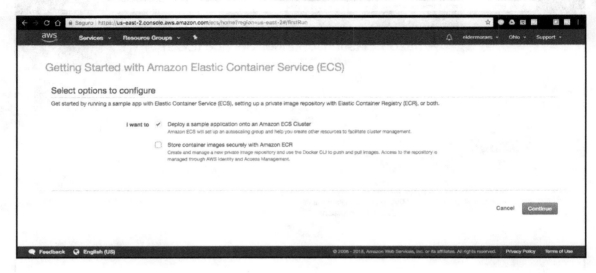

First page for ECS creation

5. Fill in the blanks as follows, paying special attention to the **Image** field, where you will use our prebuilt image:

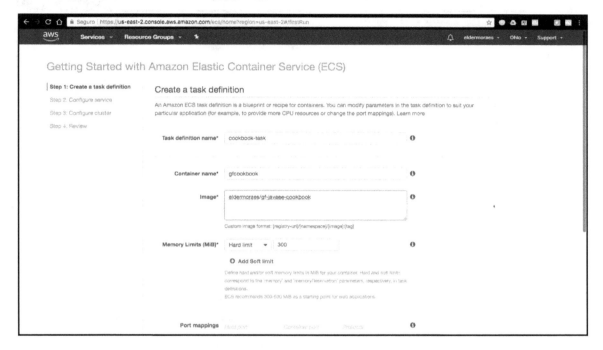

Task definition page

6. Scroll down the page and set **Port mappings** as shown here. Click on **Continue**:

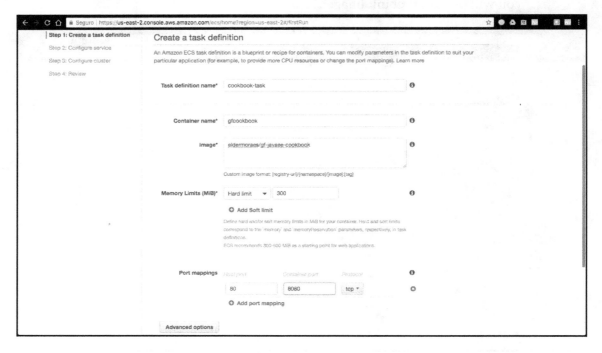

Port mappings

7. Give the service a name and set the **Desired number of tasks** to 1. Click on **Next step**:

Service and network configuration

8. Configure the cluster as shown here:

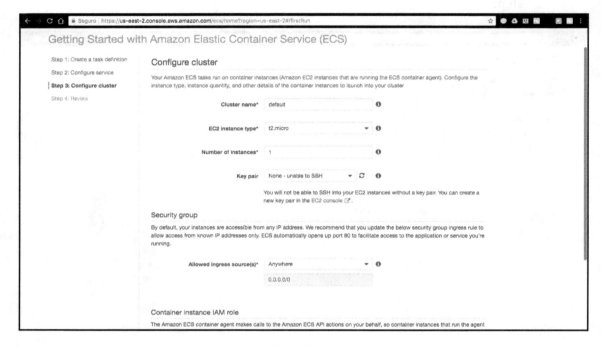

Cluster configuration

9. Scroll down to the page and click on **Launch instance & run service**:

Launch instance

10. You can follow the status of the process on the following page. When it's done, click on the **View service** button:

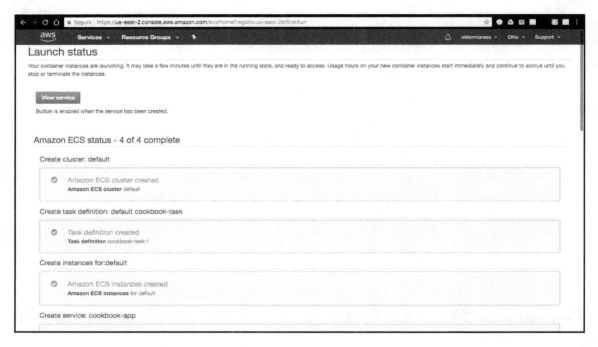

Launch status

11. You'll see the details of your service on the following page. Click on the **default > label:**

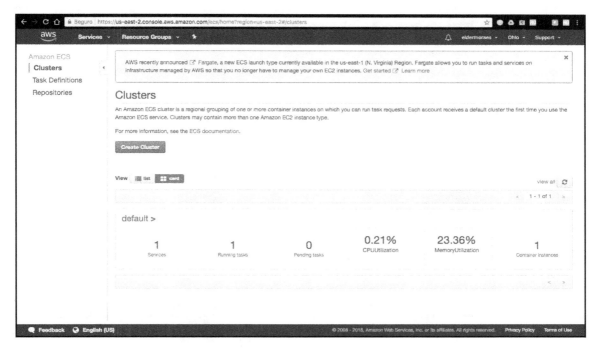

Cluster information

On the page that opens, you can see more details about the cluster:

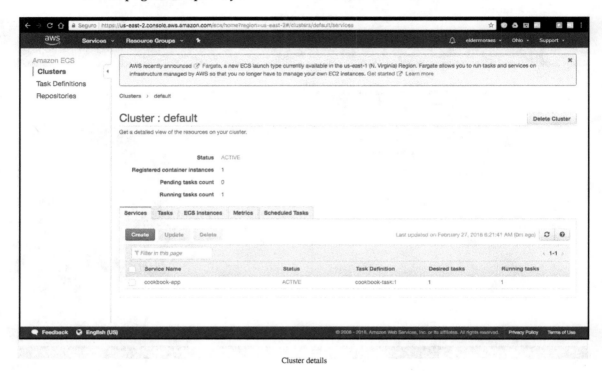

Cluster details

12. Click on the **Tasks** tab to see information about the tasks and the containers created:

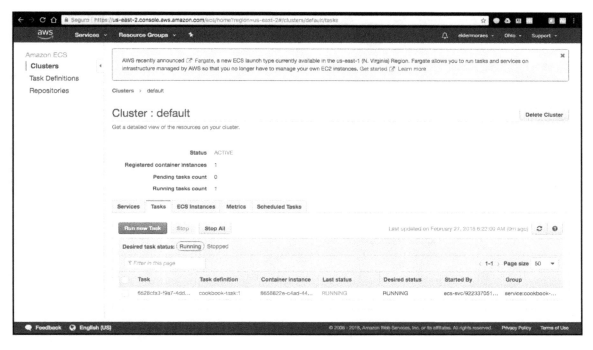

Container tasks

13. Click on the **Container Instance** label to see details about the container that has been created:

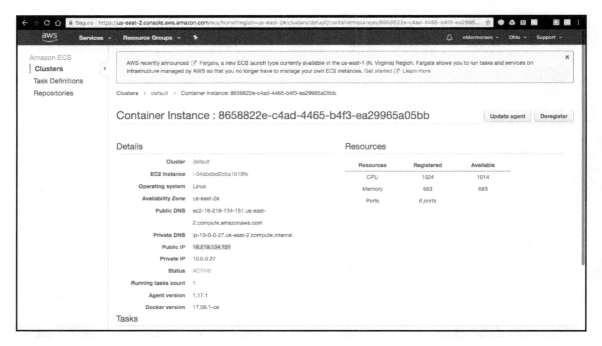

Container details

14. Check the **Public IP** label and copy the IP. It's automatically mapped to the 8080 port. Use `http://[public-ip]/app` to try it:

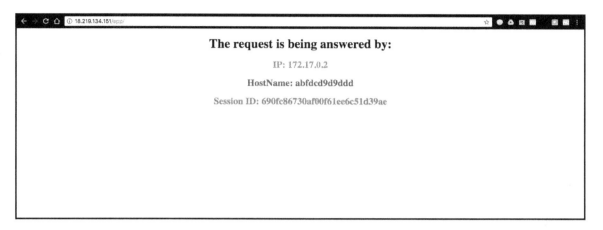

Test page for our application

If you can see the same screenshot, that's great! You are now orchestrating your container in AWS.

How it works...

The reason why it's so simple is because you are using a platform that's designed to make it simple. So, all the heavy lifting that you'd make to do it in your own infrastructure is done by the platform.

There's more...

The reason why you should use a provider to orchestrate your containers in the cloud is not only because of the ease of creating services, but also because the platform will take care of keeping it up and running.

So if your container goes wrong and needs to be stopped, restarted, or even killed and recreated, the platform will do it automatically.

12
Appendix: The Power of Sharing Knowledge

This appendix covers the following topics:

- Why contributing to the Adopt a JSR program can make you a better professional

- The secret to unsticking your project, your career... and even your life!

Introduction

Wait... career, knowledge sharing, community... in a cookbook?

Well, I should really thank my editors, who have surrendered to my charm (and insistence) and allowed me to put this chapter in this book.

The reasons why I stressed them about it were the following:

- I am sure that this content is quite important and can be life changing for you and your career
- I don't know if or when I'll write another book, so I wanted to take the chance now

I consider this content as important as the rest of the book. Actually, if you apply its principles to your own career, you could be the next one writing a book.

Why contributing to the Adopt a JSR program can make you a better professional

Did you ever hear the phrase, *"Help others to help yourself"*? Yes? This section is all about it. Believe me, I wrote that.

Maybe you've never heard about the Adopt a JSR program, or maybe you've heard about it but have no idea what it is. Or you do know it, but don't know how it could have anything to do with your career.

Allow me to have your company for the next few pages and enjoy the ride.

Understanding the Adopt a JSR program

First of all, what is the *Adopt a JSR* program?

It's an initiative intended to bring the community closer together in the process of evolving Java. By *community* we mean **Java User Groups (JUGs)**, individuals, and any other kind of organization.

To understand it, maybe we should hold on for a second and understand the Java evolution process.

Java technology is a set of standards called **JSR**, the abbreviation for **Java Specification Request**. Every API and any aspects of the language have to be written in some JSR.

Every JSR has a spec leader, an individual in charge of leading the process of building that specification. Each spec lead works with a group called an **EG**, or **Expert Group**, which works with the spec lead and does all the heavy lifting of creating and/or evolving a JSR.

In each JSR there are also contributors, people from the community who volunteer to collaborate with a JSR. They don't have the same role as the spec leader or the EG, but can also do a lot for this process.

For each JSR, there's a **Reference Implementation** (RI). The RI is the real code that JSR is working as a real Java code. It exists to bring all those conceptual lines of a specification to the real world. It's vital for proving that what was once specified really works.

Examples of RIs are Mojarra for JSF, Soteria for Security, and GlassFish for Java EE.

When we say that the RI is a proof that some JSR really works, this is not just some conceptual stuff. It is really tested. That's why we have the **TCKs**, or **Technology Compatibility Kits**.

TCKs are a set of tests designed to test the implementations specified in the JSR. So when an RI is written, it should pass in the TCKs to prove that it's really working (at least in theory).

Those three parts—the JSR, the RI, and the TCK—are the pieces ratified by the **Java Community Process** or **JCP**.

So in the JCP, you have all the working JSRs and their own processes monitored by the **Executive Committee** (EC), a group formed by companies, individuals, and JUGs that guarantee that all JSRs are working under the best practices defined by the JCP, and moving towards to the best results for the Java ecosystem and the community that relies on it.

So the next time you think *"how can I contribute to Java?"*, *"how can I make my contribution?"* or, more specific to this section, *"how can I adopt a JSR?"*, know that you can do it by doing the following:

- Joining as a contributor to some JSRs. Most spec leaders will be happy and open to accepting help with the hard work of evolving a JSR.
- Helping write the specification or at least helping with useful suggestions.
- Writing tests for TCKs or helping solve issues found in the TCK tests.
- Coding for the RIs.

All those topics you can do by yourself, but they are all much more productive (and fun!) if you do it with the community. You can do it by joining a JUG, or starting a small group in your company, or wherever you can find some people to work together. It's a lot of work, so it's better to have some company!

For more information about adopting a JSR program, you could check the following links:

- https://jcp.org/aboutJava/communityprocess/community/JCPAdoptJSR.pdf
- https://community.oracle.com/community/java/jcp/adopt-a-jsr
- https://developercareers.wordpress.com/2011/11/01/give-your-career-a-boost-by-adopting-a-jsr/

And to get to work, visit: https://jcp.org.

Collaborating on the future of Java EE

So if you are reading this book, I believe that you are interested in Java EE. And if you reach this very line, I hope that I'm beginning to convince you that you can help Java EE to move forward and it can help your career.

Yes, you can definitely help Java EE move forward, and talking from my own experience, I can assure you that you should start it right now! But, in terms of process, things are slightly different for Java EE.

A few months since the time of writing, Oracle decided to transfer Java EE to the Eclipse Foundation. So while I'm writing these lines, the transfer process is happening!

Just a little note: this is valid only for Java EE, not for Java! Other Java specifications will continue under the JCP (at least for now).

What does it change for you in terms of collaboration? Nothing. There are still groups, specifications, tests, RIs, and so on. The only thing that is being changed are the names, as the process is now owned by the Eclipse Foundation.

So Java EE was transferred to Eclipse as **Eclipse Enterprise for Java**, or **EE4J**. It's the project umbrella that holds all other projects under it. These other projects are the former JSRs. More details about EE4J are at `https://projects.eclipse.org/projects/ee4j/charter`.

The transfer process and EE4J itself has a lot of answered questions here:

`https://www.eclipse.org/ee4j/faq.php`

The project in Eclipse is led by the **Project Management Committee (PMC)**, like the EC in the JCP. More details about the PMC are at `https://projects.eclipse.org/projects/ee4j/pmc`.

The bottom line here is that you can, and I believe that you should, make your contribution to the future of Java EE. Maybe you think that you don't have what it takes. Yes, you have! Every suggestion counts, every good idea, every line of working code, every test that passes. Give it a shot and see the results!

Setting yourself up for collaboration

There are some things you need to do in order to collaborate on the future of Java EE.

Set aside a specific time for it

If you just do it when you have time for it, you may never ever do it! So make time. Define some time you are willing to do it per week (one hour per day, three hours per week, and so on). Write it down and make an appointment.

Choose where you'll concentrate your effort

It's useless to start sending emails to dozens of spec leaders asking them to join the group and collaborate. I know it, I've already done it before.

Instead, take a step back, think about what you are really interested in, and choose one single specification to start. Join the mailing list, find its repository on GitHub, and start watching it.

A great way to start collaboration on any open source project is with documentation. It's important, but often people involved with writing specification and coding don't have enough time to go deeper into the documentation. So, they are usually glad when somebody else is willing to do it.

I know many people who start collaborating this way today are committed to some of the biggest open source projects.

Do it!

Any plan just makes sense if you do something about it. So stop procrastinating and get to work! Don't wait until Monday, or after vacations, or after the end of college, or when you get a better job, or whatever.

Have in mind that you probably will never feel like you are ready for it. So stop feeling and start doing, even if you don't feel like it. If you do the hard work the results will come, be assured about that!

The secret to unstucking your project, your career... even your life!

Are you feeling stuck in your career? I've felt like that too. Let me tell you a story and a secret that made my career explode.

The year is 2002. I'm in the American Chamber of Commerce in San Paolo, attending the Sun Tech Days. The venue is full and I'm a little lost.

Maybe lost doesn't define it very well. Out of place sounds much better. After all, I'm just a tech newbie in the middle of giants.

I see some known faces. Bruno Souza, Fabio Velloso. Should I introduce myself?

Of course not... who am I? Leave the guys alone, they are too busy in a conference like this.

I read the program and see that there is a keynote in the main room. Looks like it's someone important called James Gosling. I have no idea who he is, but I go there.

I'm the first in line. Of course, I'm a newbie! Everyone is having some conversation while I'm here alone in front of the door. What are they talking about? For sure, some super technical discussion that I can't understand. Better stay here and wait.

Five minutes before they open the doors and there are 200 people after me in the line. Hey, looks like I'm a lucky newbie, huh?!

I walked in and took a seat in the second row, waiting for the keynote to start.

Holy God, that James Gosling is the Java creator! What a dumb newbie I am...

His talk is awesome! You know, he is not the best speaker in the world, but there are some things in his speech that amaze everyone in the room. Maybe it's his passion, his knowledge, or even the super cool project that he is working on: the operating system for a remote-controlled Mars rover. Damn!

It's already the end of the second day of the conference and I'm absolutely disturbed: there are so many possibilities with this Java thing. I've tried it a little by myself, but seeing all those Sun evangelists talking about real and cool projects took me to a whole new world of possibilities in my mind. My career needs to go in that direction.

After some days out of the office I'm back and can't help myself: I need to tell everybody what I've just seen during those days. You know, most of us work here with Visual Basic and Delphi... but Java brings a new set of possibilities to our projects.

Just six months since I've attended those Sun Tech Days and I'm in my first Java project. Yes! The company outsourced a project and asked me to work together with our partner.

What a terrible idea! Our partner's lead developer knows as much as I do about Java... OK, let's do this. At least I have the opportunity to work on a real Java project.

It's 2004, and I'm about to talk in a big conference for the first time ever. I have to admit, I'm terrified. But actually I'm joining in on a talk with a new friend, Mauricio Leal. He is one of the top Java influencers in Brazil and agreed to give a talk with me to the Just Java conference. Or was it me that agreed to him? Well, it doesn't matter now...

It was very hard for me to go there as my mother had started a fight against cancer just a few months before. I'm not only very concerned about her, but I also didn't have enough time to get prepared for the conference. However, she herself encouraged me to be here and said she was proud of her child talking at a big event. Thanks, mom!

We gave our talk and it was great! I have a lot to learn from Mauricio and all his Java friends. Actually, I need to keep going with this community thing: events, open source, talks, and so on.

Here I am in 2005, and I've decided to join a big project at the same company that I've been working with for the last three years. No, it's not a Java project, but it's so big that I can't miss the chance. It will be good for my career and I'll have some opportunities as a project manager.

We are in June, 2006, and my mother has just lost the fight against cancer. I'm destroyed. I never thought in my entire life that I would lose her when she was only 58 and I'm 26... Who cares about career? Who cares about the job? Who cares about anything?

The year is 2015. The month is December. I'm driving my car. My wife is at my side and my baby daughter in the back seat. I'm telling my wife that I'm very concerned about my career.

I'm not a kid anymore. I'm 36, have a good job, getting decent money from it, but... I'm stuck. Since when... 2004? I know, it was a big mistake to join that project, even though it was a big one. We all failed on it.

I tell her: *"You know, I have to do something..."*.

After a couple of sleepless nights, some hours of research on the internet, and some reading of reference books, I think I have a good list for someone who has done nothing for years:

- Write a technical article for publishing
- Give a tech talk at some small event
- Get a Java EE Architect certification

I've decided to go with Java until the end. I know a lot about it. I've being studying it and working with it for many years. I have to focus on it and I can definitely do it.

And suddenly, in the middle of this big confusion and lots of doubts, I've made it! Now I'm a partner in the company.

Well, maybe I've done something right, huh?! All these years of hard work and study finally paid off.

But... what was I thinking? I hate sales, I hate dealing with clients, I hate negotiations, I hate wearing a suit, and I hate chasing money. I hate this partner stuff!

To have my own business was always a dream, but my life right now is much more of a nightmare. This wrong decision literally made everything fall apart. The situation is unbearable to the point that I now need medicine for depression.

All this poison in my mind makes me think, *"what the hell am I doing with my life?"* That's not the path I want to follow. I mean... yes, the company is great and they are doing great, but not in a way that works for me.

I really need a change. I need to make a move. If I don't, what about my family's future? What kind of support will I be able to give my wife and daughter when I get old and retire?

It's just another terrible day and then I got an email from... Bruno Souza? The Brazilian Javaman? How the heck does this guy have my email? Oh, yes... I'm subscribed to some mailing list.

He is talking about dreams, saying that one of his friends will help him this year with a career dream, so he decided to help others too. He says: *"Tell me your career dreams for 2016 and I'll try to help you with them"*.

Well, I'm sure this guy won't even read my email, but let me reply to it anyway. At least writing down my dreams for this year will help me visualize them. I'll use that list that I told my wife a few weeks ago.

What? Just half an hour and he replied?

OK... he is saying that he can help me this way:

- **Article**: He can help me on finding a good topic and publish it at the Oracle Technology Network? Is this serious? I was just thinking about a blog post or whatever.
- **Talk**: Once we have the article, he can help me turn it into a talk. Ok, sounds interesting.

- **Certification**: He won't help me at all. I should sit down and study. Yeah, makes sense.

From all the conversations I have with Bruno one thing is always on top: sharing. Share knowledge, share what you know, share to help others, share, share, share. Seems like this guy really wants to help people.

So I manage to leave the company (and the partnership) and finally got a position that I really want: systems architect!

That's it, I love architecture, and I love to deal with all those trade offs when planning an application from scratch or scaling/refactoring some legacy application.

That's it, now I've found my place!

Not so fast, pal. Not so fast, within a month or so the company changes its CEO and the guy just decides that Java would die there and then. The focus now is .NET! OK, let's try it.

In the meantime, Bruno and I publish our first article in the OTN and it gets thousands of views in just a few days. That's awesome!

This article becomes a proposal on the same subject for *The Developer's Conference* (the biggest developer event in Latin America) and JavaOne Latin America. Both are accepted and I have the opportunity to talk with Bruno to hundreds of people at these events.

On the last day before submitting to JavaOne San Francisco I decide to give up on it. I don't have the money to afford it. Bruno almost kicks my ass and says: *"Come on! Submit it! If it gets approved you figure out how to afford it"*.

The talk gets approved and Cristina Saito, a former boss (and partner!) sends me a gift: the air tickets to JavaOne. She said she was proud of me. I could probably never thank her enough for her kindness and generosity, and I hope this mention here goes some way towards that thanks.

It's hard to believe. Just 10 months since I opened Bruno's email, 10 months since the depression medication, 10 months since the darkest moment of my career, I'm in San Francisco, California. In a couple of minutes, I'll be giving a talk with Bruno at JavaOne, the biggest Java event in the world. A movie just went through my mind. And here I am now.

The talk was great! Some stuff went wrong, but... we made it! Seems like this sharing stuff is really working. I'm feeling really confident and can't wait to be back in Brazil and getting back to work. Getting things done. Climbing my own success mountain.

So I land in Brazil, go to the office, and... get fired? Really? I thought that all this sharing stuff would help me, not cause me to lose my job... somebody lied to me!

OK, OK... let's take a deep breath... you know, I'm more confident now. No, I wasn't prepared for something like getting fired after achieving the best accomplishment of my career until now, but... I think I'll figure something out.

It doesn't take long until I get a position at Summa Technologies. Yes, sharing is working: I didn't even need to send a resume. They heard about me (because of sharing) and here I am, working with things that I've been talking and writing about.

The company is great, the team is highly skilled, and the project is challenging. But, you know... six months later and it looks like the things are getting stuck again... the results are just OK, the project is just OK, and there is no big deal to learn or to do here.

We are in May, 2017. In a few months, Java EE 8 will be released. What if we interview some top Java EE influencers from all over the world and share all the information, expectations, and news they have about it? Sounds good. Let's call it Java EE 8 - The Next Frontier.

Bruno was skilled enough to convince me to do this Java EE 8 stuff, and SouJava would give all the support needed. Actually, it was a SouJava initiative from the very first moment.

But, come on, why would all those Java EE experts give me an interview? Who am I?

It's been just three months since I've been working with SouJava for the Java EE project. We've already interviewed 15 of the top Java EE influencers. Thousands of developers from almost 70 countries see the interviews. Our playlist on YouTube is featured on the official Java channel. All the content gets thousands of views a month.

I have to be honest: I would never have imagined that the Java EE community would be so open to this initiative. I mean, it's like they were expecting this content. They are willing to consume it.

The thing I was lacking this entire time? Focus! Anything you do without focus is almost useless. It can be helpful, but won't have continuity.

These projects led me to write this book you are reading right now. In one of my conversations with Packt I asked them how they found me. They said, *"well, you've been sharing a lot of Java EE 8 content... that's what we need"*.

And just a few days after signing with Packt I got a call from... Oracle? "That" Oracle?

So I'm here, writing these lines and working at one of the biggest companies in the world, doing exactly what I'm telling you in this chapter: sharing knowledge.

I insist to you: if sharing changed my career, it can also change yours. Don't think you don't have what it takes for it: you have it! I can assure you that you know many things that other people would love to learn.

Why don't you find some good way to help them? Can I give you some suggestions on how you could help others based on what you just read here? Here they are:

- You can write a little block of code based on something you learned in this book. Share it on Twitter or in some blog post.
- Record a video explaining some insight you had when reading something in this book. Share it!
- If you don't want to expose yourself at this point, email me telling me anything that this book has taught you. I'd love to read it! Write to `elder@eldermoraes.com`.

Sharing is a habit. Exercise it!

Other Books You May Enjoy

If you enjoyed this book, you may be interested in these other books by Packt:

Java EE 8 and Angular
Prashant Padmanabhan

ISBN: 978-1-78829-120-0

- Write CDI-based code in Java EE 8 applications
- Build an understanding of Microservices and what they mean in Java EE context
- Use Docker to build and run a microservice application
- Use configuration options to work effectively with JSON documents
- Understand asynchronous task handling and writing REST API clients
- Explore the fundamentals of TypeScript, which sets the foundation for working on Angular projects
- Use Angular CLI to add and manage new features
- Use JSON Web tokens to secure Angular applications against malicious attacks

Architecting Modern Java EE Applications
Sebastian Daschner

ISBN: 978-1-78839-385-0

- What enterprise software engineers should focus on
- Implement applications, packages, and components in a modern way
- Design and structure application architectures
- Discover how to realize technical and cross-cutting aspects
- Get to grips with containers and container orchestration technology
- Realize zero-dependency, 12-factor, and Cloud-native applications
- Implement automated, fast, reliable, and maintainable software tests
- Discover distributed system architectures and their requirements

Leave a review - let other readers know what you think

Please share your thoughts on this book with others by leaving a review on the site that you bought it from. If you purchased the book from Amazon, please leave us an honest review on this book's Amazon page. This is vital so that other potential readers can see and use your unbiased opinion to make purchasing decisions, we can understand what our customers think about our products, and our authors can see your feedback on the title that they have worked with Packt to create. It will only take a few minutes of your time, but is valuable to other potential customers, our authors, and Packt. Thank you!

Index

M

managed threads
  building, with returning results 234, 235, 236
maturity stages, automation pipeline
  continuous delivery 212, 214
  continuous deployment (CD) 207, 214
  continuous integration (CI) 207, 209
Maven
  about 209, 211
  URL 209
Message Drive Bean (MDB) 159
message-driven beans
  reactive applications, building 259, 260, 261, 262
  setDeliveryMode method 261
  setDisableMessageID method 261
  setDisableMessageTimestamp method 262
messaging services
  using, for asynchronous communication 158, 159, 160, 162
MicroProfile
  about 200
  URL 200
microservices
  about 185
  advantages 185
  automated pipeline, building 206, 207, 208, 215
  building, from monolith 186, 197, 199, 200
  gateway microservice 193
  user address microservice 193
  user microservice 193
monolith
  about 197
  building 187, 189, 191
  microservices, building from 186, 197, 199, 200
MVC 1.0 code
  executing 37, 38, 39

O

objects representation
  easing, with JSON-B 95, 96, 97, 98
observers
  reactive applications, building 251, 252, 253
OpenShift

using, for container orchestration in cloud 315, 320, 326
Oracle Cloud
  URL 282
  using, for container orchestration in cloud 282, 285, 292, 298, 303

P

Payara Micro 200
programmatic security
  about 37, 135
  using 143, 145, 146, 148, 149
Project Management Committee (PMC)
  URL 346
Project Object Model (POM) 210

R

reactive applications
  building, with asynchronous servlets 248, 249, 250, 251
  building, with asynchronous session beans 267, 268, 269, 270
  building, with events 251, 252, 253
  building, with JAX-RS 263, 264, 266, 267
  building, with message-driven beans 259, 260, 261, 262
  building, with observers 251, 252, 253
  building, with websockets 254, 255, 256, 257, 258
  improving, with CompletableFuture 270, 272, 273
  improving, with lambdas 270, 272, 273
Reactive Manifesto
  URL 247
reactive systems
  features 247
Reference Implementation (RI) 174, 344
request and response management
  with Servlet 52, 53, 55, 103
Request for Comments (RFC) 6901 28
rights
  granting, through authorization 123, 125, 127, 130, 132, 133